D0780340

GARIBALDI'S

MEMOIRS

Volume I

WITHDRAWN
UTSA LIBRARIES

Bologna 26 7bre 59

I manoscritti da me rimessi a Elpis Melena sono scritti di mio pugno —
G. Garibaldi

Garibaldi, original frontispiece in pen and ink with statement:
The manuscripts given by me to Elpis Melena are written by my hand.

G. Garibaldi

GARIBALDI'S

MEMOIRS

from

his manuscript, personal notes and authentic sources
assembled and published

by

ELPIS MELENA

Edited with Introduction and Annotations
by
ANTHONY P. CAMPANELLA

VOLUME I

INTERNATIONAL INSTITUTE
OF GARIBALDIAN STUDIES
Sarasota, Florida
1981

Garibaldi's Denkwürdigkeiten
nach
handschriftlichen Aufzeichnungen desselben
und nach authentischen Quellen
bearbeitet und herausgegeben
von
Elpis Melena

Hamburg, Hoffmann und Campe, 1861. 2 Bände.
Published for the first time in English
Translated from the German by Erica Sigerist Campanella

Copyright © 1981 by Anthony P. Campanella
All rights reserved

ISBN 92-9013-003-2

The opinions expressed in this book are those of the author
and editor and are not necessarily those of the Institute
or its Board Members.

International Institute of Garibaldian Studies
1025 Shadow Lawn Way
Sarasota, Florida 33581
U.S.A.

LIBRARY
The University of Texas
At San Antonio

Garibaldi's name is surrounded by a spell which nothing can extinguish; a whole life devoted exclusively to one idea, the fatherland. A name consecrated by honorable and heroic deeds, first abroad, then at home; valor and constancy more than admirable; simplicity of life and manners reminiscent of the ancients; manly dignity in bearing the hardest ordeals and losses. Glory and poverty! Everything concerning such a man is worthy and precious.

Italia del Popolo 1850.

CONTENTS

VOLUME I

BOOK ONE

GARIBALDI'S AUTOBIOGRAPHY

From his Birth until the Year 1848

VOLUME II

BOOK TWO

GARIBALDI'S RETURN TO EUROPE

THE DEFENSE OF ROME

BOOK THREE

GARIBALDI ON THE RETREAT FROM ROME
by Elpis Melena

BOOK FOUR

ANITA

BOOK FIVE
by Elpis Melena

BOOK SIX
by Elpis Melena

*

*

ILLUSTRATIONS

INTRODUCTION
BY THE EDITOR

This volume is not intended for a novice in Garibaldian history, but as a supplementary aid to introductory studies already published. Besides, Elpis Melena was not an historian, so that her accounts of events and people are not always accurate. Instead the value of this work lies in the intimacy she enjoyed in the Liberator's confidence, as revealed in Books Three through Six of Volume II. For the novice, the biographies of Garibaldi by Guerzoni, Sacerdote, Bizzoni, J.W. Mario, Corselli and Provaglio still remain as the most trustworthy, while for the particular episodes here recounted, that is, the Latin American experiences of Garibaldi and his retreat from Rome in 1849, the reader would do well to begin first with such specialized volumes on Brazilian and Uruguayan history as those by Assis Brasil, Collor, Spalding, Varzea, H. Boiteaux, Caillet Bois, Fernandez Saldaña, Leite de Castro, Setembrino Pereda and Isidoro De Maria; for the period of the retreat from Rome, the volumes by Belluzzi, Beseghi, Bonnet, Franciosi, Guelfi, Mastri, Hoffstetter and Fonterossi still are fundamental and essential.

This is the fourth and last version of Garibaldi's memoirs published from his original manuscript. As we know, Theodore Dwight, the American writer and personal friend of the Italian revolutionary, published the first version in English in 1859 through A.S. Barnes and Burr in New York. Early the following year Francesco Carrano, Garibaldi's Chief of Staff of his voluntary army, the *Cacciatori delle Alpi* in the war against Austria of 1859, published the second version in Italian through the Unione Tipografica-editrice of Turin. Shortly after, still in 1860, none other than Alexandre Dumas, the dean of novelists and countryman of Garibaldi, published the third version in French through Michel Lévy in Paris. Finally Elpis Melena, the budding Anglo-German writer and erstwhile mistress of Garibaldi, published this version in German through Hoffman and Campe of Hamburg under the title of *Garibaldi's Denkwürdigkeiten* the following year. The translation which appears here is the first to be made from the original German.

The necessity of publishing the different versions becomes apparent when one realizes the time elapsed between the handing over at different times of the constantly amended and enlarged manuscript. Garibaldi handed it to Dwight in 1850 at the time of his first trip to New York; in 1853, after sailing around Cape Horn en route from China via Peru, Garibaldi arrived a second time in New York and handed Dwight more pages of his eventful life. By the time 1859 rolled around, Garibaldi had settled on the Island of Caprera, had resumed his career of sea-going captain in the Mediterranean and had been honored by being named a general in the Sardinian Army. The victories of his *Cacciatori delle Alpi* followed in the Austrian-Sardinian War of that year, all of which added still more pages to that life which G. M. Trevelyan called "perhaps the most romantic that history records."

Still Garibaldi's richest pages had yet to be written. In January 1860 Alexandre Dumas finally met his hero, or as he described him, "he is Ajax and d'Artagnan rolled into one, he is Garibaldi!" New episodes were recorded, even some which had not been written down by Garibaldi during his memorable twelve-year stay in Brazil and Uruguay. Ever since 1850, when Uruguayan Minister of War Pacheco y Obes had come to Paris to solicit funds for the continuation of his country's war against the Argentinian invasion and had recounted the prowess of Garibaldi in maintaining the defense against the invader, Dumas was eager to meet *el Salvador* of Uruguay. Hence the French novelist's version became the most complete and best known. In fact many were they who belittled the new episodes as figments of Dumas' romantic imagination. But such sterling historians as Alessandro Luzio, Giacomo Curàtulo and Gustavo Sacerdote proved the accuracy of Dumas' enriched version.

Similarly the Melena version introduces new facts to the Garibaldi manuscript, even if not to the extent of the Dumas version, for her association with the *Hero of Two Worlds* and *Messiah of Oppressed People* was gained through an intimate friendship which extended over twenty years. Some detractors of Garibaldi, like Denis Mack Smith and Jasper Ridley, whose writings contend that he so loved her that twice he proposed marriage and both times was refused, have apparently sought to belittle him. The truth is that in the 201 letters of their correspondence extant today in the Archives of the Museo del Risorgimento of Milan and in the International Institute of Garibaldian Studies in Geneva not a single reference exists concerning a proposal of marriage at any time.

Elpis Melena was born Marie Espérance von Brandt in Southgate, Hertford County, England on 8 November 1818, that is, eleven years after Garibaldi first saw the light of day in Nice, France. She was the daughter of a Hamburg banker who resided in England, but being born in England it legally gave her the nationality of that country, which she maintained throughout her wandering life. But after childhood she was little to see England again, residing the remainder of her years in Italy, Germany, Greece, Crete and Switzerland.

As a child she was taught almost exclusively by Espérance von Sylvestre, her maternal aunt, who was best known for having been the tutor of the Queen of Prussia at the Court of Weimar. Later Marie was brought to Geneva for her middle school education and lived for a while in Petit Saconnex, then with the prominent Dominicé family of Genthod. Before long her forte appeared in her grasp of foreign languages, three of which she learned during this period; later she added another five. Unfortunately her education was disrupted at the age of 15 when she was persuaded, much against her will, into marrying her cousin and banker Alexander Brandt.

The event was indeed unfortunate, for it was an unhappy marriage and ended on 12 July 1838, when her husband committed suicide. Still very young, she was now brought to Rome for the continuation of her education. Here, among the colorful atmosphere of an international coterie of artists and aristocrats, she was to receive her first impulses towards a creative and exuberant life. And included among her many new acquaintances was another banker, this one from Hamburg by name of Baron Ferdinand von Schwartz, whom she married on 25 September 1842.

Her second marriage was also unhappy, despite some years of adventurous travel together. Mainly on horseback, the couple visited Greece, Turkey, Asia Minor and Egypt, and while en route to Tunis, they were shipwrecked near Stora and were saved by sheer luck. However, with such a background of travel and linguistic ability, our young newly-wed Marie Espérance von Schwartz decided to become a writer under the pseudonym of *Elpis Melena*, that is, Black Hope, or the translation into Greek of her given name Espérance (hope) and her new German name Schwartz (black).

Her first literary endeavor was *Blätter aus dem afrikanischen Reisetagebuche einer Dame* (Leaves from a Lady's Travelogue of Africa), a two-volume set which she published in Germany in 1849. But branching out as a writer meant more to her than the companionate travel in elegance to which her husband was accustomed; incompatibility followed, and in 1854 their marriage was legally dissolved. Furthermore since 1849, when Melena had domiciled herself permanently in Rome, a certain Republican freedom fighter had arrived there after years of South American renown had preceded him. He was Italian, blond and the talk of the day; and as he daringly repulsed the French Army, the most highly-rated of Europe, in its attempt to destroy the newly-created Roman Republic in order to replace it with the Papacy again, Melena found herself, as did practically all the female spectators of Rome those days, madly in love with him. This hero was, of course, Garibaldi.

Still Melena did not lack excitement, if that was what she sought. After the termination of her second marriage she maintained an envious salon of savants in Rome. No less than such well-known celebrities as Ferdinand Gregorovius, the historian, Franz Liszt, the pianist and composer, Odo Russell, nephew of Lord John Russell and British agent at the Vatican, Cardinal Bedini, Internunzio and Apostolic Delegate of the Holy See, Count Clement Alertz, the personal physician of Pope Gregory XVI, and numerous others honored her intellectual soirées.

But she dreamed of Garibaldi, even though she dared not meet him at the time he gallantly defended Rome. She yearned to learn more about his life. She would write more, become a professional writer, then, who knows, perhaps interview him for a prospective biography. Verily, she followed just that plan. Her second literary work was the novel *Memoiren eines spanischen Piasters* (The Memoirs of a Spanish Piaster) in two volumes which she published in Braunschweig in 1857. The time was now ripe; indeed she could wait no longer, so betook herself directly to Garibaldi's island home of Caprera off the northeast coast of Sardinia. It was the beginning of that twenty-year friendship which was to affect both of their lives. To this man whom Melena so loved, for her professions of love for him are numerous in her writings, she was to serve at various times as mistress, espionage agent, translator, literary agent, publicist and foster mother to his illegitimate daughter Anita, named after his inimitable first wife. He represented to her the ideal man because of his healthful, courageous and meaningful life. On the other hand, as became apparent before long, in several ways she reminded one of Anita; she too was courageous, enterprising, a good horsewoman and adjusted well to his rugged individualism. More than that, she became the main disseminator of the Garibaldian movement among Germanic peoples through her articles and translations of his historical novels.

This volume is not unique as another version of the Garibaldi memoirs; in fact, because Melena condensed parts of the manuscript in her German translation, the result at times appears as historically in error. Instead, as we have already pointed out, the special value of this volume rests in Books Three through Six, excepting Four, which was written by Garibaldi himself, although unpublished elsewhere. In these Books our authoress is able to convey to us her interpretations of the events from his return to Italy in 1848 to his visit to Romagna in 1859. Especially valuable is her narration of that trip which she made with Garibaldi (*The Pineta Ten Years Later*), just as is her description of the Garibaldi March to San Marino, his flight to safety and Anita's death, even though she was aided by the notes of two Garibaldians who took part, Major Gustav Hoffstetter (*Tagebuch aus Italien 1849*, Zürich, F. Schulthess, 1851) and Colonel Gioacchino Bonnet (*Lo Sbarco di Garibaldi a Magnavacca, episodio storico del 1849*, Bologna, Soc. Tip. Azzoguidi, 1887). Nevertheless with these latter two volumes being extremely rare, the authoress' incorporation of some of their facts makes her work keenly appreciated.

No less important is Melena's *Annex* in which she succinctly lays the background for the Garibaldian Uruguayan epic. In a very simplified manner no other single volume introduces our subject as well as she does here. For this reason it perhaps should be recommended to be read before Book One, that is, before reading Garibaldi's autobiography, especially if the reader is unfamiliar with the situation of Uruguay and those of its neighboring countries prior to the advent of Garibaldi there.

Melena's friendship with Garibaldi was obviously the most cherished part of her life. Besides her own admission on this point, the majority of her literary output attests to this fact. In addition to the *Denkwürdigkeiten*, her other publications which bear on Garibaldi are: *Blicke auf Calabrien und die Liparischen Inseln im Jahre 1860* (Views of Calabria and the Lipari Islands in the Year 1860), Hoffmann and Campe, 1861, which treats a bit of Garibaldi in Caserta; *Dr. E.G.F. Grisanowski, Mittheilungen aus seinem Leben und seinen Briefen* (Dr. E.G.F. Grisanowski, Information about His Life and Letters), Hannover, Schmorl and von Seefeld, 1890, contains a good description of Rome during the French siege of 1849, besides describing the admiration Grisanowski bore Garibaldi; *Une évasion de Caprera*, an article which appeared in the "Bibliothèque Universelle et Revue Suisse," Vol. 32, 1868, LXXIIIe, being the *Fuga da Caprera* written up by Garibaldi and given to Melena at Varignano Prison on 7 November 1867; it describes Garibaldi's escape from Caprera to the home of Mme Collins on the nearby island of La Maddalena. *Excursion à l'Ile de Caprera* (Excursion to the Island of Caprera), Genève, Pfeffer and Puky, 1862, describes the island and its "Cincinnatus"; *Garibaldi im Varignano 1862 und auf Caprera im October 1863* (Garibaldi in Varignano 1862 and on Caprera in October 1863), Leipzig, Verlag von Otto Wigand, 1864; *Garibaldi, Mittheilungen aus seinem Leben, nebst Briefen des Generals an die Verfasserin* (Garibaldi, Information on His Life, as well as Letters of the General to the Authoress), Hannover, Schmorl u. von Seefeld, 1884, being the first publication of 161 letters from the general, and his secretary Giovanni Basso, to Melena; they are all translated into German, while, unfortunately, many of the originals are no longer to be found; translations of this important work exist, even if rare, in: *Garibaldi, Souvenirs de sa Vie publique et privée, avec plus de cent lettres du Général à l'Auteur*, Paris, E. Leroux, 1885; *Garibaldi, Recollections of His Public and Private Life* . . . English version by Charles Edwardes, London, Trübner & Co., 1887; and *Garibaldi Aneddotico e Romantico*, translated by Antonio Monti, Milano, Sonzogno, 1944. *Hundert und ein Tag auf meinem Pferde und ein Ausflug nach der Insel Maddalena* (One Hundred and One Days on My Horse and An Excursion to the Island of La Maddalena), Hamburg, Hoffmann u. Campe, 1860, describes the authoress' horseback ride from Rome to Lucerne to visit her brother, then to Garibaldi on Caprera Island; *Recollections of General Garibaldi, or Travels from Rome to Lucerne, comprising a visit to the Mediterranean Isles of La Maddalena and Caprera*, London, Saunders & Otley, 1860 describes in Part II the first meeting with Garibaldi in 1857; and lastly, *Kako je Garibaldi utekas s Kaprera, U Speciji, 4 novembra 1867*

(How Garibaldi escaped from Caprera, La Spezia, 4 November 1867), "Vidov-dan," Belgrade, VII/1867, b. 252, str. [2], written in Serbo-Croatian.

The remainder of Melena's literary output is more aptly termed travelogues, or as she herself calls them, "esquisses de voyage," humanitarian appeals and some novels. Concerning her humanitarianism more needs to be said.

Towards the end of 1865, her relationship with Garibaldi now being confined to occasional correspondence concerning her work as translator and press agent for his historical novels, Melena transferred her domicile from Rome to the Island of Crete in the Mediterranean, where she became a benefactor of the village of Khalepa, near Canea. Here amidst vineyards and a rustic environment she acquired a comfortable home and lived tranquilly with Garibaldi's daughter Anita until 1875, alone after that until 1896, and always occupied herself with the welfare of the less fortunate, animal as well as human. Her sacrifices in time and money were considerable; she founded hospitals, schools and asylums, besides translating German school books into modern Greek, while also translating into German, Cretan folksongs and legends. Her *Kreta-Biene, oder kretische Volkslieder, Sagen, Liebes-, Denk- und Sittensprüche* (The Bee from Crete, or Cretan Folksongs, Legends, Sayings of Love, Thought and Customs), 1874, are an example.

Particularly well known became her efforts in behalf of the protection of animals; in Canea and Khalepa she maintained hospitals for horses, donkeys and other domestic animals. Homeless dogs were fed daily and she published numerous tracts against vivisection. Her *Notes sur la vivisection* were published by J. Carey in Geneva in 1876 and gained for her European recognition in the field; it is a poignant appeal, not without a keen understanding of the pseudo-scientific arguments put forth by the medical profession in its defense, against all forms of cruelty to animals imposed in the name of progress. How closely in these humane sentiments did she also resemble her hero Garibaldi!

At Khalepa she wrote too the volumes *Der junge Stelzentänzer, Episode während einer Reise durch die westlichen Pyrenäen* (The Young Stilt-Dancer, an episode during a trip through the western Pyrenees), 1865; *Die Insel Kreta unter der ottomanischen Verwaltung* (Crete under Ottoman Rule), 1867; *Von Rom nach Kreta, Reiseskizze* (From Rome to Crete, Travel Sketch), 1870; *Gemma, oder Tugend und Laster, Novelle* (Gemma, or Virtue and Vice, a short story), 1877; and *Erlebnisse und Beobachtungen eines mehr als 20-jährigen Aufenthalts auf Kreta* (Experiences and observations of a more than 20-year stay on Crete), 1892.

Oddly enough when Melena left Khalepa in 1896 to spend her last years in Ermatingen on Lake Constance in the German-speaking canton of Thurgau, Switzerland, she took up residence in the very guest house, the Adler (Eagle) Hotel, where Napoleon III had often been a guest too. In fact the Adler was, and still is, known as the *Auberge de Napoléon.*

The future Emperor of France lived from 1825 to 1837 in the nearby Arenenberg Castle with his mother, the former Queen Hortense of the Netherlands. He was a military student then under General William Henry Dufour, graduating with the rank of Captain of Artillery. But Napoleon III and Garibaldi were each other's most bitter enemy. Among what memories Melena must have lived there during those last three years until she died on 20 April 1899!

Before closing this brief introduction, especially for the benefit of those scholars who would complete their comprehension of this interesting and versatile character, it would not be amiss to cite Melena's principal critics. The first of these was Luisa Gasparini, whose research *(Un amore di Garibaldi, Correspondenza con Speranza von Schwartz,* Milano, Treves, 1932) in collaboration with the German Consul Kruger in Canea, produced the greater part of factual data on Melena's life. While corroborating the latter's serious contributions to the Garibaldian movement and its popularization aboard, Gasparini questions the validity of the so-called Garibaldi letters translated by Melena into German. As already pointed out, the whereabouts of the originals remain unknown, while some of the actions therein reported seem to be disproven by other sources. In addition, Melena's rather affected and ornate style of writing is definitely criticized as tendentious.

Similar criticism comes from Giacomo Curàtulo, the former director of the Risorgimento Museum of Milan and outstanding collector of the Garibaldi-Melena correspondence, in his volume entitled *Garibaldi e le Donne* (Garibaldi and Women), Roma, Impr. Polyglotte, 1913.

The third of these outstanding scholars was Antonio Monti whose translation of the *Mittheilungen,* already mentioned, concurs more or less with the Gasparini and Curàtulo opinions.

Of particular interest is the volume entitled *Garibaldi nella vita intima, memorie di Francesco Bideschini* (Garibaldi in his personal life, memoirs of Francesco Bideschini), Roma, Tip. Forense, 1907. The author was the brother-in-law of Menotti, Garibaldi's oldest son, who lived for months at a time with the Garibaldis on Caprera. Bideschini calls Melena "a liar and graphomaniac." In fact all the members of Garibaldi's family voiced similar opinions, as did Clelia, the Liberator's oldest surviving offspring, to this editor in 1955.

Menotti Garibaldi, after reading Melena's *Mitteilungen* on Garibaldi which had just been released in the English version, voiced bitter contempt of the work in a letter sent to "The Scotsman" of Edinburgh, which published it in its issue of 12 January 1887.

Thus it would seem that a final judgement of Melena lies with the reader, and possibly with further research.

A word concerning the footnotes appearing in the text of this volume; they are all starred and were written entirely by Elpis Melena. On the other hand, the Arabic numerals pertain to the editor's annotations which are to be found at the end of the volume.

And a final word of gratitude I should like to express to Dr. Janet Fyfe, professor at the University of Western Ontario, for reading the manuscript and making valuable suggestions.

February 1981   **Anthony P. Campanella**
                                           International Institute
                                           of Garibaldian Studies
                                           Sarasota, Florida

THE ORIGINAL FOREWORD
BY
ELPIS MELENA

> *"Garibaldi - la più potente, la più maravigliosa individualità che nei campi dell'azione vanti l'Italia e forse il mondo.*
> *Uomo veramente straardissario! Enigma insoluto e forse insolubile!"*
>
> **Boggio**

When in the late fall of the year 1853 I took a holiday in Sorrento, and when the lengthened evenings made the presence of this or that dear guest doubly precious, Captain D[odero], my friend of long standing, would come to visit me whenever his ship, the *Lombardo*, took him to Naples. We used to sit on the vine-clad terrace of my lodging under an arbor like Anacreon's, gazing at the magnificent spectacle of the Gulf, or listening to the distant sound of a guitar or mandolin. "Beatus ille qui procul negotiis etc., etc.," epicurean moments indeed, and far into the night I listened with pleasure to the tales of the grey-haired seaman, all the more so since he himself derived no little pleasure from leafing through the book of his turbulent life.

One evening the conversation turned towards Garibaldi, the freedom fighter who was at that time already famous as a result of his South American guerilla wars and his heroic defense of Rome. In Constantinople many years ago my friend had established close relations with him and everything he told me of the heroic Nizzard inspired me with such enthusiasm, for it stood in sharp contrast with the incredible tales which had come to my ears until then, especially in Germany, that I made Captain D. promise that he would ask Garibaldi to entrust to me for publication in Germany his interesting biography.

I realized however that the fulfillment of this bold promise was problematic, for who knew at that time in which Chinese or South American waters the disappointed and afflicted patriot was cruising? Yet two years later I acquired the desired manuscript. But this was of little use to me, for it ceased with the year 1848, just when Garibaldi's activities in Europe were beginning to attract attention. During the following two years I spared no pains to persuade the General directly, and indirectly, to complete his biography. But in vain! In the meantime he settled as a true Cincinnatus on the previously uninhabited Island of Caprera, off the northern coast of Sardinia. Now for me to give up my project, which could have very well brought to that exiled man well-merited renown in Germany, in as far as my modest contributions permitted, would have been disloyal. Furthermore it was against my own love of truth and justice. Hence I took advantage of his proximity and in the fall of the year 1857 went to Caprera to win over the unyielding hero to my purpose.

I had hardly talked to him for half an hour when I sensed that this move was also doomed. Garibaldi confessed with his customary frankness that he could write nothing because he was devoting himself completely to the cultivation of his property, and in addition, did not wish to compromise anybody.

The great interest of meeting him personally did not however lessen the disappointment which I felt for my frustrated hopes. On the contrary, I so admired his patriarchal hospitality, his warmth as a father of a family, the gentle dignity of his whole being, the presentation of his humane policy, his unselfish hopes for Italy, all expressed in his melodious voice, that I was convinced more than ever that fate had destined this man to a high position and was only reserving for him many Herculean tasks to come. Thus worthier to me than ever seemed the self-appointed role to do some good in the field of literature for this man, quasi outlawed by the world, and to awaken such recognition as was his due.

A second visit I made to Caprera in the summer of the year 1858, upon his invitation, granted me many more fine glimpses into the great soul of this hero. I still found Garibaldi unwilling to pick up the threads of his biography and it was quite apparent, in fact more than ever, that he was engrossed in the growth of his plantings and in the general cultivation of his property. Despite this, during one of his rest periods I succeeded in eliciting from him a narrative, even if sketchy, of his travels and experiences from the year 1849, when he again left Europe, until he settled in Caprera in the year 1855, all of which I jotted down in his presence and used in the following pages. Furthermore the General told me that for further information I could use Hoffstetter's *Tagebuch aus Italien* [Diary from Italy], Ruggieri's *Narrazione* of his retreat and the *Storia della Rivoluzione Romana* of a Calabrian exile named Biagio da Strongoli as reliable additional sources, if I was anxious to publish his "povera vita" in Germany.

The year 1859, which brought to fruition tremendous political events, put an end to the retreat into the country and the rural occupations of the modern Cincinnatus. In January, instead of accompanying him, his children and his friend Nino Bixio to South America, as previously arranged, I met Garibaldi in Turin, where Victor Emanuel had called him. There, and in fact immediately before the outbreak of the glorious Italian war of liberation, I saw the noble warrior again, irradiated by joyous confidence and hopeful of victory, but unfortunately in lamentable health. He was almost paralyzed by acute rheumatism. On the day of his departure for the front, as I, the Marchesa Pallavicini Trivulzio and many other enthusiastic noblewomen of Turin escorted the brave leader of the *Cacciatori delle Alpi* to the railroad station, he still suffered so much in his left knee that he had to lie down on the waiting room sofa. Strangely enough, the war seemed to have brought about a miracle cure in him, for when in the following September I saw the hero again in Ravenna, crowned with new glory and new victories, all trace of his disease had disappeared.

It was not by chance that I found myself in the ancient metropolis of the exarchate. The General, anxious to gather around him for some time his daughter and a couple from Nizza, with whom he was on very friendly terms and to whom he had entrusted the lovely Teresa, had suggested to me that I join these good people. The twelve days which I spent with Garibaldi and his group during the trip through Romagna will certainly remain until my dying hour the most interesting period of my life, just as the episode of the pineta will perhaps also appear to the reader as the most gratifying chapter of this book.

Late in October of the same year I met the General once again, this time in Bologna. I cannot remember ever having seen him in better spirits; for hours he read to me from Ugo Foscolo, his favorite poet, then asked me to write down* a small poem which he composed many years ago in South America, and in parting even promised to complete his biography for me.

Scarcely had I arrived in Rome when Garibaldi informed me that he had retired from military service, that he wanted to devote his time to the completion of his biography, and for this reason asked me to send back to him his Italian manuscript which was in my possession, since he was hoping soon to provide me with something more complete. However, I was no little surprised to find out soon after fulfilling his request that he had in turn given the manuscript to Monsieur Alexandre Dumas in Genoa!

I mention this disloyalty as a fact which offended me deeply and which I do not wish to judge; nor can I explain it. Surely he who dedicates himself to the liberation of Sicily and carries deep in his breast the

---

*I give it to the reader at the end of the second volume, exactly as it came from Garibaldi's lips.

"unification of Italy" as the aim of his life, can claim a lenient judgement, even if, temporarily deluded, he permits himself to be misled into preferring the bombastic bungling and encomiums of the cleverest of French novelists to the unadorned disclosure of pure truth. Nor had I intended in any way to use Garibaldi's biography as the basis for a novel with which to rival Alexandre Dumas. The absolute truth is the only merit which I claim for the following pages, and these I offer to the reader in the hope that, despite other literary shortcomings, they will find their way to the better part of the public. Nor by publishing this biography does any pretention on my part make me believe that I am enriching literature with a well-written work. Instead I am using these means to further a noble humane purpose and to obtain well-earned recognition for an often defamed person.

Agreeing fully with Buffon's saying "le style c'est l'homme," I did not dare take the words out of the hero's mouth and let *him* tell the story, inasmuch as the material which he entrusted to me was sufficient, limiting myself to paraphrasing and to making clear to the reader certain obscure passages in the Italian original. May he not hold me responsible for errors in the spelling of foreign names and words, nor for many other literary offenses. What did not flow from Garibaldi's pen I have taken partly from reliable sources which he recommended to me, and partly from my own opinion and experiences.

I am still hopeful that Garibaldi will sooner or later enable me to complete these small volumes with a third one. But since these pages become more important with each passing day, revealing additional interesting details concerning this great warrior who, while all of Europe watches eagerly, is filling the finest pages of Italian history, I will no longer deprive the German public of them.

Deliberately have I initiated the reader into all the details of the publication of these pages in order to convince him that they fall far short of what I had hoped to provide, and for this I ask his indulgence. Yet, as even the hostile Mazzini proclaimed publicly: "Everything concerning such a man is worthy and precious."

Rome, June 1, 1860   **Elpis Melena**

BOOK ONE

GARIBALDI'S AUTOBIOGRAPHY

From his Birth until the Year 1848

Chapter I

My Parents

I cannot begin the story of my life without thinking of my good parents, whose excellent character and loving ways so greatly influenced my education and the development of my natural faculties.

My father, son of a sailor, and himself a sailor from early age, was named Dominic Garibaldi and came from Chiavari. Of course he did not have the knowledge which people of his station have nowadays, but he possessed that practical ability which is found in people who have come up from below. In his youth he sailed on ships of my grandfather, later he commanded his own vessels. His fortune was subjected to numerous changes, and he might have procured for us a richer heritage, I often heard him say.

However, I am most grateful to him for what he gave me and I am convinced that he did not spare anything which he thought necessary for my education, even in those times when the fulfillment of his fatherly obligations were not a small burden, considering his modest means. If he did not have me instructed in gymnastics, fencing and other bodily exercises, it was not so much his fault as that of the times, when youths, (thanks to the blackcoats), were invariably trained to become either priests or monks, instead of becoming strong citizens capable of serving their unhappy fatherland in some useful undertaking. Perhaps this omission was also due to the fervent love my father bore his children, precluding in this manner their exposure to the vicissitudes and dangers of military careers.

My mother could have been a model for all mothers. I say this with pride, and feel that I need not explain further. It has been a very great sorrow for me that throughout my life I was not able to cheer up her last days, especially when I recall often having made her life bitter and sorrowful as a result of the uncertainties of my destiny. Perhaps the love which she bore me was too great. Yet, was it not to this same motherly love and influence, her compassion for every unhappy and needy person, that I owe my feeling of patriotism? Were not these same feelings those

3

which enabled me to gain the confidence and sympathy of my honest, even if unhappy, countrymen? I am not superstitious, but in the gravest moments of my life, when I was spared unharmed from being engulfed by the ocean waves,[1] or remained unscathed amidst the hail of bullets on the battlefield, I saw my loving mother on bended knee and bowed head before the throne of the Almighty appealing for the life of the one to whom she had given birth. And I believed in the efficacy of her prayers.

Chapter II

The Early Years of My Youth

I was born in Nizza[2] on July 4, 1807. My early years passed like those of most children, with merry games and childish sorrows, with laughter and tears. Devoted more to pleasure than to serious occupation, I unfortunately did not profit enough from the care which my parents devoted to my education.

Furthermore my youth contains nothing extraordinary. It is certain that I was good-hearted; one day when I had caught a cricket in the fields and on taking him home had torn a leg from the poor beast by mistake, I was so upset that I locked myself in my room and wept bitterly for hours.

Another time, while accompanying my cousin on a hunt in the department of Var, I sat on the edge of a deep ditch in which hemp was put to soak and where I saw a woman washing clothes. She tripped and fell and I, although a mere lad, rushed to save her. And in every such instance, when it was a question of helping a fellow man, I was never idle, even at the risk of my own life.

Among my teachers I name Padre Giaume[3] and Signor Arena, whom I shall always remember kindly. Of course I learned little from the former, because at that time I thought more of pranks than of studies; and still I regret having neglected the English language totally, all the more so, since in later life, where chance brought me in contact with Englishmen, I often felt this lack.

The little I know I owe to the excellent Signor Arena. I am especially indebted to him because, even though late in my education, he initiated me into the beauties of my native tongue by reading Roman history. The lack of knowledge of our native language and of the conditions surrounding us are only too common in Italy, and especially in Nizza, where I was born. The nearness and the influence of the French, and even more the neglect into which our rulers let the land fall, permits only few people to know the facts and to love Italian nationality.

In addition to Padre Arena, I am also grateful to the inspiration of my older brother Angelo,[4] who from America warmly recommended to me the study of our beautiful language.

I close this first section of my life with a short description of an incident which may be termed the first taste of my later adventures. Tired of school and my regimented way of living, I suggested one day to some boys of my age that we flee to Genoa. No sooner had I made the suggestion than we were on our way. We got into a boat, took some food and gear on board for sailing and fishing, then headed eastwards. We had already reached Monaco, when a seaman, whom my good father had sent after us, caught up with our boat and brought us back home, thoroughly ashamed. A priest had betrayed us.

Chapter III

My First Voyages

How youth beautifies everything! How beautiful you were, oh *Costanza,* on which I was first to plow the Mediterranean and the Pontus![5] Your broad sides, your graceful masts, your clean deck and woman's bust on the bowsprit shall always remain engraved in my memory. How gracefully your smart sailors, the elite of the undaunted Ligurians, swarmed over your deck. With what joy I crowded into the stern of the ship in order to listen to their folksongs and melodious choruses. They sang of love, and they touched and intoxicated me, for I was then in love. But they would have delighted and edified me more, if they had sung of their native land, of Italy. But who had ever taught them to be patriotic, to be Italians? Who had ever spoken to them of the existence of an Italy, a common fatherland, waiting for revenge and liberation? Oh, we grew up like Jews,[6] in the illusion that gold is the only compensation for all suffering, the only goal in life.

My father had destined me for a safe and peaceful career. He wished I would become a lawyer, priest or physician, but he yielded to my longing, my unrelenting hankering for an adventurous life, and finally permitted me to go to sea. My grieving mother prepared the necessary items for my voyage, and I sailed on the brigantine *Costanza,* whose captain was Angelo Pesante.

Pesante was the best sea captain I ever knew. If our naval fleet had been permitted to develop according to the natural conditions of our country, Pesante would have commanded one of the first ships of the line, and it could not have been better commanded. He never had to deal with a navy, but his seamanlike and creative ability was proven on all occasions, so that he would have proved himself useful and meritorious of the glory of the fatherland on the three-master, just as he had been on the simple bark.

My first voyage was to Odessa. It was like other trips of this type, and it would be superfluous to give a description of it today.

My second trip was to Rome, in company of my father, on board his own tartan *Santa Reparata*. To Rome! to the capital of the world! the capital of a world of ruins and of relics of the past, today the capital of a sect, which formerly freed slaves and ennobled men, contained true priests, teachers and guardians of human rights — but alas, today a sect which in its degeneration is the greatest scourge of our country and which it has sold shamefully to the foreigner.

But no! Rome, which my youthful mind imagined, was not that scourge of Italy. It was the Rome of the future, it was the *eternal* city, in which was concentrated everything present, past and future. At that time Rome became dear to me above all else, and I honored it with the total fire of my soul, and even in exile, far from being extinguished, this love burned all the more abroad. Often, very often in fact, years later I begged the Almighty one further meeting with that orphaned city. For me Rome is Italy, because I see Italy only in the union of its mutilated members. And Rome is the symbol of Italian unity, whatever way you look at it.

I made a few further trips with my father. Then I accompanied captain Giuseppe Gervino on the brigantine *Enea* to Cagliari. On that voyage I was an eyewitness of a terrible shipwreck, which I shall always remember. On the way home from Cagliari we had reached Cape Noli, along with several other vessels, among which was a Catalan felucca. The seas were high, brought on by several days of a violent southeaster, and as the latter increased in intensity we were obliged to abandon our journey to Genoa and repair to Vado. During all this the felucca appeared to be holding its own gallantly, so well in fact, that our sailors had almost preferred to be aboard her. But the situation did not last. A dreadful wave overturned the vessel as we looked on hopelessly and sorrowfully. A few moments later a few of the unfortunates appeared standing on the capsized hulk, stretching out their arms forlornly to us, but only to disappear forever an instant later engulfed by a second terrible wave. All of this took place on our right where it was impossible to come to the rescue of the momentary survivors. The barks behind us were also powerless to help; and without help, nine people, all members of the same family, found their death in the sea. On board our ship tears flowed, even though they dried quickly as we realized what danger we still faced. Fortunately however, our vessel and the others escaped a similar fate and reached port safely.

From Vado we sailed to Genoa, then to Nizza, from which port I made several other trips to the Near East on board different ships for the

Garibaldi's

Denkwürdigkeiten

nach

handschriftlichen Aufzeichnungen desselben,
und nach authentischen Quellen

bearbeitet und herausgegeben

von

Elpis Melena.

Erster Band.

Mit Garibaldi's Portrait.

Hamburg.

Hoffmann und Campe.

1861.

1. Facsimile of the title page of the Denkwürdigkeiten

7

firm Gioan. During these trips we were seized and plundered by pirates three times, twice during the same trip, so that the last pirates hardly found anything worth taking.[7]

On one trip I had to remain behind sick in Constantinople. As my ship, the brigantine *Cortese* commanded by Carlo Semeria,[8] sailed away, I realized that I was in serious circumstances, especially since my illness persisted for some time. But it is not in my nature to lose courage in worries and danger; in fact, I almost always have been lucky enough to meet good people who took an interest in me. I shall never forget among these Signora Luigia Sauvaigo[9] of Nizza, one of those women whom I have often considered, (regardless of whatever some men may think), to be the most perfect creatures of creation. As a mother and wife she gave happiness to her excellent husband and her charming children, whom she educated with unsurpassable care.

The war which had broken out at that time between the Porte and Russia contributed to lengthen my stay in the Turkish capital. I earned my living by giving lessons. Introduced by a Dr. Diego to the widow Timoni, I came to her as a tutor for her three sons and where I remained several months.

Finally I went to sea again and sailed on the brigantine *Nostra Signora delle Grazie*. This ship was the first I commanded as captain, taking her to Port-Mahon,[10] Gibraltar and later back to Constantinople.

I will skip over the details incurred during my last trips to the Levant, since nothing of importance occurred on them. I should only mention some acquaintances I made, inasmuch as they exerted a decisive influence on my life.

Chapter IV

Young Italy

From earliest youth I was an enthusiastic admirer of Italy and my most ardent wish was to be initiated into the secrets of her political rebirth, as well as into all books and writings which dealt with Italian freedom, seeking at the same time men who were devoted to serve her. The first one who gave me some information about the course of our patriotic cause was a young Ligurian[11] whom I met on a trip to Taganrog. Truly Columbus himself could not have found greater satisfaction in the discovery of America than I, when it was granted to me to find a man whose mind was turned towards freeing the country, and who assured me that thousands of others were also working on the liberation. From that moment on, my life had a purpose. I became completely absorbed in the national effort, although I felt that it had always been part of me.

On another trip I made aboard the *Clorinde*, I met a number of St. Simonists whom Emile Barrault was taking to Constantinople. I approached the leader, introducing myself as an Italian patriot, and was initiated by him into the ideas of the sect of St. Simonists,[12] who had until then been unknown to me. The conversations with Barrault were not without influence on my ideas, so that the cosmopolitan theories of St. Simonism swept away the one-sided view of my patriotism, and led my gaze from nationality towards humanity.

In 1833 I returned from the Orient to Marseille.

At that time the insurrections[13] of upper and middle Italy had just been betrayed to the governments. Spies had sneaked in among the insurrectionists, and the Piedmont police was working full time. Many people were arrested, while military tribunals condemned 76 conspirators to heavy punishment and 12 death sentences were carried out. But the blood of the martyrs aroused only feelings of revenge, and Mazzini[14] quickly decided to risk a new attempt at insurrection.

The expedition undertaken from Switzerland into Savoy[15] is already known, as well as its failure, thanks to the incompetence, or cowardice, of Ramorino. I had been given a part in the movement which was to follow this expedition. In Marseille I had become friendly with a person named Covi, who introduced me to Mazzini and had announced that I could be relied upon. I joined the Piedmontese Navy as a seaman first class on the frigate *Eurydice*. My task[16] was to proselytize among the crew and if the movement should succeed, I, along with my companions, were to take over the frigate and put it at the disposal of the Republicans.

My propaganda on the *Eurydice* was successful, but despite my burning eagerness, the operations assigned to me did not suffice. In the meantime I found out that in the harbor of Genoa, where we were anchored, an insurrection was about to take place and that the police barracks on Sarzana Square were to be seized. Consequently I left the taking over of the frigate to my companions, put to sea in a boat at the house where the revolt was to start, and landed at the customs. From there I rushed to Sarzana Square.

I waited about an hour, but in vain; there was no gathering of people. Then I heard that the affair had failed, that arrests had been made, and that the Republicans had fled. Thus, since I had joined the Sardinian Navy only in order to further the Republican cause, I thought it useless to return aboard my frigate. Instead I began to ponder my own flight to safety, especially as troops approached and began to encircle the Square. There was no time to lose.

I fled into a fruit shop and confessed my difficult situation to the owner. The excellent woman [17] did not hesitate. She hid me in an installation in the rear, got me some peasant's clothes, and at seven in the evening of February 5, 1834 I left the city of Genoa via the Lanterna Gate disguised as a farmer, proscribed.

9

Without knowing the way, I turned towards the mountains. Luckily I managed to escape through gardens and over walls, then taking Cassiopea as my guiding star I made my way into the mountains of Sestri. After a march of 10 days, or rather of 10 nights, I reached Nizza. Here I went straight to the house of my aunt and begged her to inform my mother of my arrival, lest she become unduly frightened. I rested a day in Nizza and the following night set off with two friends, Joseph Jauno and Angelo Gustavini. When we came to the Var River we found it swollen by continued rains. My friends remained behind while I swam across to safety.

Now confidently I approached a customs post, told the soldiers my name and why I left Genoa. To my dismay they immediately proclaimed me their prisoner and was placed in custody until further instructions came from Paris. Eventually I was taken to Grasse and from there to Draguignan. In the latter place I escaped from my captors. It happened as I was being led to a room on the first floor[18] where there was a window looking out onto a garden, and as I approached the window and noticed that it was open, I jumped out. The soldiers however, in order to catch me, preferred going down the long way via the staircase. By that time I had reached the street and scurried into the mountains.

I decided to head for Marseille although I had no idea of the route to take. Nevertheless being a sailor, I orientated myself by means of the stars. On the way I came to a village, whose name I no longer recall, and entered an inn and asked for some food. The table was being laid for supper and the young innkeeper and his wife asked me to join them. I readily accepted, found the food and wine good, the fire warm and cozy, my hosts apparently trustful so that I felt safe enough to relate to them my flight and the reasons which motivated it.

To my astonishment the face of the innkeeper darkened as I spoke, so much so, that I enquired about his uneasiness. In brief he explained that he was obliged to arrest me, upon which I laughed, so as to show him that I did not take his threat seriously. Also I was not for a moment afraid, being one against one. "Ah," I finally asked calmly, "you want to arrest me? Very well, I guess after dinner there will be plenty of time for that. Allow me to finish my meal, then I shall pay you double." With that I rattled the coins in my pocket, then continued eating, without appearing worried in the least.

But soon I observed that the innkeeper would have no lack of helpers to secure my arrest. Young people from the village came in, good friends of the innkeeper who came to play cards, drink and sing. The innkeeper now merely kept an eye on me and spoke no more of arrest, obviously relying upon these fellows if necessary, since there must have been at least 10 of them.

A good idea saved me. As one of the drinking fellows finished singing and while the resultant bravos subsided, I quickly raised my glass and exclaimed: "Let me sing also," and I began to sing Beranger's *God of*

Good People.[19] I ascribe it not to my passable tenor voice, but to the verses of Beranger, the popularity of the poet, the fraternal spirit of the refrain, and perhaps the pleasant manner in which I sang, that all the audience was carried away. In fact I was obliged to repeat two or three stanzas; then the company finally embraced me and shouted: "Long live Beranger! Long live France! Long live Italy!"

After that there was no more talk of arresting me. My host ignored the matter completely. Instead for the remainder of the entire night we sang, played and drank. At daybreak the whole of that pleasant company offered to accompany me and we parted only after a walk of several hours.

During this journey I also saw for the first time my name in print. It was my death sentence published in the newspaper *Le Peuple souverain* of Marseille.

Chapter V

Wanderings

After living a few months in Marseille in idleness under the assumed name of Pane, I was accepted by captain Francesco Gazan and embarked again aboard the ship *Unione* as second in command.

One evening as I had just dressed up to go ashore, I was suddenly aroused by a noise in the water and rushed, followed by the captain, on deck. An unfortunate chap was drowning under the stern of our ship. I jumped into the water, and in sight of a cheering crowd, succeeded in rescuing the young Frenchman from the water and from premature death. The saved one was a fourteen-year-old boy named Joseph Rambaud.[20] His mother was so grateful that her tears wet my cheeks, while the felicitous blessing of the whole family was bestowed upon me. In the port of Smyrna a few years previous I was equally fortunate in saving my friend Claudio Terese.

I pass over the trips which I made aboard the *Unione* to the Black Sea, another later aboard a frigate of war built for the Bey of Tunis from Marseille to Tunis, and finally one aboard a brigantine from Nantes under a Captain Beauregard in a voyage from Marseille to Rio Janeiro. I stopped for the last time in Marseille when I returned from Tunis on a Tunisian brig of war. The city was at that time infested with cholera which brought terrible devastations. Ambulances were set up and many people volunteered their services. I also signed up with one of them, occupying myself for the few days of my stay in Marseille[21] with watching and taking care of cholera patients every night.

11

On arriving in Rio Janeiro I did not have much time to look for friends. Still without seeking I found one. Rossetti, whom I had never seen before, met me on the *Largo do Passo*; our gaze met, and it seemed as if it were not for the first time. We smiled at each other, and we became brothers, inseparably and for life! I mention elsewhere the warm loving soul of this individual, but I wonder whether I shall die without having been lucky enough to plant a cross in the soil of America where the bones of that noblest and warmest friend of my country lie.

After spending some months in idleness, we decided to begin a trading business. But neither Rossetti nor I seemed born traders. So soon tired of this undertaking, we decided to accept a proposal of Zambeccari, who was secretary to Bento Gonçalves,[22] President of the Republic of Rio Grande. The secretary, as well as the President, were Brazilian prisoners of war and imprisoned in Santa Cruz, a fort at the entrance of the harbor of Rio. Zambeccari introduced us to the President, and he gave us letters of marque against Brazil. We outfitted for fighting a small vessel of about 30 tons, the *Mazzini*, with which we had plied our coast-wide trade, and went to sea.

Chapter VI

In the Service of the Republic of Rio Grande

Under the banner of freedom on the wide open ocean with 16 brave companions I challenged an empire, I alone, the only representative of the Republic of Rio Grande, flew her flag from my mast!

Off Isola Grande we came across a brig loaded with coffee and overpowered her. The *Mazzini* was set afire,[23] since there was no pilot aboard her who could have led her further in the open sea. Not all my companions were like Rossetti, of pure and gentle manners; indeed, some of them had an exterior which did not inspire much confidence. Then, in order to frighten our innocent enemy, they had made themselves look especially wild and cruel, although on my part, I did everything possible to lessen the fright of our prisoners.

In boarding the brig from our barque, one of the captured passengers, a Brazilian, approached me imploringly and offered me three valuable diamonds in a little box. I refused them, and ordered immediately that the captive crew and passengers were not to be touched. This procedure I followed on similar occasions later and have always suc-

12

ceeded in having my commands observed. The passengers and crew were taken ashore north of Cape Itapecoria. We gave them the boat of the *Luisa,* our captured brig, and permitted them to take along not only their personal effects but also foodstuffs of their own choosing.

We steered south and arrived safely at the Rio de la Plata in the harbor of Maldonado, where the friendly reception by the authorities and the population augured well. Rossetti went to Montevideo to sell the captured freight and improve our finances accordingly, while I remained behind alone for about eight days. These were as many feast days for me and my crew. On the eighth day however, I had to put an end to the festivities, lest the end become tragic, the local police become less complacent and I less lucky.

Oribe, the President of the Republic of Montevideo, gave the highest official in Maldonado the command to arrest me and to capture my brig. But that official was a friendly man; he let me know that not only the flag of Rio Grande was not recognized, contrary to my instructions, but that even a formal order for our arrest had already been issued. Thus I had to hoist sails again and, in spite of a heavy storm, I promised to depart that very night.

Before that, however, I set a money matter in order. I had sold some bags of coffee from the freight of the captured ship to a merchant in Maldonado, in order to buy food. Until now I had not received the money, and it was reasonably sure that in case of departure I would never get it. Towards nine o'clock at night I took my pistols, wrapped my cloak around me, had myself put ashore and walked to the house of the dilatory payer. The merchant was standing in the doorway relaxing from the stress of the day in the moonlight. He recognized me from afar, made signals with his hand to indicate that I was in danger and entreated me to rush back to my ship. I took no notice of his gestures and words, approached him directly, put my pistol to his breast and merely said: "My money." He wanted to explain and gave excuses. When I insisted with the simple request: "My money," he asked me to step into the house and counted out the 2000 patagones which he owed me. With the money well under my cloak, I returned aboard the brig.[24]

From an acquaintance I found out that word about the outcome of Rossetti's deals in Montevideo would reach me at Punta de Jesús María. Later we sailed; it was twelve midnight. Heading up the La Plata River, we sailed without a fixed destination. After a burdensome trip and only with difficulty avoiding being shipwrecked off Piedras Negras, because the compass went out of order due to its proximity to the rifles and had led us almost into the cliffs, we finally reached Punta (or Point) de Jesús María, but unfortunately without finding the desired news. Yet our food was finished and we had no boat with which to land. Still the hunger of twelve men had to be appeased.

One day although we were four miles from land we clearly spotted a house on the shore. Immediately I decided to reach land on a plank[25] and to bring back food at any price. The winds were blowing from the pampas, making it difficult for one to approach the coast and land. Hence we brought the vessel as close as possible to the shore and cast a double anchor for greater safety.

A raft was then improvised from a table and with a sailor by name of Maurizio Garibaldi we climbed onto it; in this manner we could not sail, but rolled and swayed in the surf of those inhospitable shores. In spite of this, we arrived safely, pulled our half-wrecked craft ashore and leaving Maurizio as guardian, I set off alone for the sighted dwelling.

The sight which confronted me for the first time is worth describing. The vast and rolling fields of the east shore of the Uruguay River (and precisely because of the location on the river, which flows by on the west, this region is called the Banda Oriental) present a new and truly astonishing sight to the European, especially the Italian, who grows up in a country where every handful of earth is covered with houses, hedges, fields and works of the human hand. In Uruguay there is nothing of all that. The creole leaves the surface of that country in the same condition in which the natives, previously exterminated by the Spaniards, left it to him. The plain is covered with gigantic grass, and only on the shores of the river's arroyo do wooded hills arise. The horse, the bull, the gazelle and the ostrich are the only inhabitants of that wilderness. Only rarely does man appear, the *gaucho,* who shows himself like the centaur, in order to remind the savage animal life of his superiority. It happens that the warlike stallion, or the angry bull, dares to cross the path of the intruder to affirmatively express to him his anger and contempt. Instead in my unhappy country I have seen how hundreds let themselves be enslaved and kicked by one single German appearing in their midst. Yes, I even saw how they hid their displeasure, afraid to compromise themselves! O God! why do you allow so much cowardice among your creatures! Is not that stallion of the pampas a thousand times more beautiful and noble?[26] His lips never felt the cold hateful steel of a bit and his shiny back is never burdened by the weight of a rider as he scampers over the fields, proudly escaping the yoke of men, neighing to the scattered mares and surpassing the wind in lightness and speed. A true sultan of the desert, he audaciously chooses the most beautiful of odaliscs without the intermediary of eunuchs, those most wretched of creatures.

Who can imagine the feelings in the breast of our twenty-five-year-old[27] European in midst of that wild nature, which for the first time unfolded her rich scenery before his eyes? The bull and the horse, unaccustomed to seeing pedestrians, stood still as stone at first sight and then appeared puzzled with curiosity and astonishment. Subsequently, perhaps in contempt of the smallness of their beings, they encircled the strangers with joking gestures. The horse never wounds, but you cannot always trust the bull. The gazelle and the ostrich fled at the sight of us with the speed of a horse, then stood still on some height, after turning around suddenly to check their supposed enemy.

Fortunately the battle front was far away from these regions at the time, and the animal world could display itself undisturbed in all its diversity.

Chapter VII

An Idyll and a Battle

In the meanwhile I reached the *estancia,* the isolated dwelling on the shore which we had seen. There was nobody at home except a woman, the wife of the *capitaz,* or overseer of the *estancia,* and since he had gone out to catch a bullock, I had to wait. Also it was late and in any case, I would not have been able to bring anything aboard the ship until next morning.

There are moments in life which dominate the imagination and which remain forever in one's memory. Here I met in that wilderness the wife of a half-savage man, at least from his external appearance, while in his young spouse I discovered a well-bred lady, in fact, a poetess! At the age at which I was then, one likes to emphasize the poetic aspect of every situation and in my place many a young man might have verily believed that he was dreaming. When I had exhausted the small stock of Spanish words of which I disposed, and the faltering conversation became progressively difficult, my friendly hostess pulled out a book and began, to my astonishment, to speak Italian. They were the poems of Quintana,[28] which not only afforded us the opportunity to speak at length about poetry, but also encouraged my hostess to recite some of her own poems, in which I found much that was beautiful and well-done.

I enjoyed the company of my gracious hostess until the return of her husband, a man, as we have said, of rough exterior yet with not too-unpolished manners, who promised to get me a *rez,* that is, a slaughtered bullock, the next morning. And thus it happened. At daybreak I took leave of my interesting poetess of the pampas and returned to the place where Maurizio was waiting for me. He had spent the night not without worrying about me; he knew those regions better than I and was well aware that there existed also tigers and other beasts, more harmful than either the horse or bull.

Soon the *capitaz* appeared leading a bullock on a lasso; within a few minutes, so great is the skill of these people in such bloody doings, it was slaughtered, skinned and cut up. Now it was the problem of transporting the butchered bullock from the shore to the ship through an agitated line of breakers at least 1000 feet long. Quickly Maurizio and I set about our task. Two empty barrels, which I forgot to mention in the previous description of our landing, were fastened on the right and left sides of the gastronomical vehicle. With great care the quarters of the bullock were tied to a board,[29] which served at the same time as a mast, while holding the meat above the water.

Each of us held a stick in his hand which was to serve simultaneously as oar and rudder, and stripped of clothing as much as possible, we found ourselves above the hips in water when the waves lifted up the raft. We were off!

We were pleased with this rather clever means of boating, in fact, proud to brave such danger. The American shouted encouragement and in view of our watching companions, who probably prayed more fervently for the safety of the meat than for us, we braved the enormous breakers. In the beginning it went quite well; but as we reached the most distant and highest breakers, and although we were several times completely submerged by them, we somehow managed to overcome them. Then hardly had we succeeded when we fell prey to a bigger and much more serious danger; a strong current suddenly carried us off towards the south, removing us forcibly ever further from our ship. There was no other recourse except for the brig to chase after us under full sail, until she was near enough to throw us a line. After that we were saved and with us all our provisions of meat, which our starving companions attacked with a voracious appetite.

The next day, as our vessel was swaying aimlessly to and fro, two barks finally appeared from Jesús María Bay, which at first we took to be friendly. But since they did not fly the prearranged signal, a red flag, I wondered whether it was not advisable to hoist sails and wait for them with weapons in hand. This precautionary measure was in no way superfluous, since the larger of the vessels upon approaching us demanded that we surrender in the name of the government of Montevideo. First we saw only three sailors aboard the bark, but when only a few feet separated us from them, thirty other armed fellows suddenly appeared on deck. Our situation was pretty nigh hopeless. At once I ordered the hoisting of the sails, and at that very moment a volley was fired at us, depriving me of one of my bravest Italian companions, Fiorentino by name. I reached for a rifle, which I had brought up from the stores below, and ordered fire. A stubborn battle ensued. The *lancione,*[30] that is the name of this type of vessel in South America, had come alongside our starboard side and some of the enemy was already climbing aboard our ship by grabbing hold of our rigging. A few shots and saber strokes however, soon drove them off. All this happened in a few minutes.

Soon there was panic among my crew, unaccustomed as they were to such fighting. My command to hoist the sails had not been carried out, even though some of the men pulled the halyards on the port side upon my command, while nobody did so on the starboard side, and the whole operation was in vain. Fiorentino, who observed the command, and who was at the rudder, rushed to starboard to complete the manoeuvre, when suddenly an onrushing bullet rendered him a corpse.

Now no one was steering, so I grabbed the rudder, happening to be there firing my rifle, but at that moment I was hit in the neck by an enemy bullet and fell unconscious. The remainder of the battle, which continued for about another hour, was fought mainly by my devoted aid Luigi Carniglia, by the pilot Pasquale Lodola and by the seamen Maurizio Garibaldi and Giovanni Lamberti, two Maltese. Our prisoners and the negroes, five in number, hid themselves in the hold. I could not move, and although conscious again soon after, remained unable to fight. Finally we succeeded in getting rid of the enemy with a continuous fire and could tack away to seek asylum in the center of the current.

One can readily imagine my condition during those critical hours. Mortally wounded and unable to move, without help or advice of an aid who knew the land or the waters, I could only cast my dying glances upon our ship's chart, which had been brought to me in order that I might indicate a destination for our journey and course to follow. I pointed to Santa Fe on the Paraná River, simply because the name seemed to me to be printed in larger characters. None of us had ever navigated in that river except Maurizio, who once before had been there. The men, with exception of the Italians, let this be mentioned for the sake of the truth, were overwhelmed with fear and confusion at the sight of my dangerous condition and Fiorentino's body. They were so afraid of being captured and treated as corsairs; consequently they took the first opportunity to desert.

The remains of the unfortunate Fiorentino, after the customary ceremony aboard, were dumped into the river on the second day, since it had been impossible to land anywhere. I must confess that this burial at sea, which at that moment might have happened to me as well, made me feel somewhat uneasy, and I even confessed as much to my loyal Luigi. I remember quoting to my incomparable companion, among other beautiful phrases, these lines from Ugo Foscolo:[31]

Un sasso che distingua le mie dalle infinite ossa
Che in terra ed in mar semina morte.
[May a stone distinguish my bones from those innumerable ones
Which death strews over the earth and in the sea.]

With tears my good friend promised not to bury me in the waves. Who knows whether he would have been able to keep his promise and whether my body would not have, after all, served as food for some beasts of the River Plata?

In that case I would never have seen Italy again; I would never have fought for my country, never have fulfilled the greatest wish of my life. Still the humiliation would have also been spared me of seeing Italy fall back into shame and slavery.

Who would have told good Luigi at that time that a year later he would be engulfed by furious breakers and that I would search in vain for his body in order to bury him in foreign soil, or to hang a stone onto his body in commemoration! Poor Luigi! Like a mother, you took care of me during all my wanderings and in all my trials and tribulations. The sight and nearness of this person, sent to me by God, was my only consolation.

Chapter VIII

Luigi Carniglia

I want to speak of Luigi Carniglia, and why shouldn't I? Because perhaps, he was not of high rank? Yet high and noble was the soul of this man, high and noble was he to justify everywhere and at any time the honor of the Italian name, high and noble he was too to brave the storm and to fight danger, and high and noble was his love for his friend, whom he protected, nursed along and watched over like a child.

When I was incapable of moving, near death, abandoned by all, even by my own consciousness, Luigi remained at my side, persevering with the patience of an angel. He has a right forever to my tearful remembrance! O Luigi, your bones which now lie scattered in the depths of the ocean truly deserve a monument, where your grateful friend, the outcast and persecuted, could dedicate to you at some time a tear of friendship!

Luigi Carniglia was born in Deira, a small town on the Riviera di Levante. He had had no schooling, but was partly compensated for this lack by his brilliant intelligence. Without the nautical knowledge which is indispensable to a pilot, he guided the *Luisa* to Gualeguay, without ever in his life having been there, with the intelligence, skill and good orientation of a skilled sailor. In the battle against the cruiser it was with thanks primarily to him that we did not fall into the enemy's hands. With his speaking trumpet in his hand and posted at the spot of greatest danger, he knew how to command respect from the attackers, since of tall stature and strong build he combined remarkable strength with extraordinary agility.

In ordinary circumstances, through his open and friendly manner, he was popular with everyone and esteemed by all.

He was also a martyr for freedom! O that Italians should be destined to serve everywhere except in their own unhappy fatherland!

Chapter IX

Imprisonment

We arrived in Gualeguay after a journey of several weeks, where we were received very well, thanks to Captain Luca Tartabull[32] of the goelette *Pintoresca*[33] and his passengers, all natives. Already off the heights of Ibicuy[34] we had met the goelette, and since Luigi had asked for some provisions from her, she offered to accompany us for some distance. In addition, they gave us recommendations to the governor of the province of Entre Rios, Don Pascual Echague, who, even though he himself had to leave, kindly left me his personal surgeon Ramón dell'Arca, a young Argentinian, who extracted from my neck the bullet which had passed in between my clavicle and throat, and made me completely fit in a short time.

During the six months of my stay in Gualeguay I lived in the home of Don Jacinto Andreus[35] and was indebted to the family of my noble host for many attentions. Unfortunately I was not free, despite Echague's good will and the sympathy of the honest population of Gualeguay, since I was not allowed to leave the place without the permission of the Dictator of Buenos Ayres, from whom, however, nothing was ever heard.

Recovered from my wound, I began by taking walks and short excursions on horseback within a distance of ten to twelve miles around, as permitted. In addition to my living expenses, one Spanish piaster daily was granted me, a good salary for those countries, where little opportunity exists for spending. Still all this could not replace my freedom. Some people, (I did not know whether friend or foe), gave me to understand that it would not displease the government if I should disappear; so soon my decision was taken to flee the place of my imprisonment, an undertaking which seemed easier to me than it actually was and whose consequences I did not believe I had to fear very much.

The governor of Gualeguay, a certain Millan, did not treat me badly, a procedure the government had required of him. I really had no reason to complain of him, although he had in fact shown me little sympathy. Hence I decided to leave and for this I made the necessary preparations.

One night in very stormy weather I headed for the dwelling of an old man, whom I used to visit and who lived about three miles from Gualeguay. I informed him of my plan and asked him to find me a guide who would accompany me with his own horses as far as Ibicuy,[36] an estancia (farm), on the River Ibiqui, from which point then, I hoped to get to Buenos Ayres and Montevideo incognito. The guide in question got the horses, and so as not to be discovered, we avoided the road and rode cross-country.

We covered 54 miles in less than half a night, almost always at a gallop. At daybreak we were within sight of Ibicuy,[37] that is, the estancia of this name, which perhaps was about a half mile beyond. The man who acted as my guide instructed me to wait for him in the forest in which we were, while he would scout the house. Thus it happened; I remained alone, descended from my horse and tied its bridle to a tree. But having waited a good while, and as my guide did not return, I ventured towards the edge of the forest to see if I could discover him, when suddenly the hoofbeats of approaching horses surprised me. I turned around and saw a group of riders rush upon me with bared sabers. Being already between me and my horse, an attempt to escape, as well as an attempt to resist, would have been futile. They fastened my hands behind my back, and after mounting me on a small[38] horse, they also fastened my feet under its belly. In this manner I was led back to Gualeguay, where much worse treatment awaited me.

Chapter X

Torture

I shudder with horror whenever I recall this shameful happening of my life. Brought before Governor Millan I was asked by him who had provided me with the means of escape, and when he was convinced that I did not intend to divulge anything, he drew near with whip in hand and began to whip me, shackled and helpless as I was. Then when I insisted in my refusal, he had a cable fastened to a beam of the prison and ordered that I be suspended from it with my hands tied above me. For two hours that shameless individual ordered such torture for me. My suffering cannot be described; my body glowed like a burning oven. When I was released I even lacked the strength to complain. I had almost become a corpse; still in this condition they shackled me again!

I had covered 54 miles through a swampy region where, especially in this season, the insects were quite unbearable; now with hands and feet tied I not only had to endure the terrible bites of the mosquitoes, but was subjected to the tortures of the cruel Millan. Already I had suffered much! and now I was in chains next to a murderer!

In the meantime Andreus, my benefactor, had also been imprisoned and consequently all the inhabitants of the area became terrified. But thanks to the aid of a courageous noblewoman, Señora Alemán, who, ignoring all fear, helped the poor prisoner; I lacked nothing in my prison. After a few days I was taken to Bajada,[39] the capital of the province, where I stayed two more months in prison. Then the governor had me notified that I could leave the province.

Although I belonged to a different political party than the one to which Echague adhered, and although I had fought for a cause which was inimical to his, I cannot forget his many acts of friendship. I should like at some time to show him my gratitude for all the good which he did in my behalf, especially in having me regain my freedom.

In Bajada I embarked on a Genovese brigantine commanded by a Captain Ventura, a man who had considerably distinguished himself from among the masses of our countrymen in that region. In most of these, thanks to the Jewish education which they received from their fatherland and invariably bring along, self-interest suppresses every other feeling.[40] Ventura treated me with knightly courtesy. I travelled with him as far as Guazu, where I embarked on a cutter belonging to a certain Pasquale Carbone and proceeded to Montevideo. Carbone likewise treated me with great respect and friendliness.

Chapter XI

Military Campaigns

Lucky as well as unlucky events usually happen in series, and so were those that were to happen to me too at this time.

In Montevideo I found a great number of friends, among whom Cuneo and Castellini should be mentioned particularly. Rossetti was also in Montevideo; he had just returned from a trip to Rio Grande, where the Republicans had received him with the greatest warmth and honor. In Montevideo the orders for my arrest were still in effect, since the affair sustained with the two cruisers of that state had not as yet been concluded satisfactorily. Thus I was forced to hide in the house of my friend Pesente,[41] where I remained a whole month. This voluntary imprisonment however, was made agreeable because of the contact I had with many of my countrymen, who were very prosperous amidst the flourishing conditions prevailing in Montevideo at the time and who missed no opportunity to show their friendship and hospitality to the new arrival.

21

Only the war, which was to follow, and the consequences of the last siege, embittered somewhat the existence of these good people.

After a 30-day-stay in that town I set out with Rossetti towards the Republic of Rio Grande and it was here for the first time that I took such a long trip on horseback, filling me with great satisfaction. Upon arriving in Piratinim I was received by the government of that Republic in a flattering manner. Almeida, the Minister of Finance, did the honors. President Bento Gonçalves, as well as his secretary Zambeccari, had just marched away at the head of a brigade to fight Silva Tavares,[42] an Imperial Brazilian Captain who had crossed the canal of San Gonzales stirring up a part of those provinces. Previously both Bento Gonçalves and Zambeccari had succeeded in escaping from Rio Janeiro after I had left that city.

Piratinim, at that time the seat of the Republican government, was a small village, but agreeable because of its pleasant and rustic location. It is the capital of the district of the same name and is surrounded by warlike peoples very loyal to the ruling form of government. Since I had nothing to do in Piratinim, I proposed that they accept me in Gonçalves' operative troops, a request which was immediately agreed to by the president.

I was presented to Bento Gonçalves and was received very well by him. For quite a long time I was very intimate with him; he was a man whom nature had endowed with her greatest gifts, although luck had not always remained with him. In his actions, as well as in his appearance, he was a true model of a venerable and noble warrior, even though at the time of our acquaintance he was over 60 years old.[43] Tall and slim he rode his fiery steed with the ease and skill of a youth and could have put to shame the best horsemen. I do not believe that with his noble purpose and lack of pretention that he had put himself at the head of the war for freedom in Rio Grande for selfish and ambitious reasons. Sober and frugal, as are all the sons of that warlike land, during the campaign he shared the modest portion of the common soldier's *asado,* which I too often shared with him in friendly confidence, as if we had been equals in age and rank. Bento, inevitably because of his qualities, was to become popular quickly and the idol of his fellow citizens. And yet, he remained unlucky in battle always; which makes me believe that luck and circumstances play considerable roles in the fortunes of war.

I followed Bento as far as Canudos,[44] a crossing point of the Canal San Gonzales which connects the Patos and Mirim Lagoons. There we encountered the first brigade of the Republican Army, unsuccessful in overtaking the hastily retreating Silva Tavares. Hence, the president decided to abandon further pursuit and head back towards Piratinim with his followers, including myself.

Soon after we heard of the battle at the Rio Pardo, where the Imperial Army had been defeated by the Republicans.

Chapter XII

Manuela

I was entrusted with equipping two cruisers (*lanciones*), which were in Camucuan,[45] so I got myself ready and went there with a few sailors who had come from Montevideo. Rossetti remained in Piratinim, in charge of editing the newspaper *Povo*. In Camucuan I betook myself to the estancia of the president, where the two cruisers were. We equipped both ships; I took over the command of the larger one, the *Rio Pardo*, while we named the other *Republicano* and gave its command to a North American by name of John Griggs, whom I found on the spot and who had eagerly helped us in outfitting the ships.

Each ship had two small cannons. The crews of both amounted to seventy men, thirty Europeans, the rest negroes and mulattoes. The *Rio Pardo* weighed from 15 to 18 tons, the *Republicano* 12 to 15 tons.

We left Camucuan, descended the river of the same name on which it is located, began crossing the Lagoon dos Patos, when we soon captured a rather large and richly laden vessel, which we unloaded on the west coast of the tributary of the lagoon near Camucuan and burned, after removing everything which seemed of any use to our small arsenal. This first capture contributed no little to the development of our small navy. The crews, until then poorly fed and scantily clothed, now became suddenly wealthy, not only in provisions but also in clothes, which we needed almost as much.

The Imperialists, who had until now despised us, began to feel our importance on the lagoon and used their numerous warships, nearly 30 sailing ships and a steamship, to pursue us. The life which we led was a very active one, and very dangerous as well, because of the many enemies. At the same time it was a good life, for it suited my taste and inclination. Nor was it restricted to the waters of the lagoon; we had saddles with us, horses we found everywhere, and when it was necessary, within a very short time we transformed ourselves into a cavalry, if not brilliant, warlike and dreaded.

Several estancias were located on the shores of the lagoon, which as a result of the war stood solitary and empty. There we found cattle of all kinds; the horses we used for riding, the cattle for food. In addition there were in those properties many *rozas*,[46] that is, cultivated fields with plenty of corn, vegetables, sweet potatoes and often even very good oranges, which grow extremely well in that region.

The crew which I led, a truly cosmopolitan group, consisted of individuals of all nations and colors. I treated them perhaps, unacquainted as I was then with the weaknesses of human nature, with exaggerated kindness. They were not lacking in courage however, and for me that sufficed. They obeyed me exactly, and such fortune I always had in my life, without having gone to much trouble.

In the region of Camucuam by the river, where we had our arsenal and where the Republic had its origin, lived the family of President Bento Gonçalves, his brothers and his many relatives. Innumerable herds of cattle grazed on these fine fields, fortunately spared during the war because of their distant location. Here also the products of agriculture were available in great surplus.

One should know that perhaps nowhere in the world is practiced a more extensive and more cordial hospitality than in this part of Rio Grande. The patriarchs of the families met us with their friendly goodwill and expressions of sympathy, as we were received with indescribable cordiality in their homes. The estancias to which we came most often, both because they were situated nearest the lagoon and because we were received there with particular warmth, were those of Doña[47] Antonia and Doña Ana, both sisters of President Bento Gonçalves; the first estancia was situated at the mouth of the Camucuam, the second on that of the Arroyo Grande.

I do not know whether in those days of my youth I perhaps beautified all things, especially under the influence of my imagination. However that may be, I can certify that no single happening of my life do I recall in my memory with rosier colors than those days which I spent in such pleasant company. The house of Doña Ana was at that time a true paradise for me, for even though she was no longer in her youth, this lady had something enchanting in her manner. In her house also lived an emigrant family from Pelotas, whose head was Don Paolo Ferreira; his three daughters, each more beautiful than the other, were the main ornament of that happy place, and one of them, Manuela, had completely conquered my heart. I never stopped loving her, although I knew that my love was hopeless; she had gotten herself engaged to one of the sons of the president. I only worshipped an ideal in this angel-like being, and my love had absolutely nothing profane about it. I also had the joy to discover in a moment of great danger that she was not completely indifferent to me, and this was enough to console me for the impossibility of possessing her.

The women, as well as the inhabitants of Rio Grande in general, were of great beauty. Also the colored female slaves, of whom there were so many on these farms, were of a more pleasing exterior than elsewhere, and seemed quite worthy of cultivation, even though less sublime. It seems hardly credible, and yet it is true, that every unfavorable wind, every storm, every expedition on land, in short everything which brought us close to these shores, was regarded on our ships as cause for celebrating. The small grove of Jerba[48] trees (a kind of palm) which marked the mouth of the Camucuam, and the orange grove which indicated the mouth of the other river, were greeted with loud joy whenever we saw them again. Similarly when it was a question of taking our pleasant hostesses to the Camucuam, where they wanted to visit Doña Antonia and her charming housemates, there was no end of joy, and we exhausted ourselves in attentions directed towards our graceful travelling companions. We actually competed in unbelievable efforts to gain the favor of these ravishing creatures.

Between the Arroyo Grande and the Camucuam there are several sand banks which are called *puntales*, which beginning here on the west coast of the lagoon, extend almost perpendicularly into the lagoon until they nearly reach the far shore with their eastern tip, thus making room for the mouth of the so-called *Canal dos barcos*. If we had been obliged to sail around those banks, our trip would have been considerably prolonged. Hence we decided, whatever effort it might cost us, to traverse the banks by freeing the ships of as many passengers as possible, then shoving them with shoulders and hands across the flats. This procedure, usually pursued by Brazilian cruisers and which we often carried out ourselves in the past, we executed with particular pleasure since in this manner we were able to shorten the way for our lovely travellers. In fact when our ships struck a sand bank and the command *al agua, patos* (into *the water, ducks*) was sounded, all jumped overboard and the maneuver was carried out with the greatest glee, if not with loud rejoicing. If however, our luck and passengers abandoned us as storms and thunderstorms harassed us from all sides, we sometimes had to spend the whole night in the water without protection, amidst surging waves and cold pouring rain. Our sense of humor also left us, and our situation became so embarrassing and painful, that all our youthful ardor was needed to withstand the adventure.

Chapter XIII

A Surprise Attack

After the previously-mentioned taking of the enemy ship, the Imperial trading ships did not venture to come into the open waters of the lagoon except in pairs and groups, rendering such attacks very difficult. Consequently the assignments of our cruisers were restricted to some unsuccessful raids in the lagoon, while the Imperalists now pursued us on water, as well as on land.

It was on such an occasion, when surprised by Captain Francisco de Abreu,[49] that our two ships, as well as their commanders, might have almost found their end. At the mouth of the Camucuam there was, opposite the galpón de charqueada,[50] a large storehouse for salted meat and maté herb (a kind of South American tea, sometimes called *Paraguay tea)*. This establishment belonged to Doña Antonia, the president's sister, and since as a result of the current war no provisions of salted meat were being collected and the galpón was only half-filled with maté herb, we decided to use this spacious building as an arsenal. Therefore we pulled our ships, which incidentally needed repairs, ashore between the storehouse and the river bank.

There were carpenters and smiths in the establishment, and there was no lack of coal,[51] since we were surrounded by forests rich in wood. Even iron was to be had, for the building which, in spite of its present devastation, still bore the marks of its original splendor. It contained in many of its parts iron and steel, which was most useful for our small ships. And whatever else our new arsenal could not provide, we fetched, when we needed it, in full gallop from the surrounding settlements.

With courage, a firm will and perseverance no undertaking is impossible; and here I cannot but render justice to my comrade John Griggs, who with unending zeal knew how to overcome all difficulties, such as he encountered in the building, outfitting and commanding of our vessels, and especially during the stay in the galpón.

He was still young with excellent qualities and of a courage which nothing could shake and an endurance which nothing could wear out. From a wealthy family, he had nevertheless in laudable unselfishness dedicated his services to the liberation of a republic in the making; and when later letters from his relatives called him back to North America to take over an enormous inheritance, he had already ended his earthly career gloriously in the service of an unlucky but brave and noble people. I myself saw the corpse of my dead friend hacked into two parts! the upper part remaining upright on the deck of the *Cassapava*, his brave face daring and flourishing, as if he were still alive; the lower part however, torn and splintered into hundreds of pieces, were scattered around in the water. A cannon shot fired close by had smashed my brave friend during the last fighting we had to endure in the lagoon.[52] Alas, I saw him on that day when I, accompanied by another, boarded the ship Griggs had commanded and was still being fired upon by the enemy. By order of General Canabarro I was charged with delivering it to the flames.

So we pulled our ships ashore and worked cheerfully on repairing them. Part of the crew was busy repairing the sails, others preparing coal in the forest, when we were notified of a threatening surprise attack. Francisco de Abreu, called *Moringue* (that is, the *marten*) because of his cunning, had on various occasions announced his desire to surprise us. His attempts, however, had been in vain until now, although he did not cease causing us some worry. This time he surprised us in a really masterful way. After the news we set up all-night patrols and the crew (I had at this time in service on both cruisers approximately 50 men) was assembled in the galpón with loaded guns. Next morning there was a thick fog, and no one dared go out; but when it finally cleared up, very detailed investigations were made outside the camp.

The ninth hour had already passed, and since nothing unusual had been discovered, work was assigned to the men, the greatest part of whom were put to chopping wood at a considerable distance away. I was seated by the fire with nobody else except the cook, who was busy preparing breakfast outside the galpón door, when all of a sudden, and as if over my head, I heard a volley of gunfire as a troop of enemy horsemen rushed upon me. Barely had I time to jump up and reach the galpón door, when an enemy spear pierced my *poncho* (coat). Luckily all the guns, still loaded from the previous night, were standing ready inside the building. I seized one and fired; then I seized a second and a third rifle and so on, fired so quickly that outside they could not believe that I was alone, for three of them had already fallen. Colonel Moringue was indeed deceived; he withdrew his men about 100 paces from the galpón, ordering the firing continued from that distance. This saved me. I let the cook, who was not a very accomplished rifleman, only reload the fired guns for me while I continued my firing without stopping. It was now less a question of killing the enemy's people than to calling the attention of my crew to the shooting in order that they might rush to help me.

Soon Ignazio Bilbao from Brescia and Lorenzo Natal from Genoa,[53] both brave fellows, rushed up, as later did also Edoardo Mutru,[54] a native, Rafaele Procopio (who had already been wounded), Francisco and several others of our brave companions, all of whom I would gladly name, if I still remembered their names. Thirteen in number we were and after six hours of battle, from nine in the morning until three in the afternoon, we beat back the enemy strong of 150 men.

After killing and wounding many of our enemies, we finally succeeded in forcing them to retreat. Among them were 80 Germans,[55] who used to accompany Moringue in such operations; they were all trained soldiers on foot as well as on horseback, and as soon as they reached our hiding place and dismounted, surrounded the house, cleverly using the terrain by hiding behind the nearby bushes and shrubs from which they began their murderous fire against us. But such operations which lack the audacious sweep of attack, are often foiled by small means. If the much superior enemy, instead of remaining in his hiding places, had marched determinedly upon the galpón, we would without doubt have been lost, since our little group was too small against the predominance of the enemy, and since in addition the side doors of the building, through which we used to drag in our materials on hand carts, were standing wide open. Instead in vain they squeezed themselves against the front wall of the galpón and in vain they climbed atop the roof in order to destroy it, then to throw broken pieces, stones and burning torches on our heads. But with few rifleshots they were dislodged from the roof and with spear thrusts we quickly bored some holes in the wall, which soon became fatal to the enemy. Finally, in order to deceive the enemy about our number, we sang as loud as our throats would permit the Republican Hymn of Rio Grande. Thus, together with our rifle fire, we made a terrible uproar, as if we numbered hundreds.

At last towards three p.m. the enemy retreated. Among their many wounded was also their leader. Six bodies we found in front of the galpón wall with many more further distant. We, fourteen in number, had not less than eight wounded, three of whom died soon after. However these battles were more murderous to us, for we had neither a doctor nor a surgeon. We treated the wounded with cold water compresses, which were changed as often as possible. Rossetti and many other comrades were far away and were unable, which they themselves regretted the most, to help us. Some of our men had to save themselves by swimming across the river, others escaped into the thick of the forest, where only one was caught by the enemy and executed.

This battle, so dangerous yet so brilliantly fought, instilled not only in our own men an unlimited confidence in us, but also in the inhabitants of those shores, who for a long time had been disturbed by the expeditions of that cunning and daring enemy. Moringue was without doubt the best leader among the Imperialists and was especially skilful in similar surprise attacks in which he made use not only of his cunning and daring, but also of his thorough knowledge of the country, the terrain and the inhabitants. Although born in Rio Grande himself, he hurt more than anybody else the Republican cause and the Empire unquestionably can thank Moringue principally for its success in conquering that province.

In the meantime we celebrated our victory and basked in the happy thought that we were safe from such a dangerous storm. In the estancia, which was 12 miles distant from the battlefield, a maiden grew pale at the news of the attack on my group and prayed for my life; and sweeter than the victory was this news to my heart. Yes, you, most beautiful daughter of the continent, proud and happy I was to belong to you, although you had promised yourself to another! But fate had meant for me another daughter of Brazil, who later meant all to me, whom I still bemoan today and for whom I shall weep to the end of my life. She met me in misfortune, me the shipwrecked one, and it was probably more my misery than my merit which caused her to give herself to me forever.

Chapter XIV

Expedition to Santa Catarina

After this skirmish nothing unusual happened during our stay in the lagoon. Two new cruisers were built, partially from materials from our earlier booty, partially from the contributions of the surrounding inhabitants, who were always helpful and friendly to us.

When the shipbuilding ended we were called to Itapua[56] to operate jointly with the army besieging the capital Porto Alegre. Unfortunately the besiegers did not accomplish anything, nor were we able to be of use during the whole time that we spent in that part of the lagoon. At last an expedition was decided upon to the province of Santa Catarina in which I was ordered to take part at the side of General Canabarro. The two small cruisers under the command of Zeffirino d'Utra[57] remained in the lagoon, while I, with the two larger ships accompanied the Division Canabarro; the latter was to operate on land, whereas I was assigned the sea as my field of activity. At my side I had Griggs, who was now inseparable from me, and the elite of my companions.

The Lago dos Patos is about 45 leguas (135 Italian miles) long and 15 to 20 miles wide. Near the end of the southern shoreline the territory of Rio Grande begins and extends as far as the opposite shore. The two fortified places, Rio Grande and San José, lying at the exit, as well as Porto Alegre, were all in the hands of the Imperialists, who thus had the key to the entrance of the lake in their hands.

To get by the forts and out of the lagoon into the open sea was for us an impossibility, and since we had no other maritime exit, nothing else remained for us but to construct our own cradles on which we could transport our fleet overland. Considering the size of our ships, the magnitude of our task can be appreciated.

At the northeast[58] end of the lagoon there is a deep bay called Capivary,[59] which gets its name from a small river which flows into it. This small river, more exactly its right shore, was chosen as the most suitable place to load our ships. An inhabitant of that district called Abreu was to deliver eight wheels of great solidity, two each of which were joined by an equally strong axle and 200 draft oxen. We then neared the shore as close as possible with our barks and placed the wheels into the water at the required distances from each other so that their position coincided exactly with the heaviest point of the load. The axles were pushed under the ships from the side and all this was managed so skilfully that the wheels had free play. Eventually the strong oxen, harnessed with strong towlines, pulled the ships of the Republican Navy ashore as if on wings. Later the teams were sorted out with more care, so that they moved along successfully for a distance of 54 miles without the least difficulty, offering the inhabitants of those regions a definitely new and strange spectacle.

In this way we reached Lake Tramandai, which lies between the Lagoon de los Patos and the Atlantic Ocean. On its shores the ships were launched again and in a short time equipped with everything necessary for our expedition. Lake Tramandai is fed by waters which originate on the eastern slope of the mountain chain called Serra do Espinasso and is connected with the Atlantic Ocean by a very shallow exit. Here at the mouth of the lake the water level reaches a mere four feet, and that at high tide; added to this difficulty is the fact that on this open and shallow outlet the ocean is never protected from the winds, hence it is almost always rough and stormy, so that even at a distance of many miles the thunderlike roar of the surf is heard.

After several days we were ready to depart and only waited for the hour of high tide. The method I used to observe in such cases proved here also to be effective: we pushed the ships into the water as far as possible, and I do not know how we could ever have floated the ships without this maneuver, since even in moments of highest tide our barks would not have found enough water. After tremendous efforts we were able at dusk to throw anchor in the open sea beyond the furious surf, and had thus solved a problem whose solution no one had succeeded in before us, in fact, no vessel had ever braved the shallows of the Tramandai.

Towards eight o'clock p.m.[60] we lifted anchor and the next day at three o'clock p.m. we were shipwrecked not far from the mouth of the Araranguá,[61] which begins at the Espinasso mountain range and flows into the sea between Torres and Santa Maura. Sixteen of my companions found their death in the waves of the ocean.

Ever since the previous evening the wind, carrying heavy clouds with it, had turned south and doubled its force every hour. The *Rio Pardo* was heavily loaded with 30 persons, a heavy 12 pounder and a hundred other important objects, which at this moment brought us more peril than help. Steering towards an enemy shore, having approached the coast more than was desirable, not knowing what fate was in store for us and our ships, thrown about by a raging storm whose waves often closed above us for minutes at a time, that was a situaion which indeed could be called perilous and desperate!

In that moment I was atop the bosunmast, hoping from there to discover a point on the coast where landing would have been less dangerous. Suddenly my vessel turned onto its side and I was thrown far off into the sea. Although I was in a most perilous situation, yet I remember that the idea of death remained distant from me. I knew that many of my companions, newcomers on the sea, were lying down seasick, and tried now to save them from disaster by grasping as many oars, boards and similar matter floating around as possible so that, if at all possible, they could hang on to them and be saved. In fact I succeeded in getting these boards near the ship and called to the unfortunate ones in order that they might throw themselves into the water and grab the pieces of wood for safety.

The first one whom I saw was Edoardo Mutru, clinging to the ship's ropes; I threw him a speaking trumpet which I had caught up with, imploring him not to let it out of his hands for anything. My valiant Luigi Carniglia, who was at the steering wheel during the catastrophe, had tied himself to it, and in fact, on the side away from the wind; unfortunately in doing this, he had entangled himself in his own clothes to such an extent that it became impossible for him to remain upright. He waved to me and in using all my strength I swam near to help my soul friend. I actually succeeded in getting near the ship and in heaving myself up. I carried a small knife in my pocket and began to cut Luigi's encumbrances. Another few cuts and he would have been saved from his entanglement, when a tremendous wave rolled over the wreck and tore us from each other. I myself sank into the depth of the sea, and when I came up again, stunned by the blow and the choking whirl of the wave, my unfortunate friend had disappeared forever!

Some of my companions appeared again on the surface and all tried to reach the shore. I was among the first to land and scarcely had I set foot aground I looked around for them, discovering Edoardo not far from me. Unfortunately he had lost the speaking trumpet which I had entrusted to him, for the force of the waves had torn it away from him. He was able to swim but the effort expended was too great and had gone beyond his strength. I saw him in a pitiful state and unconsolably looked on, for alas! my spirit was still soft and not yet hardened by the icy storms of life! I swam towards him to hand over the board which had helped me in swimming. In fact I was quite close to him with my strength doubling because of the purpose of my effort, when a tremendous wave crashed over us both, depriving me of my hearing and sight. I came up again, luckily, and called desperately to my friend, but in vain! He had been swallowed up in the waves of that sea whose dangers he had wanted to share with me in the service of freedom. He was also a martyr of the good cause and his bones had earned him a stone as a monument and marker on foreign soil!

The bodies of sixteen of our companions were carried away by the waves, probably 30 miles further to the northern shores of the bay, where the sand of those vast dunes buried them. Fourteen survivors reached the shore; but in vain I looked among them for an Italian face; of the seven compatriots who belonged to our crew I was the only one to be saved. The world seemed a desert to me, and I could not fathom the caprice of fate which had dedicated those six valiant swimmers to death, while it had saved many others who neither knew how to swim nor were they seamen.

With us a little barrel of spirits had floated ashore, which seemed to me a good find. "Let's open it," I said to Manuel Rodriguez, "and try to revive our spirits a bit." They turned to immediately, but just during this small business such an icy cold engulfed us that, leaving our barrel, we felt compelled to warm up by running, lest we collapse from the cold and exhaustion.

We ran and ran almost mechanically on towards the south along the shore, encouraging each other from time to time. The seashore formed a small wall here, whose inner slope is washed by the Araranguá which flowing north and almost parallel to the coast, flows into the sea about a half mile distant. After we had advanced four miles along the right bank, we finally found an inhabited place and an hospitable reception.

Fortunately that part of the province of Santa Catarina where we were shipwrecked had risen against the Empire as soon as the approach of our flotilla became known. We were therefore received not only in a friendly manner, but truly enthusiastically, and found immediately, even though not everything we still needed, all that those poor people could muster for our relief. We were soon able to get in contact with the advance guard of Canabarro, commanded by Colonel Teixeira[62] and advancing in forced marches towards the lagoon. Our other vessel commanded by Griggs had resisted the storm because of its better construction and larger dimensions and was safe.

Having arrived with the troops in front of the small fort which dominated the lagoon of Santa Catarina, we besieged it for a short while only, since its occupants consisting of 400 men surrendered before long. Three of the enemy ships became preys of the flames[63] after short resistance. I myself went aboard the goelette *Itaparica*, which was armed with seven guns.

Fortune was in those days smiling especially on the Republicans; the Imperialists did not know, and also did not expect, such a sudden invasion, hence sent weapons, munitions and soldiers to the lagoon but unfortunately they arrived much later than we, and fell hopelessly into our hands. The Catarinians greeted us as brothers and liberators, appellations which really during our stay among those good people we did not wholly deserve.

After the month of July, during which we had entered and set up the Republican government, Canabarro established his headquarters in a town on the lagoon which the Republicans called Villa Giuliana. For the first president of the young state an honorable priest of good reputation was chosen, while Rossetti, with the title of Secretary of State, was the real soul of the government; in fact, nature had predisposed him for such a post.

All went superbly. Colonel Teixeira had pursued the fleeing enemy with his brave column, had even encircled them in the capital of the province, and taken over on the way the greatest part of the villages and the territory of the province. Everywhere our men were received with open arms and their ranks swelled by a large number of deserters who exchanged the Imperial banner for the Republican one.

A thousand marvellous plans were drafted by General Canabarro, who even though rough and hasty, especially in those times of good luck, proved himself a loyal warrior. He liked to say that out of the lagoon the hydra of the Republic would appear, and perhaps his word would have been confirmed, if he had led the end of that fortunate expedition with more care and moderation. But our arrogant demeanor towards the Catarinians, as well as the small means at our disposal, made us soon lose again the fruits of that truly brilliant campaign.

Chapter XV

In Love

The General had in the meantime ordered that I should go back to sea with three armed vessels, in order to harass the Imperial fleet along the Brazilian coast. Without delay I got ready to execute this order and prepared all that was necessary.

At this time occurred one of the most important events of my life. Until then I had never thought about marriage and indeed thought myself quite incapable of it because of the independence of my nature and the unrest of my shifting career; to have a wife and children seemed to me unreconcilable with the character of a man who had devoted his whole life to one principle; then, even in the most favorable circumstances, I could never find that peace which is necessary for a family man. Fate decided otherwise. After the loss of Luigi, Edoardo and of my other companions I remained in total isolation and it appeared to me as if I stood alone in the world. Of all those friends none remained with me, and the friendship of my new comrades was too recent to be intimate, although they were valiant and true companions. Rossetti was as dear to me as a brother, but it was not my lot to see him often, let alone to live near him, and even though I was still young I had enough knowledge of life and of men to know how rare is a true friend. In addition the change in my situation had been too sudden and too stormy not to have left me shaken. In short, I needed a soul to love me and without which my existence seemed to become unbearable to me.

What I searched for, what I needed, was a wife. I had become used to considering women as the most perfect creatures of creation, and whatever one may say against this, it surely is easy to find among them a loving heart.

Sunk in these observations, I once was walking to and fro on the deck of my ship and by chance cast my glance towards the groups of houses which adorned the Barra, that is, the east side of the entrance to the lagoon. Not far from the shore I clearly saw a young girl standing. I ordered to be brought ashore in a boat and hurried towards the houses in which the object of my attention must dwell. It was impossible for me to find the girl. Nevertheless by chance I met a man from the village whom I knew since our arrival. He invited me to have a cup of coffee in his house, and I accepted the invitation. The first thing I noticed on entering the house was the sought-for girl, whose sight had drawn me ashore from my ship.

"You must become mine," I said in greeting her, and with this I had tied a bond which only death could sunder! I had discovered a hidden treasure, a treasure of incredible value, to be sure! If there was guilt in it, it was exclusively mine, and certainly I was guilty, for the love in which our hearts united broke the heart of a poor innocent person who had more rights than I! But Anita is dead, and he is avenged![64]

When there at the mouth of the Eridanus,[65] hoping to tear the loved one away from death I locked her in my arms, I felt the whole enormity of my guilt. I wept tears of despair and wandered alone and abandoned through the world! God, protector of innocence, pardon me and protect the children of the unfortunate woman and the banished one! But you, my children, when at some time you are questioned about your parents, reply:

"We are orphans for the sake of Italy." But love Italy, for she is so unfortunate!

Chapter XVI

A Combat at Sea

The three vessels assigned to the previously mentioned expedition were the *Rio Pardo*, which I commanded myself, the *Cassapava*, commanded by Griggs, and the *Seival*, commanded by an Italian named Lorenzo. I embarked accompanied by Anita, who from now on never left me on my campaigns.

The mouth of the lagoon[66] was blockaded by Imperial warships. In spite of this, we got through unharmed under cover of the night without being noticed by the enemy, and tacked northwards. Off Santos we met an Imperial corvette which chased us for two days in vain. On the second day we landed on the Island Abrigo, where we captured two sumacas (a kind of Brazilian goelette[67]). Nor was there any lack of prizes as we continued our cruise. On the eighth day we started back to the lagoon.

I had the worst premonitions about the state of our affairs there, inasmuch as before my departure a bad atmosphere was evident among the inhabitants of Santa Catarina. Also it was known that a strong detail of troops led by General Andrea was approaching; he was ill-famed from the days of the conquest of Para and for the cruelty which he showed there. Off the Island of Santa Catarina, not far from the destination of our return, we came upon a Brazilian warship, a kind of schooner. Since the *Cassapava* had lost us several days before during a dark night, we were reduced to the *Rio Pardo* and the *Seival*. By the time we sighted the enemy ship from the bridge, there was no time to flee; therefore we attacked it by turning our broadside towards it and opened a violent fire. The enemy responded eagerly, but the whole battle came to no decisive result because of the height of the waves.

We only lost some of our prizes, due to the timorous leaders of those ships, who, frightened by the superiority of the enemy, lowered their flags, while others decided to gain the shore and flee. Only one of the prizes, commanded by the valiant Ignacio Bilbao, was retained safely and reached the harbor of Imbituba without mishap. The *Seival*, which had sprung a leak and from whom during the fight a cannon had been dismounted, headed in the same direction. Consequently I was forced to follow these two ships. As we entered Imbituba the wind was blowing from the southeast, turning later entirely southward. In such a wind it is impossible to enter the lagoon. Furthermore we probably had to fear an attack from the Imperial ships stationed near the Island of Santa Catarina and already notified of our movements by the *Andurinha*[68] (the ship with which we had just fought).

Hence we had to prepare for a new attack. The dismounted cannon of the *Seival* was placed atop a promontory which arose in the eastern part of the bay and on which we built a parapetto gabbionato[69] (a hidden gallery).

By daybreak already we discovered three Imperial ships heading towards us. The *Rio Pardo* went to meet them and opened the unequal battle against the far superior enemy. The winds blew seaward thus favoring the Imperialists who were easily able to tack with their sails while directing a terrible fire against the poor small goelette which I commanded. Nevertheless we defended ourselves with the greatest persistance, something we could do more readily since we were near enough to the enemy to use our carbines. Our deck became full of corpses and mutilated bodies, the flanks of our ship were riddled with holes like a sieve, and our sails and masts shot through. But I had decided to defend myself until death and was strengthened in this resolve by the imposing sight of my Brazilian wife, who not only disdained to be put ashore, but took part in the glorious battle herself, gun in hand.

While we fought bravely on our part, the help of the stalwart Manuel Rodriguez was not to be underrated. From the above-mentioned land battery he fired well-aimed and successful shots on the enemy ships. Thus the enemy was attacked from two sides, even though he directed his whole attention upon our goelette and several times came so close that I thought he sought to board us. Finally, after several hours of violent fighting, he had to withdraw. Later it was said that this retreat had brought death to the commander of the *Bela Americana* (one of the enemy goelettes). The rest of the day we spent in burying our dead and in repairing the major damage done to our ship. The next day the enemy stayed away in order to prepare for later battles.

At nightfall we took aboard the cannon we had placed ashore, weighed anchor, then set sail for our return to the lagoon. By the time the enemy noticed our departure, we were already far enough away not to be hit anymore by the few shots which he sent after us the next morning. When we reached the lagoon's coast we were hailed vociferously by the people; stupefied, they could not understand how we had been able to escape from the enemy, who was so much stronger than us.

Chapter XVII

A Plundering

In the lagoon other matters which preoccupied us no little awaited our return. The enemy, who was considerably superior to us on land, had incited several localities to rise against the Republican authority. This was not difficult to do as a result of our demeanor in Santa Catarina, which was not to be approved. Among others, the locality Imaruhy,[70] located on the deepest bay of the lagoon, had deserted us. Canabarro gave me the embarrassing order to retake the place and as a punishment to have it plundered. The garrison, as well as the inhabitants, had made preparations for its defense on the sea side so that I preferred to land at a distance of three miles, thus by-passing Imaruhy, and to make a surprise attack from the mountainside. The garrison soon fled before us in wild flight and we were the lords of Imaruhy.

I wish for myself and for everyone else, who has not ceased to be a human being, that he may never be in the situation of being ordered to sack. However vivid and true the descriptions of such horrors may be, it is quite impossible to describe their complete atrociousness and meanness.

Never in my life have I had such a regrettable day! God save me from a second one! I did everything that was in my power to prevent cruelty against persons, and I believe that in the end I succeeded. But concerning property I was not able to put a halt to the worst devastation and plundering. The authority of my command and the threatened punishments assured by me and my few officers were powerless against the unleashed lust for robbery. Nor of any effect was the threat that the enemy might return in doubled strength and perpetrate a terrible massacre among the uncontrollable and drunken plunderers. This prediction was soon literally fulfilled in one part, for the village, in spite of its small size, unfortunately had enormous provisions of spirits, so that there was general drunkenness in a short time. In addition the crew which had landed with me was newly engaged personnel whom I did not know at all and who knew nothing of discipline and order. Indeed, 50 men of the enemy would have been sufficient to overwhelm us. Finally, but only after many threats, shoves and beatings, the beastly horde re-embarked and, richly provided with provisions and brandy for the division, we returned to the lagoon.

In the meantime our advance guard under Colonel Teixeira disengaged itself from the enemy who was approaching on the double and with a strong detachment. We began to transport our baggage onto the right shore of the lagoon and very soon it seemed necessary that the troops themselves follow suit.

Chapter XVIII

Defeat

On the day of the retreat to the right shore of the lagoon I was extremely busy, for even if the number of men was small, the war materiel and the horses were very numerous. Added to this was the fact that there was a strong current near the exit of the lagoon and so wide was it that one could hardly avoid it without getting too near the coast. From early morning until late afternoon I was busy transporting the division to the right shore, after which I went to the coast in order to observe the enemy ships, which had started moving at the same time as the land forces. Before I climbed the mountain at the mouth of the lagoon, I had General Canabarro notified that the enemy apparently was moving to force the entrance of the lagoon. I was able to spot the enemy ships already while I steered along the Barra, so that when I climbed the promontory, I found only the confirmation of my supposition. There were 22 enemy ships, all equipped for the shallow water of the Barra. Immediately I repeated my message; but whether the general himself was hesitant and undecided, or the troops really needed rest; in short, nobody arrived. If our infantry had arrived at the right time, reinforced by the battery set up on the eastern shore, it could easily have created a great defeat among the enemy, even though that battery itself did not do much damage because of the lack of the cannoneers' knowledge and the bad quality of the cannon. It was equally bad with our three Republican vessels under my command; the crew which in itself was small, was partially dissolved that day on account of the troop transport, then many had remained ashore, not wanting to expose themselves to the coming murderous battle. I took my station on board the *Rio Pardo*, where my incomparable Anita, already with her own hand, had fired the first cannon shot and had encouraged the frightened crew with her calls. The battle was short but fearful. If not many died, it was because we were only few. Still of all the officers of our fleet, I alone remained alive. The enemy squadron, favored by the wind and the current, forced the entrance to the lagoon under devastating fire, and anchored at cannon shot distance from our ships, firing upon them incessantly. I sent to Canabarro and asked him for men to continue the battle, but the answer given was that I should destroy the ships and retreat with all that I could save and take along. I had entrusted Anita with the mission to the General, with the request to remain ashore; and yet it was she who brought back the answer to me on board. Surely it was due only to the great courage and cold blood of my incomparable wife that our war munitions were saved.

Meanwhile the enemy continued to harrass us with his fire, while I readied our small flotilla for the flames. My vision was beclouded by the saddest spectacle, as I went from one ship to the other carrying out my orders. On the decks of all the ships I found the corpses and torn-off limbs of my brave fighters. I found Juan Enrique,[71] the commander of the *Itaparica*[72] stretched out with smashed chest and struck down by a cannon shot. John Griggs, the commander of the *Cassapava,* had been shattered by another cannon ball, so that only the upper part of his body lay on deck, reddened in the face from the excitement of the battle and by chance leaning against the ship's railing, he seemed to me asleep.[73]

After a few moments the remains of these brave ones were submerged by the waves, and gone were those unfortunate but terrible enemies of the empire, who in Canabarro's expression had wanted to swallow it. Smoke enveloped the ships and soon they were consumed by the flames.

It was night when I assembled the small group of my survivors around me to hasten toward the headquarters on the Rio Grande, on that same road along which we had come only a few months before in triumph and with hearts full of hope.

Chapter XIX

A Soldier's Life

In the many storms of my life there has been no lack of fine moments. Such it was as I, at the head of the small group of men who remained after so many battles and who rightfully deserved the name of heroes, rode at the side of my beloved Anita, now the admiration of the whole world. I moved towards a new career which was almost more tempting to me than life at sea.

What did I care that I owned no other clothes than those I had on my back? What did I care that I served a poor republic which could not pay anybody? I had nothing but a sabre and a carbine which I carried over my saddle. My treasure was my Anita, who was aflame no less than I for the holy cause of the people. She had conceived battles as a pleasure and the hardships of the soldier's life as a pastime. Whatever then might come, the future was smiling at us; and the more wild the endless American steppes extended before us, the more pleasant and beautiful they seemed to us. It was a comfort to me to know that in all battles and warlike activities I had done my duty to the best of my ability.

We retreated to Torres on the border of the two provinces and pitched camp. The enemy, content with the taking of the lagoon, did not pursue us. In agreement however with the Division Andrea, the Division Acunha approached via the Serra, having come from the province São Paulo and turned towards Cima de Serra,[74] a mountainous terrain belonging to the province of Rio Grande.

The inhabitants of the Serra, overrun by a superior force, begged General Canabarro for help; he sent out an expedition under the command of Colonel Teixeira to assist them. We also took part in this expedition and, with the people of the Serra assembled under the chief command of Colonel Aranha, we completely defeated the enemy troops near Santa Vittoria. The enemy general lost his life on the River Pelotas, and the greater part of his troops fell into our hands. This victory subdued for the Republican banner the three districts of Lages, Vacaria and Cima de Serra.[75] A few days later we entered Lages triumphantly.

In the meantime in Misiones, as a result of the enemy invasion, the Imperial party had gotten into power again, and Colonel Melo had been able to increase his corps in that province by about 500 cavalry. General Bento Manuel, who was sent against him, could not reach him, since Melo had retreated in the direction of San Paolo, where First Lieutenant Portinhos was also supposed to pursue him. Our position and power would have enabled us not only to resist a thrust of Melo, but also to annihilate completely his whole following. But it was not to be; Colonel Teixeira, not sure whether the enemy would come via Vacaria or via Coritibani, divided his troops into two parts and sent Colonel Aranha with the good cavalry from the Serra to Vacaria, while he himself, with the infantry and a cavalry consisting mainly of prisoners, marched to Coritibani. It was also this direction which the enemy took. But the splintering of our troops was soon fatal to us. Our recently won victory, the impudent character of our commander and our information concerning the state of the enemy, whom we thought to be powerless and demoralized, made us look down upon him with pride and disdain.

After a three-day march we reached Coritibani and took up positions not far from the Pass of Maromba,[76] through which in our opinion the enemy must pass. Along the way, and also on all side roads, sentinels were placed. Towards midnight the sentinel in the pass itself was attacked by the enemy and with such fury that he barely was able to save himself after exchanging a few gun shots. We were ready for the battle. At dawn the enemy approached, crossed the River Maromba and took up his position not far at all from ours.

Realizing the superiority of the enemy, anybody else but Teixeira would have tried at once to bring about a reunion with the column of Aranha while attempting to hold off the enemy at any cost until then; but the hotheaded Republican seemed to fear that the enemy, and with him a fine opportunity to vanquish him, would escape. "To the attack!" he cried, unconcerned about the advantageous position of his opponent. The latter, in using the unevenness of the terrain, had posted himself in battle order on a rather high hill, in front of which a valley opened which was deep and unpassable because of underbrush. On his flanks he posted several cavalry squadrons and in such a way that we could not see them. Teixeira ordered him attacked with an infantry column and believed he could take advantage of the difficult terrain of the valley. The attack took place and the enemy made a semblance of retreat, but while our column, after crossing the valley chased the enemy under violent fire up the hill, it was suddenly attacked on its flank by one of those hidden squadrons, and was obliged to retire in extreme disorder. One of our most able officers paid for this encounter with his life. In spite of this, our column assembled again, and more ready and decided for battle than before, proceeded to the second attack.

This time the enemy really withdrew, leaving one dead behind. There were not many wounded, since altogether only few troops were involved.

We pursued the enemy fleeing in wild flight for nine miles with continuous artillery bombardment, for our infantry, even in forced marches, had not been able to continue the pursuit very long.

After reaching the Maromba Pass, we found out from the commander of our advanced guard, Major Giacinto, that the enemy was in the greatest haste to transport his *ganado*[77] and *cavalladas*[78] across the river, in our opinion a sure sign that his flight was meant seriously.

Chapter XX

A Combat

The hot-blooded Teixeira did not hesitate an instant but commanded our cavalry to galop ahead, while ordering me to follow with the infantry on the double. The sly enemy however had so far only made a slight maneuver; he had slipped out of sight as the main body of his troops had swiftly disappeared. At the same time on reaching the river, as a feint, he had his oxen and horses put across while concealing his troops entirely behind a small hillock. He also left a squadron of cavalry to cover his firing column and as soon as he observed that we, in unwise manner were leaving our infantry behind, he turned right and attacked us with his columns on our left flank by falling upon us from a less deep valley. Our mounted division, which was left behind for the protection of our infantry and was attacked by the enemy on the flank, was the first to notice our error, but did not have time to correct it and was completely routed.

Three other columns of our cavalry shared the same fate despite the courage and firmness of General Teixeira and many other brave officers from Rio Grande. Attacked in small groups, they were only able to offer little resistance and even our cavalry fleeing singly would have been totally annihilated in this manner. I had never been pleased with the far separation of the infantry from the vanguard, especially since the latter did not consist of good elements. Most of them were from the number of cavalrymen we had taken prisoner in San Vittoria. Because of this, I drove the infantry under my command forward with great effort in order to reach the battlefield with them; but in vain. Arrived atop a hill, I witnessed the defeat of our men, and realizing that it was too late to have any influence on the outcome, my only thought was not to lose everything. I called, and a dozen of the bravest and quickest of my older comrades rushed towards me on the double, while one of the officers (Major Peixotto)[79] took over the command of the rest. With my twelve braves I took up positions on a hill protected by bushes and shrubbery.

There we began to face the foe and to teach him that he had not won everywhere. At this point Colonel Teixeira fell back, after trying with great courage, to halt the fleeing enemy. But the infantry joined us, and now began the battle for the defense which became dreadful and murderous for the enemy. Many of our infantry fell and many fugitives were killed by the enemy. We however, favored by our position and 73 strong men, outfought the enemy, who not only was deprived of his infantry, but also was not very much accustomed to fighting against foot soldiers. Still, in spite of our favorable position, we had to look for an even safer refuge, so as not to give the enemy time to reunite his troops, nor let the eagerness for battle die down in our men.

We spied a so-called *capón,*[80] that is, a group of trees standing close together, at a distance of about one mile. We began retreating in that direction, while the enemy tried to surround us and, as often as the terrain permitted, to harass us. On this occasion it was very advantageous for us that our officers were armed with carbines, and being skilled marksmen, they beat back the attack of the enemy with sheer bravery. Finally we succeeded in reaching the *capón*, where we were safe from the enemy. We then penetrated into the middle of the forest and selected an open spot; here, with loaded guns, we waited for nightfall. Outside we heard the enemy yell: "Surrender!" but we remained silent.

Chapter XXI

In the Forest

At nightfall we prepared for the march back, but in so doing some of our wounded created great difficulties for us. Among these was also Major Peixotto, wounded in the foot by a bullet. Hence we prepared the wounded for travel as well as possible, started off at 10 o'clock at night and by leaving the capón on the right, we marched along its edge in order to reach the nearby *matto*, that is, a large forest.

This forest, perhaps the largest in the world, extends from the delta of the Plata as far as that of the Amazon, crowning the heights of the Serra do Espinasso, that spinal column of Brazil. Its width is of 34 degrees; its length I cannot cite exactly. The three districts of Cima da Serra, Lages and Vacaria form so-called *campestres* amid this forest, that is, fields bordered by the forest. Coritybanos,[81] located in the District of Lages was the scene of action of my narration. The name of the place comes from Corityba[82] in the province of S. Paolo, from where emigrants came to settle down here.

As I said, we followed the edge of the capón to reach the large forest, then took the direction for Lages to find the corps of Aranha, which unfortunately had separated itself from us. As we left the capón, one of those cases happened which show man that he depends on chance, and that even the most undaunted courage can be broken by frightening panic.

We were marching along in the deepest silence, but also ready to pounce resolutely upon the foe, if he should bar our way. On our approach, even though we were silent, a horse which happened to be at the edge of the wood became frightened, bounded and fled. "The enemy!" unfortunately a voice cried, and immediately our whole troop fled into the thicket, those same 73 who had beaten 500 of the enemy with much bravery. The fright was so great and so deep did they flee into the forest that even after a three hours' search it was impossible to find all of them; consequently some had to be left behind to their fate.

After we had collected ourselves together again as well as possible, we started up once more, reaching the edge of the forest by daybreak. The enemy pursued us the next day but, of course, without finding us.

The day of our last battle had been terrible with hardships, deprivations and strain; but at least one was fighting, and this idea suppressed all others. But in the jungle, where all food was lacking, we had to spend four whole days without any other food than herbs and roots. Indescribable are the hardships which we had to endure to break a path for ourselves through the thicket, since not even footpaths existed, and nature, freer and more lavish than elsewhere, under the colossal pines of the forest, has let the gigantic reed grow wild, the so-called *taquara* whose decaying remnants place against the feet of the intruder unsurpassable hurdles. Many of our people lost courage; some even deserted, and it became necessary to call everyone together and to tell them clearly that it was better to say openly whether they wished to accompany the expedition further, or if otherwise, that no one would hinder them from parting from us. This procedure had an incredible effect: from that moment on, nobody deserted any longer and all were full of courage and hope again.

Only on the fifth day did we come upon the *picada*,[83] that is, the path hewn through the forest, where we soon found a hut and halted to allay our hunger with two freshly-slaughtered oxen. We even made a few prisoners in this hut, for it belonged to the same enemy who had given us so much trouble. After a day of rain we reached Lages.

Chapter XXII

A Stay in Lages

The locality of Lages, which had received us joyfully on our victorious arrival, had deserted us again on the news of our defeat, and some of the most decided ones had not hesitated to declare themselves in an open proclamation for the Empire. These fled on our appearance, and since they were mostly merchants, their well-filled storehouses fell into our hands; this was of great use to us, for our troops were lacking in many necessary things.

In the meantime Teixeira had written to Aranha commanding him to unite with him. On that day we also heard from Colonel Portinho, who had been sent out by Bento Manuel to pursue the troops of Melo, those same troops which we unfortunately encountered in Coritybanos.

In the Americas I have served the cause of the people and have devoted myself to it with all my heart, because I have everywhere fought absolutism. I loved the system which agreed with my convictions and hated the opposite, but only the system. The people I have pitied more than hated, for I can make allowances for the egotism of our nature. Now, being far away from the scene of those happenings which I am about to recount, I can, I suppose, be considered as an impartial reporter.

Brave and undaunted were the sons of the Amerian continent, who in Lages had to prevail over an enemy ten times superior. Many days passed before Aranha and Portinho could arrive with their forces and during this time the enemy was kept at bay by a handful of men. But as soon as our reinforcements arrived, we bravely marched on the enemy. However, he did not accept the offered meeting and withdrew slowly, always depending upon the region of S. Paulo, from where considerable reinforcements of infantry and cavalry joined him. Now we felt very clearly our great weakness, which is inherent in almost all revolutionary armies: however brave and courageous the people are from whom such armies are formed, they still do not know how to remain under arms patiently when the prospects for battles and skirmishes are not near. This weakness became our undoing in that moment, so that a more enterprising foe could easily have taken advantage of it and annihilated us. First the Serra people (people from the nearby mountains) left our ranks, taking with them not only their own but also the horses of the division. Soon after, Portinho's people, who partially came from the province of Misiones, followed their example; and in short time our ranks were decimated to such an extent that we were forced to leave Lages and return to Rio Grande, taking care to avoid the enemy. The small remnant of our troops was not in very good shape and suffered from lack of clothing, a condition which was felt all the more since the cold had begun earlier than usual in those high regions. The discouragement became so great that I often heard the men complain in loud voice that they wished themselves back in their homes.

Colonel Teixeira was therefore forced to act upon these complaints and commanded me to descend the Serra and unite myself with the main army. But this descent was surrounded by great difficulties, partly because of the bad condition of the roads and partly because of the enmity of the local inhabitants, who proved to be the most bitter enemies of the Republicans. Sixty in number we advanced via the Pelufo Picada and were obliged to face such dangers that it was only due to the courage and endurance of the men whom I led that we escaped unharmed. The path which we had to follow was extremely narrow and enclosed on both sides by inpenetrable thickets. The enemy, native of this country and knowing the terrain, always picked the most dangerous and difficult places of our road to hide themselves in the thickets, then to pounce upon us while raging and shouting, and to pursue us with rifle shots as far as he could. In spite of this, we suffered only small losses; one single horse died, and among the men there were only a few wounded.

We finally reached headquarters in Malacara, 12 miles from Porto Alegre, where we met President Bento Gonçalves (also commander in chief at the time).

Chapter XXIII

The Battle on the Taquari

The Republican Army was just getting ready to march. The enemy troops, which had gone to Porto Alegre after the battle near Rio Pardo, had vacated the place again on the command of old General Giorgio and had taken up positions on the shore of the Cahó,[84] in order to meet with General Calderón, who had left Rio Grande with a strong division of cavalry and was supposed to join them by crossing the country. Again we felt the defects mentioned above of Republican armies, which are most obvious when the enemy is not in sight: we lost much time in protecting our men from total dissolution, and when finally General Netto, who was to surround the enemy troops, had gathered the necessary number of men, Calderón had already gotten in touch with the main part of the Imperial Army and threatened his Republican attackers with superior might.

It was indispensable for the president to connect with the Netto Division, for alone he was in no condition to confront the enemy army; and the successful manner in which he effected this maneuver speaks highly for the military talents of Bento Gonçalves.

Heading towards San Leopoldo we marched with the army from Malacara passing only two miles distant from the enemy, and after an uninterrupted march of two days and two nights we reached the region of the Taquari, where we joined General Netto who came to meet us.

On this whole march we were never able to eat in peace, since the enemy, who knew our movements, pursued and repeatedly attacked us. This usually happened when we rested or roasted our dried meat (the only food of South American armies) over the fire. Then head over heels we had to pick up our belongings and postpone the eagerly-awaited meal for a more propitious occasion. In Pinheiriño,[85] six miles from the Taquari, we finally halted and all preparations for the battle were made.

The Republican Army consisted of about 5000 cavalrymen and 1000 infantrymen. They occupied the heights of Pinheiriño, the heights of a landscape overgrown with coniferous trees, as the name indicates. The infantry formed the center and was commanded by the old Colonel Crescenzio; the right wing was under the command of General Netto; and the left one under that of Canabarro. Both wings thus consisted only of cavalry, which, without exaggeration, I can call just about the best in the world, although it was called *farrapa,* "clothed in rags." Our infantry was also very good and fired with the urge for battle. Colonel Juan Antonio formed the reserve with a cavalry corps.

It was rumored that the enemy had 4000 infantrymen and 3000 cavalrymen, in addition to some pieces of cannon, and were taking up positions on the far side of a small forest brook which separated the armies from each other. Also his demeanor commanded respect, for they were the best troops of the Empire commanded by General Giorgio, who although old was very able. Furthermore the enemy had come here in forced marches obviously to pursue us, because he had already taken the necessary measures for a regular attack. Soon two of his batallions had crossed the dry river bed and set up two cannons on its edge with which they opened a strong fire against our cavalry ranks. The First Cavalry Brigade under Netto's command had already drawn their sabers and were waiting only for the trumpet signal to hurl themselves against the two enemy batallions. These braves were full of hope for victory, for Netto and his men had never been defeated. Also our infantry, stationed in small units atop the hill, was eager for the beginning of the battle.

Then the dreadful lancers of Canabarro made a forward movement surrounding the right flank of the enemy and forcing him to turn and retreat in the greatest disorder. The brave Republicans, proud of their success, felt stronger than ever and with their forest of lances and smart horsemen presented a truly beautiful sight. They were, except for the superior officers, all negroes freed from slavery by the Republicans. The enemy never saw the backs of these true sons of freedom; their lances, whose length exceeded the usual dimensions, their pitch-black faces, their strong limbs steeled in battle and hardships, their military bearing and discipline invariably filled the enemy with fear.

"Today each one of us will fight as four," reverberated in our ranks the encouraging cry of the commander in chief, who was gifted with all the qualities of a "Gran Capitano," except for his luck. Our hearts beat faster, eager for battle and our breasts were full of hope for victory! Truly a more beautiful day, a more grandiose spectacle I have never again experienced.

Posted in the center of our infantry on the highest peak of the hill, I could clearly see both armies; the terrain in front of me was overgrown with low shrubbery only and presented no obstacle to the eye. Every detail, every smallest movement could be followed. There at my feet within a few minutes would be decided the fate of the greatest part of South America! These massed ranks, these strong columns were to be thinned and torn apart! These strong youths were to smear the green of these fields with their blood, their maimed limbs, their corpses!

Now the signal for battle was urgently awaited, but in vain. So this was not to be the battleground? The enemy general, intimidated by our strong position and our firm demeanor hesitated to begin the battle, withdrew the two advanced batallions and stayed on the defensive, giving up the idea of attacking.

General Calderón had just been killed while scouting. Perhaps this was the cause for the indecision of our enemy. But how about us, what were we to do? Shouldn't we attack, since we were not attacked? This was the opinion of the majority. To be sure, to await an attack in our high position would give our side all the advantages; but if we should give up this position in order to inflict upon the enemy some damage, we would have to cross the bed of the mountain stream, which even though dry, was difficult. We would then, without doubt, be obliged to feel the numerical superiority of the enemy infantry. Finally it was decided not to fight, so we remained facing each other, without indulging in other than a few small skirmishes.

In the meantime in our camp the meat began to run out and especially the infantry suffered considerably from hunger. Water was also lacking, and thirst was even more unbearable than hunger. But these people seemed to be created for a life of hardships. The sole complaint heard was that which reflected the unsatisfied eagerness for battle.

O Italians! if you were united and sober, as the sons of this continent, then the foreigner would no longer tread your soil with despotic foot, would no longer disfigure your hearths, and Italy would reach its place again among the first nations of the world!

During the night old Giorgio had vanished, and by morning the enemy could nowhere be discovered. Only when the morning mist had lifted, towards ten o'clock could we see the enemy troops in firm positions on the Taquari. Soon thereafter we heard that his cavalry was crossing the river, thus leaving no further doubt that he really was retreating. Now it seemed propitious that we should attack him, and our general did not hesitate for a moment. He let us go ahead with determination.

Although the enemy cavalry by means of several Imperial ships posted there, had already crossed the river, their entire infantry was still on the left bank, where thanks to the warships, they had taken up a rather advantageous position. Our Second Infantry Brigade, consisting of the second and third batallions was destined to open the attack. They carried it out with all possible bravura, but the enemy unfortunately outnumbered us too much; our brave soldiers, after brilliant proofs of their courage, had to retreat without effect, even though the First Brigade, which consisted of the first batallion of marines and a few artillerymen, unfortunately without cannons, came to help their hard-pressed comrades.

Terrible fighting ensued, especially in the forest. The explosion of shots, the rustling of the traversed underbrush and the noise of the fighters caused a truly infernal uproar, which became even more gruesome through the thick smoke which covered everything. Not less than 500 dead and wounded were bemoaned by each of the warring parties. On the banks of the river corpses of brave Republicans were found; this far had they pursued the enemy. Unfortunately these important losses were without advantage for us, since night fell after the retreat of our Second Brigade and forced us to halt the fighting, while it permitted the enemy to cross the river unmolested.

Bento Gonçalves, notwithstanding his brilliant character traits, was incredibly slow in making decisions, probably as a result of the little luck he had had in his previous operations. Many of us thought that the action once begun should now be completed, and suggested to have not only the whole remainder of the infantry, but even the cavalry take part on foot. Indeed such a procedure might easily have procured us a brilliant victory, if we had surprised the enemy from the back at the moment he embarked. However much this suggestion seemed plausible, the general still hesitated to gamble with the whole, the only infantry of the Republic. Therefore that bloody affair remained for us nothing but a clear loss because we were not able to replace it, for, unlike the enemy, we did not have the possibility of acquiring new foot soldiers.

The enemy remained on the right bank of the Taquari, while we did not dare contemplate another attack. Instead we returned to Porto Alegre to take up the siege again. Later the conditions of the Republic worsened and we were sent to San Leopoldo, then to Malacara, our old camp which we now transferred to Bella Vista. Here the general conceived a new plan of operations, the success of which he was convinced should move us into a very favorable position.

Chapter XXIV

The Attack on San José do Norte

As a result of the operations in the open, the enemy had to commandeer many of the garrisons from his fortified places. Such a place was San José do Norte, a fort situated on the northern shore of the mouth of the Laguna dos Patos. It was the key to the lagoon, and its possession might have given matters a different turn, principally because it would have made it possible for our troops to obtain sorely needed provisions of food and clothing. This point was important not only because it dominated the entrance into the lagoon and the province, but also because of the *Atalaya* which was located there, that is, the signalling mast which indicated to approaching ships the depth of the water in that shallow ford.

The expedition which we undertook there unfortunately ended in the same way as that to the Taquari. It started with the greatest astuteness and secrecy; but again remained fruitless for us because we neglected to drive the last blow.

An eight days' march in which we covered 25 miles daily brought us below the walls of the fort. It was one of those winter nights, when shelter and a little bit of fire are true gifts from heaven. The poor soldiers, tired and exhausted with stiff limbs, who had been exposed during almost the entire march to a heavy rain and a cold wind, silently sneaked up to the well-manned towers and walls. The officers' horses were left behind at some distance, and when each one had rolled up his small bundle, the attack was prepared. The *who goes there* of the enemy sentinel was the signal for our attack. We found only little resistance on the walls and in the forts; the artillery also was not used much. At one hour after midnight the attack began and at two o'clock already we were masters of the trenches and three of the forts which protected them. We had stormed them with our bayonets.

After we had overwhelmed these forts and penetrated into the town, one should have thought that we would remain masters of it. And yet! this time also we were to lose out. The star of the Republic was setting and luck seemed against our commander. As soon as the soldiers were in the town they thought of nothing else but of robbing and plundering. The Imperial troops in the meantime had gradually recovered from their fright and massing in a fortified part of the town resisted us. We attacked them again, but were beaten back; and when our fighters looked for each other to renew the attack again, they found it impossible. Some were full of wine and others heavily laden with booty. Still others had damaged their rifles, lost their flints, and what not.

But the enemy made use of his time and soon several warships which were in the harbor had now taken up suitable positions and swept the streets which we occupied with their fire. In the meantime we also received relief from Rio Grande which stayed on the opposite side and was strong enough to hold the conquered forts with the exception of one, which fell into enemy hands.

The largest fort, called *Imperial*, which was situated in the center of the line of fortifications and had cost us much blood, was rendered unusable soon after its capture by a terrible explosion of gunpowder. Thus again we had to mourn quite a few dead and wounded. In the end our glorious triumph was to change into a shameful retreat, not to say a flight. The bravest wept with rage and despair. Our loss was tremendous; our infantry only a shadow. The few cavalry who had taken part in the expedition covered our retreat, and while the division took up its quarters in Bella Vista, I remained behind in San Simon with the division of marines now reduced to about 40 men.

Chapter XXV

Anita

My remaining in San Simon had the purpose of collecting some boats in order to make connections with the other side of the lake. However during the few months that I spent there no canoe ever appeared, so that the whole idea of my stay came to nought. Hence instead of using boats, we busied ourselves with horses, since there were nearby a large number of colts which served to train my sailors as horsemen and trainers.

San Simon lies in a very beautiful and wide valley; it is a landed property which was idle and deserted at the time and I believe belonged to an exiled Count of San Simon. He, or his heirs, were outlawed because of their opinions which were opposed to those of the ruling system. Since we found no one belonging to the Count's family, and the owner at that time belonged to the party of our enemies, we confiscated the property. Still taking over consisted in merely eating, drinking and breaking in horses, all of which became for us a source of great pleasure.

It was during this period that occurred Anita's first confinement. The survival of my first-born, whom I called Menotti and who was born on 6 September 1840,[86] was a real wonder, for during the course of her pregnancy the heroic mother took part in numerous battles and suffered untold hardships and strain. The small head scar with which the boy was born is certainly the result of his mother's repeated falls from horseback.

Anita waited for her confinement in the house of a colonist in the region of Mustarda, where she received all imaginable care and nursing, and forever I shall remain grateful to those good people for this. It was good that my poor Anita remained in that house, because the misery and privations in the army had reached their highest mark at this time. I did not even have enough to provide the dear young mother and baby with clothes and linen. So I decided to travel to Setembrina where I knew that a few friends, especially the good Blingini, would bring me the most essential. I actually set out although all the fields of that alluvial soil were flooded in that season and often had to ride for days in the water up to the belly of my horse. Passing through Rossa Velha I met the captain of our lancers, Massimo, who was in charge of the safekeeping of the horses and who, as a good comrade, received me well. That evening I arrived in the village during a violent rainstorm, spent the night there, and since the next day the bad weather was raging even more strongly, the good captain insisted at all cost that I stay longer. Nevertheless my mission was too important to be postponed, so again I ventured forth, however much they warned me of that sea of flooded fields.

I rode for a few miles when I heard shots from the direction I had just taken; I became suspicious, but felt I could do nothing else but ride on. Finally I reached Setembrina, bought some linens and turned back towards San Simon.

When I returned to Rossa Velha I learned the reason for those shots and the sad happening which had occurred immediately after I rode away. Moringue, the same who had surprised me in Camaquan, had attacked Captain Massimo by surprise, and in spite of the most heroic defense, almost all the lancers of the garrison, about thirty, as well as Massimo himself, were killed. Then most of the horses of the cavallada were embarked, while the rest were all destroyed. Moringue had carried out this expedition with warships and infantry.

By first transporting his troops by water, then disembarking and reenforcing them with some cavalry, he drove through the country as far as

51

Rio Grande del Norte, surprising and scaring all the small troop units which were scattered in that region and had thought themselves safe. Among these were also my few soldiers, who were forced to seek refuge in the forest. Even my poor Anita, on the twelfth day after her confinement and during that terrible tempest, had to flee with the soldiers, holding her infant on the saddle in front of her. I no longer found my men and my family where I had left them but at the edge of the forest, camping in complete ignorance of the movements of the enemy.

We returned to San Simon, remained there a while longer, then transferred our quarters to the left bank of the River Capivari. This river is fed by several springs which trickle down from the numerous lakes that adorn the northern part of the province of Rio Grande between the seashore and the eastern slope of the chain do Espinasso. It gets its name from *Capivara,* an amphibian, which is very frequently found in the rivers of South America. On the Capivari and the Sangrador* do Abreu we had made two boats (canoes) and frequently made trips along the western shore of the Lago dos Patos in order to transport persons and baggage.

Chapter XXVI

La Selva das Antas

The situation of the Republican Army however, deteriorated from day to day; the needs became greater and the possibility to satisfy them lessened. The two engagements of Taquari and San José do Norte had decimated the infantry so that our battalions were mere remnants of their former strength. All the rest was demoralized by misery and the lack of success in war. Now the inhabitants were tired of their troubles, as usually happens in long conflicts, and reserved for themselves the right of neutrality towards both armies.

This was the state of affairs when the Imperialists made offers of settlement, which considering the desperate situation of the Republicans, were very favorable; even then, they were not accepted by our side. This declining of the peace offers, which emanated from the better disposed part of our troops, created much bad feeling among the rest, who were tired of fighting. As a result it was decided to give up the siege of Porto Alegre and to retreat. The Division Canabarro, to which the marines belonged, was to lead the march and open the passes of the Serra occupied

---

*A Sangrador is a canal which connects a swamp and a lake.

by General Labattue. Bento Gonçalves, with the remainder of the army, was to form the rear guard and cover the movements of the army corps.

At that time our incomparable Rossetti died, an irreplaceable loss. He had remained behind with the main body of troops garrisoned at Setembrina, which was to leave last, when he was surprised by Moringue and lost his life by falling from his horse while fighting bravely.

Is there any corner of the earth where the bones of a brave Italian do not rest and who does not merit to a full extent the tears which his people shed in their most just grief? Italy will feel the lack of those noble ones on the day when she rises triumphantly on the corpses of these birds of prey who are now gnawing on her!

Rossetti was from Genoa and destined by his parents for the calling of the clergy. But because of an aversion against this calling he went abroad and arrived, after much wandering, in Rio Janeiro. There he began a business. But Rossetti was not a business man either; he was the most generous and extravagant man I have ever seen. Nor was he lacking in the necesary business sense; but he was too good-natured. His house and his purse stood open for each unfortunate one, indeed for every Italian. He did not wait until an exile looked him up, he himself went to look him up, as soon as he heard of his arrival. If he himself was not able to help, he let the newcomer wait in his house, rushed to his friends and ran around until he gathered together a sum of money.

I had met Rossetti in Rio Janeiro and a firm bond of friendship united us. Death cut this bond also, as so many others!

The retreat through gorges and forests began in the middle of winter in almost incessant rain, the worst that I can remember. Our total provisions consisted of a few cows, which we dragged behind us, since on the steep paths made impassable by the rain no other provisions could be transported. The many rivers which we had to cross were unusually swollen and a large part of our baggage was carried away by the floods. Soaked to the bones and hungry we marched and had to camp in the same circumstances. Those who marched behind with the cows still had meat to eat, while the others, and in particular the poor infantry, could not even help itself out with horse meat. Of course many conflicts and some very gruesome scenes arose. According to the customs of the land, many women and children followed the army; but of the children most had to be left behind in the forest and only a few were taken along by riders who followed, as some infantrymen had been lucky enough to catch a horse and with it from time to time save a child left behind by a dead or dying mother.

Anita shuddered at the thought of losing our Menotti, whom we saved only by a miracle. At the most difficult places of the road I carried my poor little one, who was hardly three months old and whom I tied around my neck with a cloth, in order to warm him as much as I could with my breath. Of the twelve horses and mules which we used for carrying loads and riding and which we had taken over upon entering the forest, only two of each were left, the others having been abandoned by us because they had become tired and unusable. To complete our misfortune our guides lost the way, and this proved the greatest obstacle of all, for it rendered more difficult our exit from that dreadful *Selva de las Antas.* *

When after endless trekking we were still not able to reach the edge of the forest, I remained there with the two mules, which also began to fail, and sent Anita ahead with the two horses, a servant and the baby to find a clearing in the wood where they might find food. Anita's courage and endurance saved my most precious one. Anita was lucky enough to reach the end of the forest and meet some of my soldiers warming themselves before a fire, a treat which had only seldom been granted us in the almost incessant rain. The soldiers quickly dried a few rags and wrapped them around my half frozen child, which revived through the long deprived warmth, after his poor mother had already given him up. With the most loving care these good people then looked for some food to strengthen mother and child.

In the meantime I tried in vain to save the exhausted mules by gathering for them Taquarra leaves, a kind of reed. But it was useless; I was obliged to abandon them, for, exhausted and hungry myself, I still had to find the exit from the forest and join my wife and child, which eventually I did after a long search. By the ninth day after our entrance into the forest the rear of our division had hardly reached the end of the forest and only a few horses of the officers were still alive.

The enemy who had preceded us in his flight had left behind in the Selva de las Antas a few cannon, which however, we were not able to take along because of the lack of transportation. Who knows how long they will remain in that jungle!

The thunderstorms seemed to have settled over that forest, since hardly had we descended from the high plateau of the Cima da Serra, when we encountered beautiful weather. Also we found here cattle and other animals which served us as food and let us forget the endured hardships. We came to the District of Vacaria, where we remained a few days and waited for the Division Gonçalves, which reached us in separate groups and in a desolate condition.

The untiring Moringue, informed of our retreat, had followed that division closely and attacked it repeatedly, aided by the inhabitants of the mountains, who had always been hostile to us. This gave General Labattue time to effect his retreat and to reach the Imperial Army. But in doing so, he arrived almost without soldiers, for most of them, exhausted by the forced marches and the hardships of the journey, had deserted. Along the way a rather peculiar misfortune happened to him: as he had to pass during his trek the two forests known by the names Mattos

---

*Antas are animals of the size of a donkey and harmless; their meat is excellent and their leather is used for many strong and elegant products.

Portughez and Castellano, he came upon some Indian tribes called Bugrés which are counted among the wildest in all Brazil. These Indians, informed of the Imperialists' march, in several places of the forest surprised and inflicted no little damage to them. Towards us, the Republicans, those Indians were friendly and did not disturb our march; in fact, on our passage through those forests we did not have to suffer at all. We did find some *foges*[87] though, that is, those pits which are usually carefully covered with underbrush into which the careless wanderer easily falls, but none of them was covered.

During that time a woman was found not far from the forest, who, kidnapped in her childhood by the savages, used our presence to save herself; she was in a pitiful state.

Now, since we neither had to fear nor pursue an enemy, we advanced slowly; also we were almost entirely lacking in horses and those which we had, had only been caught en route and were not broken in yet. The lance corps which had almost no horses anymore, could only become mounted again by capturing colts. It was a beautiful sight to behold almost every day many of those young men as they tore through the fields climbing on the backs of those wild runners, while the untamed animals shied and shook themselves to get rid of their unwanted loads. The riders kept their seats with admirable strength, skill and daring and, then with blows, spurs and pulling of reins tired out the proud sons of the desert. The colt comes in from the field, is caught, saddled, bridled, broken in by a rider and within a few days gets its bit; in a short time it becomes a wonderful horse, although the animals rarely leave the hands of the soldiers well tamed, especially during the marches when one can devote only little care to this training.

After wandering through the two forests Portughez and Castellano we came to the province of Misiones and turned towards Cruz Alta, the capital of the province. This well-built small town lies on a plateau in charming surroundings, just as that part of Rio Grande is characterized by its beauty. From Cruz Alta we marched to San Gabriel, where we made our headquarters and erected barracks for the army. I also built a hut for myself, in which I lived for some time with my small family.

My last six years had been full of danger and hardships and the great distance from relatives, friends and connections with my country (of which in these far regions, cut off by the war, I had no news at all), had awakened in me the desire to get to a place where I might find out some details concerning my people, especially about the fate of my parents, whose love I could disregard for a time, but whose memory was always vividly present in my soul. Also I had to give thought to improving my own condition, as well as that of my dear companion and child. I therefore decided to go to Montevideo, at least for some time, and upon my request obtained from the president permission for the journey, as well as a herd of cattle for my expenses. With this herd I left.

Chapter XXVII

A Cattle Herder

So after a *condottiere* I became a cattle herder!

In an estancia named Corral de Pedras I succeeded, with the permission of the Finance Minister, to round up 900 cattle in about twenty days; and if it had been difficult to gather such a number, it was much more difficult to lead the herd to Montevideo.

Innumerable obstacles I had to overcome during my journey; the very worst was the flooded Rio Negro, where I came close to losing my whole capital. Then, in spite of my inexperience and the cheating of my helpers, whom I hired for the transport of the cattle, I saved about 500 head; these however, exhausted by the long trek, the lack of food and the hardships of crossing the river, were deemed incapable of reaching Montevideo. It was therefore decided to slaughter these animals in order, at least, to be able to use their hides, for which the natives have their own word *cuerear*.

After a 50 days' journey, which had become unpleasant to me because of difficulties of all kinds, the cold, hardships and accidents, I finally reached Montevideo with a few hides, the only remnant of my 900 cattle and from which I could clear only a few hundred scudi, just enough to take care of the most necessary needs of my family. In Montevideo I stayed at the home of my friend Napoleone Castellini, who was very kind to me; also at that time I owed much to my other friends there, such as Cuneo, Antonini and Risso. I was in the situation of having to look out for the living costs of three persons, without having the means to do so. The bread of others has always tasted bitter to me, although often in my changing life I have had to take refuge in another's aid and luckily always found friends who offered it to me.

I finally decided on two occupations; they did not bring me much profit, still they assured me a living for some time. I became a broker, and on the side I taught mathematics in the house of Mr. Paolo Semidei; this activity lasted until I joined the Army of the Banda Oriental.

The question of Rio Grande was moving towards a solution, and I could do nothing more for this state, nor could it do any more for me. Soon however I was offered an activity by the República Oriental which was more suited to my nature, namely as commander of the war corvette

Constitución. This brought me into conflict with the Republic of Buenos Aires.

The fleet of the Oriental Republic was commanded by Colonel Coe, the enemy fleet by General Brown, and already some skirmishes, even if indecisive, had taken place. But at the same time a man like Vidal was appointed Minister of the Oriental government, with whom unfortunately only sad memories are connected: in fact, the first thought of this despicable man was to free the Republic of its fleet, declaring it a burden for the state.

This fleet which had cost endless sums and was maintained with all possible care, could have assured at that time an imposing position for that state in the La Plata region; instead, it was ignominiously destroyed by throwing away the wood and remaining materials at unworthy prices.

I was engaged to serve a republic whose lot could only be an unhappy one due to the inexperience and wickedness of the participants.

Chapter XXVIII

In the Service of the Republic of Uruguay

With the *Constitución,* a corvette with 18 cannon, the brigantine *Pereira,* a two-decker also of 18 cannon, and a transport ship, the goelette *Procida,* I was to go to Corrientes, an allied province, to help it in operations of war against Rosas.

Before I continue my narrative however, I think I should first give some explanations about that war and its causes.

The Republic of Uruguay, like almost all South American republics, was torn by inner strife. The cause of it was the jealousy of two generals who vied against each other for the presidency. Fructuoso Rivera, the luckier one, finally succeeded in overthrowing General Manuel Oribe, who had until then held the president's chair. Oribe fled to Buenos Aires where Dictator Rosas received him, as well as other emigrants from Uruguay, and used them against his own enemies at home led by General Lavalle.

In this new situation Rosas saw a desirable opportunity for the realization of his vast plans: namely, to first use Oribe and his followers against Lavalle and thus annihilate the opposing Unitarians at home, who also favored the Rivera regime of the Banda Oriental of Uruguay, then when this was accomplished, to turn the Oribe faction against the Rivera government itself in Montevideo. In this manner Rosas planned to destroy the Uruguayan Republic most surely by injecting it with the germ of a frightful civil war, thus establishing his exclusive supremacy over the entire La Plata region.

At the time I commanded my ship up the La Plata River; the Army of the Republic of Uruguay was in San José del Uruguay, while Oribe's army was in Bajada (or Paraná), the capital of the province Entre Rios, and both were preparing for battle. The Army of Corrientes was preparing to unite with that of Uruguay.

I had to ascend the Paraná River as far as Corrientes, a distance of more than 600 miles from Montevideo, along which I could land nowhere except on islands or steppes. The first battle I had to fight since my departure from the capital was against the batteries of Martín García, an island which lies close to the junction of the two large rivers Paraná and Uruguay, and by which one must pass very close, since the surrounding channels are not navigable for large ships. I had some dead and wounded, among others the valiant officer Pocaroba, an Italian, who was decapitated by a cannonball.

Three miles beyond Martín García, the *Constitución* went aground in the sand and unluckily just at the beginning of low tide. It cost us endless trouble to get the ship off again and then to ward off a near annihilation which threatened our small fleet. While we were still occupied in transferring the heavy objects aboard the *Procida*, the enemy fleet appeared on the other side of the island and headed for us under full sails. Never before had I been in so frightful a situation: our largest ship aground and lacking its cannon, which now stood on the deck of the *Procida* crammed together in great disorder. Both ships were thus incapacitated for combat and only the *Pereira* remained, whose brave commander with the largest part of his crew had helped us in our labors.

In the meantime the enemy advanced upon us with seven warships, proud and sure of victory amidst the shouts of approval of the island population. My nature does not tend to despair; I have never known this feeling; but that my situation was an embarrassing and painful one everyone can easily judge. It was not only a question of life, for which in that moment I cared little, but also in fighting and dying it was difficult to save our honor, since in our situation it was almost impossible to accept battle. But once again providence held her hand protectively over my fate, and that was enough. The enemy's admiralship also went aground in the sand near the island, and the daring of the enemy was weakened by this. We were saved! The bad luck of our enemy heightened our courage and doubled our strength; within a few hours the *Constitución* was free and could take aboard again her batteries and other material.

"One piece of luck, good or bad, rarely comes alone," so goes the saying. A very dense fog soon enveloped the whole region and did us great service; it hid from the enemy the direction which we took. How much the enemy was mistaken about our route could be seen from the fact that his soldiers pursued us swimming as far as the Uruguay River, into which we had not sailed at all. In this manner the enemy lost many days before he was able to find out exactly the direction we had taken. In the meanwhile I reached the Paraná, protected by the fog and favored by the wind.

I was fully aware of the difficulties of my undertaking while believing that it was the greatest one of my life. But on that day the joy at the surmounted danger and the eagerness for the undertaking itself were no little embittered through the apathy and stubbornness of the pilots. Until that moment they had believed that they were steering towards the Uruguay[88] and pretended not to know the Paraná, hence refused all further responsibility. I really did not care much about their responsibility, what I needed was a pilot, the quicker the better. After a few questions it was learned that some of them actually had knowledge of the river, but were trying to get away from us because they were afraid. However, knowing this was enough; I quickly cleared up all obstacles with my sword. Soon we had a pilot. A favorable wind soon after blew us close to San Nicolás, the first little Argentinian town on the right bank.

There we found several merchant vessels, and since we very urgently needed smaller transport ships and helmsmen, we seized both on a nocturnal expedition. A certain Antonio, an Austrian, who had been trading on the Paraná a long time, fell into our hands as a prisoner and rendered us extraordinary services on our subsequent voyage.

As far as Bajada, where the army of Oribe was, nothing remarkable happened. We landed several times en route to take on fresh provisions which consisted mainly of cattle. This booty was often contested by the inhabitants and by the watchful cavalry, and often some skirmishes occurred which turned out at times good, other times bad. In one of these I lost the excellent officer Vallerga[89] da Loano, a young Italian of extraordinary courage and promising character, who, like so many other sons of Italy, had hoped at some time to shed his blood for the freeing of his unhappy fatherland.

In Bajada, the so-called capital of Entre Rios where the army of Oribe was stationed, we found the most terrible preparations awaiting us, so that before long we were engaged in a battle whose beginning made us fear the worst. However it turned out indecisive, for the favorable wind and our great distance from the enemy batteries made the cannonade, which had already begun, harmless for both parties. In Las Conchas, a few miles above Bajada, we managed a landing which netted us 14 oxen in spite of the most violent resistance of the enemy. Our men fought on this occasion with great bravery, even though the enemy artillery gave us considerable trouble by following us along the shore and using the counterwind, while the narrowness of the river exposed us to their fire for a long time.

In Cerrito, a strong point on the left bank, the enemy had placed a battery of six[90] cannon. The wind was favorable however, but weak, and just at that point blew towards us, because the many windings of the river obliged us often to change direction. We thus had to cover a distance of about two miles under fire from a battery which seemed to hang over our heads.

The battle was brilliant. The largest part of our crew was occupied with the small ships, the others with the cannon; we fought and worked with the utmost cheerfulness, although we had to deal with a proud enemy who had just been victorious and soon after was to defeat the two united armies of Montevideo and Corrientes at the Arroyo Grande. In the meantime we sustained small losses which were easily endured. We had silenced all enemy fire mouths and dislodged several pieces of artillery. Also several merchant ships which had come from Corrientes and Paraguay in order to place themselves under the protection of the enemy battery, fell into our hands.

Chapter XXIX

Sea Combat on the Paraná

So we continued upstream. The enemy got tired of putting obstacles in our way, and after having gone aground several times, we reached Cavallo,[91] where we joined the flotilla of Corrientes. The latter consisted of two sloops and a cutter armed for war. In consequence of this junction we came into possession of fresh provisions and our situation became satisfactory in every way, even acquiring helmsmen and some troop reinforcements, who although small in number helped to encourage and revive our crew. Thus we reached the Costa Brava and had a short layover because of the shallowness of the river, which at this spot had four palm-widths less water than was necessary for the draft of the *Constitución*. This circumstance began to instill in me worries about the success of our expedition. I knew well that the enemy had left nothing untried to thwart it, for once we reached Corrientes it would mean a tremendous disadvantage for him because we would then be in command of the entire river and would proceed to destroy enemy trade between the inner provinces and Paraguay on the one hand and the capital of the Argentinian Confederation on the other.

Thus it was understandable why the enemy tried to get rid of us at any price; and in this he was aided in quite a remarkable way by the incredible shallowness of the river (which according to the indication of Mr. Ferré, Governor of Corrientes, a similar shallowness had not been known for half a century). Therefore because it was impossible to advance, I decided at least to defend the flotilla as best as possible. Towards the left bank where the water was deeper, I drew up a line of ships beginning with a small vessel, on which I had mounted four cannon. The *Pereira* formed the center and the *Constitución* the right wing, so that our order of battle was vertical in the direction of the river and turned towards the enemy the strongest side. This line-up was not without difficulty because of the strength of the current which, in spite of its shallowness, was so strong that we had to tie up the ships, particularly the deep-draft *Constitución* with all its cables and chains.

Our labors were not quite completed when the enemy appeared in front of us with seven ships; he was not only superior to us in number, but also had the advantage of being able to receive reinforcements and provisions at every instant, while we, distant from Corrientes, the only place which might have helped us, had not the least possibility for reinforcements. Still, and first for the sake of honor, we had to accept battle. The enemy led by General Brown, the foremost maritime celebrity of South America, advanced against us confident in its might. I believe it was on 15 June 1842; the wind was favorable to the enemy, but weak, and through our left wing which was based on the left river bank, we dominated this shore. Consequently we put ashore sailors and marine troops unnecessary on board to contest step by step the warping being undertaken by the heavier enemy vessels in order to advance along the same shore. Our men fought bravely and very considerably retarded the progress of the enemy until he, having put 500 men ashore to oppose us, forced our numerically inferior group to return aboard under cover of our ships' cannon. Major Pedro Rodríguez, who had saved himself from the shipwreck off Santa Catarina along with me, commanded our landing troops and fought in this affair with great daring and skill.

After the enemy had posted his sentinels toward evening, he prepared for battle the next day. The sun had not risen yet, when he opened fire against us with all the artillery he had overnight been able to bring up, and until nightfall the battle was continued by both sides with the greatest violence. The first victim to fall on board the *Constitución* was again an Italian officer by name of Giuseppe Barzone, whose funeral I unfortunately could not attend, for the violently raging battle absorbed me. The losses on both sides were great; our ships were shot to pieces, the corvette had a considerable leak although we tried hard to plug the smaller holes, and was hardly able, in spite of incessant pumping, to stay above water. The commander of the *Pereira* had been killed on land by an enemy bullet; in him I lost my best and bravest comrade.

Although we already had many dead and wounded and the crew was tired and exhausted, we could not allow ourselves any rest since we still found powder and bullets on board, so had to continue fighting, not in order to win, but, I repeat, to save our honor.

We were fighting 600 miles distant from Montevideo surrounded by enemies on all sides, weakened, but not discouraged despite bad luck, hardships and battles, almost certain of our defeat, while Vidal, the Prime Minister of the Republic, was scraping together doubloons in order to cut a brilliant figure in the salons of European capitals. That's honor! Such is the world! For what did so many brave Italians shed their blood, who through the misfortune of their fatherland were driven to these far regions? Why was Colombo put in chains, Castelli decapitated in Buenos Ayres, Borso di Carminati shot in Spain? Thanks for such sympathy we received outside of your walls, O Rome, when your eternal neck wanted to shake off the shameful yoke, which your children and pupils, O Mother of Nations, had imposed on you! Of course they trembled when you shook your mane and only through deceit, disunity and the alliance of hell were you compelled to fall. But you are still great, O Italy, and the day will come when the hungry and cowardly vultures that gnaw on you will be chased away.

During the night of the 16th to the 17th the whole crew was busy making bullets, having almost expended those we had previously made, by breaking up anchor chains to replace needed cannonballs, and in pumping out the dangerous water. Manuel Rodríguez, the same Catalan officer who had saved himself with me from the shipwreck off S. Catarina, busied himself with a handful of picked men setting up small merchant ships as torches to direct towards the enemy ships with the greatest quantity of inflammable materials. This measure harrassed our opponents throughout the night but could not, despite all our efforts, achieve the desired end, because of the exhaustion of our men, the worst drawback we had to suffer.

But of all the mishaps of that hellish night, that which made me the saddest was the desertion of the Corrientes flotilla. In fact Villegas, its commander, a show-off like a thousand others, was so afraid of the impending danger that our allied ships, all manned by very good men and because of their lightness very suitable for service in the river, were of no use to me. I saw that Villegas was intimidated and commanded him to take up a position behind our line of battle next to the small vessel which we had converted into our hospital ship. Towards evening he sent word that he was going to alter his position somewhat (for what reason I do not know), but since I needed his cooperation badly for the setting up of the burning ships, I had him fetched, only to receive the shocking news that his squadron was not to be seen anywhere. I could not believe him capable of such treachery, so went over with a small ship to convince myself. Nevertheless, after sailing for a mile towards Corrientes and being unable to discover him, I returned unwillingly and saddened in heart. Indeed my grief was not without foundation, for since the greater part of our small ships had been destroyed in battle, I had counted on those from Corrientes to save our wounded and provisions during the inevitable retreat. This was so important, since we were a considerable distance from the inhabited border of Corrientes.

All my hopes were now gone, thwarted by the disloyalty and desertion of our allies in the hour of danger, the most ignoble of all crimes.

I returned aboard even before dawn. I had to fight and saw around me nothing but tired and exhausted men, heard nothing but the wailing of the wounded who, unable to fight, begged to be brought to the hospital. Still I had reveille sounded, let the men gather around me on one of the ship's pumps, then addressed a few words of comfort and encouragement to them. These words were not in vain; in the souls of my poor comrades I found a truly edifying strength of decision. An unanimous battle cry followed, then each one of these braves went to his post.

At first we thought that we had the advantage, but again on that day the worst was to happen to us. Our new bullets contained the most miserable powder, our cannonballs of heavy calibre being used up, we replaced them with smaller worse ones, so that our 18-pounders, which on the first day had harmed the enemy so much, now gave forth only weak uncertain shots. The enemy was informed of our condition through some deserters and became so daring as to make a front with all his ships, something he had not succeeded in doing the previous day. Thus while his position improved with every moment, ours deteriorated and we seriously had to think of retreating, not in our ships, for it was impossible to set them afloat, but individually, and try to save the weak remnants of our crew. I ordered that the wounded, the weapons, the munitions and provisions be brought to some small remaining ships. In the meantime the battle continued on, although weak on our side, it was stronger than ever on the side of the enemy.

We hardly had time to put the torch to our ships, when I went ashore accompanied by a small group. Naturally the enemy had noticed our landing and pursued us with his whole infantry. We were quite willing to fight but realized that such a battle would have been too uneven, partly due to the numerical superiority of the enemy, partly due to the greater skill of his infantry which was familiar with the terrain, and lastly, because we had to cross rivers of unknown depth. Fortunately the burning of our ships and the explosion of the powder magazine had caused such fright among the enemy that he soon desisted from pursuing us further. It was a terrifying and imposing sight to see the wreckage of the blown-up ships flying overland. At the spot of the explosion the river remained smooth as a mirror, while the debris crashed down destructively on both shores with a frightful din.

Chapter XXX

The Battle Near Arroyo Grande

$\mathbf{T}$owards evening we crossed the river Espinillo and camped on its right bank. To reach Esquina, the first little town in Corrientes, we took three days, marching constantly between islands and swamps; a small ship-biscuit was our daily ration. Our situation improved considerably in Esquina: the wounded found shelter and we all enjoyed a hospitable reception among the good inhabitants of the small town. In general though, the few months which we spent in the province of Corrientes did not offer anything of interest.

The government of the province had intentions of setting up a flotilla of armed vessels, but in fact nothing came of it and I sacrificed my time there uselessly. In the meantime I received from the government of Montevideo the order to march with my troops to San Francisco in Uruguay and to put myself at the disposal of General Rivera, who was near that place with his army. We thus crossed the whole region of Corrientes from Santa Lucia as far as Higos[92] Pass above the Uruguay River. After clearing out of that place we moved down to San Francisco partly by water and partly by land, where I found some of our warships, the command of which I took over.

General Rivera had gone with his army to Entre Rios to join the Correntinian troops and jointly to attack the army of Oribe. On 6 December 1842 at Arroyo Grande the memorable battle took place in which the cause of tyranny triumphed and three peoples were defeated who fought for the most holy rights. I shall not explain the cause of this disaster, for this would lead me afar; let it only be said that it was the eternal discord of a few, nourished by ambition and egoism, which brought those noble nations into misfortune and delivered them to the fury of annihilation by an implacable foe. What had happened in Italy we see repeated in the Plata states and for the same reasons; it was the pernicious elements which God in his wrath, or the devil himself, sows among men.

In San Francisco I remained only a short time because soon I received orders from General Aguyar, who was there for his health, to go with all available forces and a few hundred so-called *aguerridos* (that is, soldiers of Colonel Guerra) to the Vissilac Pass to cooperate with our main army. But when I reached Vissilac with the ships I found only a few traces of the existence of our troops, but not a single living being. I sent out some sentinels, but in vain, for it was the fatal 6th of December and every last man had been called to the battle being fought at a distance of 18 miles on the shore of the Arroyo Grande. There is in the depth of our souls something above our intelligence which is hard to define or describe, but yet exists and whose hidden feelings cause happiness or pain in us; our spirit looks to the future, for a divine breath blows through it and makes it immortal.

On that day something solemn, even though sad, hovered over us. One saw the unfortunate ones lying on the field of glory, trampled by the hoofs of horses and by those of an implacable victor. At this sight we all felt an indescribable disquietude which spoke less of sadness than of an evil foreboding. We found nobody who could give us information about the army, and since the promised commands of General Aguyar did not come, it was decided to put ashore the whole crew, leaving behind only a small group, so as to better search for our people. I want to mention here in passing that it was invariably my system never to march without cavalry. This system I followed also on this occasion, by putting together from my amphibious comrades an excellent contingent of cavalry. Some of the men in fact were excellent riders, former cavalrymen who had been dismissed for military misdemeanors but who fought well, even though they needed strict discipline and sometimes hard punishment. We soon found some abandoned horses to which my soldiers quickly helped themselves; this is readily understandable, considering the abundance of horses in those countries and the fact that war operations are greatly facilitated with them.

We were all ready to march when an order from General Aguyar recalled us back to San Francisco. Luckily for us! for certainly we would have fallen victims to that fate which had befallen our army which, defeated and dissolved, was no longer to be found, besides falling hoeplessly into the arms of the victorious enemy. Without knowing the cause for the new order and without having received the least information concerning the happenings there, we embarked again. On my arrival in San Francisco I received from Colonel Esteves[93] a note which began with the depressing words: "Our army has suffered defeat." In the meantime General Aguyar had marched along the left bank of the Uruguay River to round up fleeing men, while I was ordered to remain in San Francisco to protect the war materiel.

Chapter XXXI

Reflections

The time between the battle of Arroyo Grande and the beginning of the siege of Montevideo was a time of unclear brooding and plan-making; there was nothing but fears, desertions and undecidedness which however, emanated more from single individuals than from parties, for the people as a whole remained firm and answered with heroic energy the call of those brave ones, who seeing the fatherland in danger invited all citizens to save it. In a short while a new army was formed, less numerous and well-disciplined than the previous one, but more buoyant and enthusiastic, and wholly imbued with the sanctity of the cause to be defended. It was no longer a question of an agitator who incited the masses, the star of this man [Fructuoso Rivera] had set in the last battle and in vain tried to rise again, it was a question of the nation, in the face of which all hatred and disunity were silenced. The foreign enemy was threatening the territory of the Republic and every citizen rushed to the country's banner with arms and horses to repel him. The more the danger increased, the greater became the zeal and devotion of that stout-hearted people. Not one voice arose for negotiations, for desisting. I have to blush when I think what we in Italy did after the battle of Novara. And yet all Italy was longing for liberation from foreign yoke and thirsted to attack the enemy! I have the firm conviction that our people, as well as any other, is capable of steadfastness and patriotic revival. But the causes of our political misfortune . . . alas, those causes are innumerable![94]

Chapter XXXII

Montevideo Prepares for Oribe's Attack

Meanwhile I received the command to dispose the largest ships of our squadron in the tributaries of the river where the enemy fleet might arrive. Soon after the order was countermanded and I was instructed to burn the vessels. For the third time I was to sacrifice a fleet to the flames, only this time without even having fought!

Having turned into foot soldiers again, we remained a few more days in San Francisco in order to load the remnants of some army materiel destined for Montevideo; whereupon we directed our march there also, since all forces were to unite near the capital. On this march little or nothing important happened, except that I met General Pacheco who was at that time a colonel in Mercedes. This man began just at that critical time to give the most brilliant examples of courage, energy and capability, and without doubt was the most outstanding fighter in that gigantic struggle of his country against the invasion of the foreigners, a struggle which can serve as an example and model to all future generations unwilling to bow down before presumption. God save the brave people of the Banda Oriental!

Montevideo at that time presented an astonishing sight. Oribe, the victor, advanced without stopping at the head of an army which had already taken over the dissident Argentinian provinces with lightning rapidity. This Coriolan of Montevideo would certainly not have given in to kneeling priests and weeping women. The thought to chastise the city which had banished him, which had seen him flee, smiled upon the soul of the cruel one like the kiss of a lover. On the way already he killed whatever fell into his hands.

The army of Rivera was dissolved and only small disconnected remnants of it remained scattered over the Republic's territory. The squadron was destroyed, weapons and munitions just about used up. The state treasury reduced to nothing! And still a minister like Vidal thought of nothing else except raking together golden ounces, the most transportable travel money for his coming flight! And in the meantime we were supposed to defend ourselves! Rivera's party was indeed large and it insisted on national defense. But he had no power to restrain it, since it consisted partly of people who were tied to him through offices and connections for personal gain. On the other hand, the nation and the people saw in Oribe not only the opponent of Rivera but also the leader of foreign intruders, whose inroads were studded with death, destruction and slavery.

The army was placed under the command of General Paz, "the man of victories." General Paz, whom envy and jealousy had removed from command, did not hesitate to follow the call of the fatherland in need of him. Rushing towards the capital with his troops, he quickly created from recruits and freed slaves that army which has remained for seven years the chief defense of the country and still stands unassailable today opposite the most powerful enemy of South America. Many famous leaders, forgotten or neglected in wars which were directed by personal interests, reappeared again in the ranks of this army and augmented the soldiers' confidence and enthusiasm.

All around the town, and especially on the most exposed side, a string of fortifications were erected and completed before the approaching enemy. Arsenals, cannon foundries, assembling halls and the like were called to life as if by magic. The cannons, which had been regarded as superfluous since the days of the Spaniards and had been set up as curb-stones between the sidewalks and the road, were dug up and put into shape. Finally the arrival of General Pacheco from Mercedes and his taking over of the war ministry crowned in a way the defense preparations.

I was entrusted with the organization of the fleet and quickly had some ships built. A lucky circumstance favored me greatly in this task: namely the *Oscar*, an enemy brigantine which used to cruise at night near the shore, was stranded near the Punta del Cerro (a mountain west of Montevideo, the base of which forms the western part of the harbor) and was unable to get off, in spite of the greatest effort, and had to be abandoned by the crew. We immediately took advantage of this shipwreck, although the enemy at first wanted to dispute our right of booty, and his warship *Palmar* received us with fire. In the end he had to give us a free hand, as a result of the ineffectiveness of his fire and our unshakable energy. Among the many objects which we salvaged were five cannons which served us for the arming of the three small ships (the first ones of our new fleet) and thus also for the coverage of the left flank of our fortifications. This event seemed to me a good omen for the terrible battle of defense about to begin.

Chapter XXXIII

The Siege of Montevideo

It was the 16th of February 1843. The fortifications of the city had just been completed when the enemy appeared on the neighboring heights. General Rivera, at the head of his cavalry, did not feel strong enough to meet the enemy, so left the city in order to line himself up in the rear of the invader, thus by-passing his left flank. This brilliantly executed maneuver really put him into a position to begin the war with an advantage.

General Paz remained at the head of the troops in the capital. These were numerous in comparison to the small stretch of coast to be defended; but when one considers the condition of this newly recruited mass and the dangerous seeds which it encompassed, then one can only admire the astuteness, the courage and the endurance of this general, who withstood with these troops, engaged and disciplined by himself, the first and most dangerous tempests of the siege.

Despite the enthusiasm of the inhabitants there was no lack either of potential cowards and traitors. Vidal, the Prime Minister, had sacked the treasury and packed his things. Antuña, the Chief of Police, had gone over to the enemy with many officials and employees. A corps of the previously mentioned *aguerridos* (foreigners in the pay of the Republic) had deserted us in small sections; in fact, while occupying the advanced posts, they had even endangered the safety of the city through their treachery. These examples found imitators also among other individuals, who under different pretexts left the ranks of the defenders to go over to the enemy.

Our affairs did not go at all well in the beginning, and I could not understand why Oribe, who certainly must have had knowledge of these things, did not take advantage of our embarrassment with a strong attack on the city. Instead he limited himself to scouting and some false attacks at night, while establishing a camp one hour from the city.

In the city we gained time by this hesitancy to arm the foreign legions. Whatever may have been said about the spirit of these French and Italian groups, an enthusiastic response to the call "to arms" and an heroic zeal to defend the land of their exile from the invasion of the enemy cannot be denied. Certainly later many individuals also sneaked in whose aims were very different, but always the legions did great service to the besieged city. The French, who were more numerous and more easily carried away by their thirst for action, provided in a short time not less than 2600 men, the Italians only 500. Even though this latter number seems small in proportion to the representations of our nation amongst the populations of these countries, it was still much larger than I had expected, considering the present-day education of my countrymen. However its number increased and subsequently rose to 700. A Spanish Legion was also formed, although this was composed predominantly of Carlists who went over to the enemy after a few months.

General Paz used these reinforcements of his troops to set up a line of troops outside the city a cannon shot's distance from the wall. From this moment on the defense was carried on systematically and professionally, and the enemy was no longer able to approach the city. The organization of the fleet also proceeded as desired under my command.

Chapter XXXIV

Continuation

As commander of the Italian Legion I had proposed a certain Mancini, who was in fact accepted. The first action the Legion undertook was a sortie which, as was to be expected, did not cut a very brilliant figure. It was seized by terrible fright at the sight of the enemy and ran away almost without firing a shot.[95] Already people in Montevideo were mocking Italian courage, and I, almost dying of shame, had to take these bitter reproaches calmly!

A littler later the Legion was commanded to participate in an expedition at the Cerro. I was with them. General Bauza, a good soldier grown grey and already senile,[96] commanded the expedition. We were standing in sight of the enemy maneuvring back and forth without plan or decisive result. Perhaps it was not wise to attack the enemy with so few and little trained fighting forces. Still I believed that I had to incite the old General to attack, although for a long time I found no willing ear, until fortune sent us General Pacheco from Montevideo. The mere sight of him gave me courage and hope, for I knew him to be enterprising and anxious for battle. I approached and asked him with the familiarity permitted me to be allowed to drive the enemy out of his threatening position, since we were separated only by a ditch.

He not only seconded my proposal, but ordered General Bauza to have the Italian Legion advance. We attacked the left wing of the enemy who did not seem to fear us, but waiting for us firmly, received our attack with a terrible fire. However the Italian Legion was destined to win that day: many of the men collapsed wounded without hindering the Legion in its advance. Fearlessly we advanced and came head on thrusting our bayonets, when the enemy took flight and were pursued by us for a good distance.

Our center and left wing were also victorious, so that, not counting the dead and wounded of the enemy, 42 prisoners fell into our hands.

This feat of arms, although insignificant in itself, had extremely beneficial effects on the morale of our troops; it raised their self-confidence, while decreasing the courage of the enemy. It was the beginning of the renown to be achieved by the Italian Legion and its arms, the precursors of a thousand other deeds of our compatriots, from now on invincible.

The next day the Italian Legion was drawn up on the largest square of the capital and in sight of the whole population received the praise of the General and Minister of War Pacheco, as well as the vociferous acclamations of the crowd, which reverberated upon it like an echo of the strong words of the General. Never have I heard more touching words, never words more suited to arouse feelings of patriotism. Let it be mentioned here that with that Italian Legion the well-known Giacomo Minuto fought for the first time and with distinction, the same who later as a captain of cavalry in Rome died of a bullet wound in the chest because at the news of the entry of the French he tore off the bandage from his wound.

From this day on until the appearance of Anzani I only left the Legion when my duty as commander of the flotilla forced me to do so. I mentioned Anzani and must stop a moment at this time.

Anzani was at that time in Buenos-Ayres and came to Montevideo at my request. I had met him on that adventurous trip to Montevideo during which I led with me the 900 oxen. In San Gabriel I heard many stories of an Italian officer who, an exile like myself, had fought in France and in Oporto and now had dedicated his services to the young South American republics. Many proofs of his courage, his coolness and his bodily strength were recounted, but among others the following incited extreme admiration from me.[97]

When Anzani arrived in America he brought with him a letter of recommendation to the Messrs N. in V. of a commercial house in a South American city. The heads of this house, likewise Italians, received him hospitably, became fond of him and employed him in their business. Soon he became indispensable to them; he took over the job of cashier, of bookkeeper, advisor, in short he was the leading spirit, the real chief of the business.

71

As is the custom in South American commercial houses, the Messrs
N. dealt in almost everything, that is, anything that could be considered a
commercial commodity. The city in which they lived however was located near a forest and it happened that the Bugrés Indians, who have
been mentioned once before, also bought or sold there.

The chief of one of these Indian tribes by the way had become the terror of the small city. Twice a year he used to come and rob at will, without the people daring to resist him. At first he appeared accompanied by
two to three hundred of his men, later with a hundred, then with fifty;
but when he saw the fear in which he was held, he came each time with
fewer companions and at last usually quite alone. But the fear which
preceded him remained the same. When the cry "the chief of the mattos" was heard, all windows were closed, all doors barred and the streets
were deserted at once. This bothered the chief very little, perhaps he even
felt flattered by it. He used to pick out one house or another, knocked on
the door, which was opened tremblingly, took what he liked, then went
off without anybody placing an obstacle in his path.

Anzani had heard of this chieftain, but had not seen him yet. One
day, after he had been in the store for about two months, the cry was
heard again: "The chief of the mattos!" As usual all doors and windows
were quickly closed. Anzani happened to be alone, busy closing the accounts of the week, and finding in the cry no reason to let himself be
bothered, remained quietly seated behind his desk with windows and
doors wide open.

The Indian stopped astonished in front of this house which had all
signs of a complete lack of worry on the part of its inhabitants in the
midst of the general panic caused by his arrival. He entered and saw at
the desk a person with a quiet bearing who was filing his bills. He
stopped again, this time directly in front of him and gazed with visible astonishment and arms crossed.

Anzani raised his head. "What would you like, my friend?" he asked
the Indian with maximum politeness.

"What do I want?" the Indian retorted.

"Well, yes," explained Anzani, "when one steps into a store, he
wants to buy something."

The Indian started laughing. "So you don't know me?" he asked
Anzani facetiously.

"How can I know you? I see you for the first time."

"I am the chieftain of the mattos," answered the Indian ostenta-
tiously uncrossing his arms and exposing four pistols and a dagger stuck
in his belt.

"All right, then, Chief of the mattos, what do you desire?"

"I want something to drink."

"And what will you drink, Chief?"

"A glass of brandy."

"Nothing could be simpler; pay first, and then I'll give you your glass." The Indian again burst into laughter. Anzani wrinkled his brow, then pointed out calmly: "For the second time you laugh in my face instead of answering. I find this impolite and therefore warn you. If it happens a third time, I'll throw you out of the door!" These words were uttered with such certainty that anyone but an Indian would have known definitely that the speaker meant it. The Indian perhaps knew it too, even though he acted as if he did not, and repeated:

"I told you to give me a glass of brandy," and in so saying knocked on the desk with one of his pistols.

"And I told you to pay first; if not, you don't get anything." The Indian threw a furious glance at Anzani; but Anzani's glance met his. Then casting down his eyes before this determined face, the chief felt the superiority of his opponent. In fact, he felt somewhat embarrassed, hesitated for a few moments, then decided to have a drink in order to re-enforce his courage.

"All right, here is half a piastre; pour me a drink!"

"It is my business to pour for people who pay," and Anzani handed over a glass of brandy. The chief drank it up in one gulp, then called:

"Another!" Anzani poured a second one, then a third, and so on as the chief kept gulping down the drinks and crying "Another!" As long as the money was enough to cover the bill, Anzani made no remark; but as soon as the chief had drunk as much brandy as could be given for the coin, Anzani stopped.

"Well?" uttered the chief. Anzani calmly counted up the bill, while the savage impatiently urged him on, crying: "Pour!"

"Pour? No money, no brandy!" was the answer.

The chief had presumed correctly; the five or six glasses of brandy had brought back his courage, which had first vanished at Anzani's leonine stare. "Brandy!" he cried again, putting his hand on his pistol. "Brandy, or I'll kill you!"

Anzani was ready, for he had long suspected that the scene would end in this manner. He was a man of five feet nine inches in height, of remarkable bodily strength and suppleness. He leaned his right hand on the counter, then suddenly leaped over it and landed with his full weight upon the Indian, his left hand grabbing the right arm of the latter before he had time to fire his pistol.

The Indian could not withstand the attack; he fell backwards with Anzani on top of him, who nailed him quickly to the floor with his knee on his chest. Then with his left hand pressing the chief's right to his side, so that the weapon was rendered harmless, Anzani tore the pistols and dagger from his belt with his other hand and threw them into the store. Then he wrenched the pistol from the chief's hand, grasped it by the barrel and battered the savage's face with the hilt. When he finally thought the latter had had enough, he got up, shoved him out of the store with kicks, rolled him to the brook alongside and left him lying there. The Indian indeed had had enough; after a while he staggered to his feet and was never seen again in San Gabriel.

Anzani had fought in Portugal under the assumed name of Ferrari, had excelled and earned the rank of captain. There he received two wounds, one on the head, the other in the chest. The head wound was a sword stroke which had cracked his skull; the chest wound was a shot through his lung which sixteen years later caused tuberculosis. But when one spoke with Anzani and praised the wonders of bravery which he executed under the name of Ferrari, he would smile and remark that that Ferrari and he were two different persons.

Consequently what was more natural than my wish to meet this man! I was told in San Gabriel that he was absent on a business trip about twelve miles distant. So I mounted my horse to look for him. On the bank of a small stream I found a man with bare torso washing his shirt. I spotted him at first glance; he was the one I was looking for. I rode towards him, introduced myself, then stretched out my hand. From that moment on we were friends.

At that time he was no longer engaged by the commercial house but, like myself, had joined the service of the Republic of Rio Grande. He had commanded the infantry of the division of Juan Antonio and, like myself, left this service and was on the way to El Salto. We spent a day together and promised each other on parting not to undertake anything of importance without letting the other know.

To characterize this man I need only describe one more trait. Anzani owned only one shirt but two pairs of trousers. I was as poor as he in regard to shirts, but he was richer than I by one pair of trousers. We slept the night under one roof, although Anzani left before daybreak and without waking me in the least. When I awoke I found the better pair of his trousers on my bed.

On my request then, Anzani came from Buenos Ayres to Montevideo. Soon he became indispensable to the Legion and earned great renown for disciplining it. As much as Mancini and Danuzio, the second chief, hindered him, for they were unable to see eye to eye, he still persisted in organizing the Legion, as far as circumstances permitted, according to his system which was based on the most profound military and administrative knowledge.

Chapter XXXV

Continuation

The fleet under my command was not without merit in the defense of Montevideo, notwithstanding its smallness. Stationed on the extreme left of the line of defense it not only covered this flank completely, but also threatened the right flank of the enemy in case he should try an aggressive movement. Likewise it connected the important position of the Cerro with that of the Isola della Libertad and thus supported and facilitated all movements undertaken against the right flank of the enemy.

For a long time the enemy had been casting an eye on the Isola della Libertad and the squadron of General Brown made earnest preparations to seize it. We therefore decided to furnish it with artillery and I was entrusted with the task of transporting two eighteen-pounders there. It was around 10 o'clock in the evening when we executed this action and, after stationing a company of Italians on the island, I returned to Montevideo. This occasion is also characterized by one of those incidents in which I tend to recognize the hand of fate.

The Isola della Libertad is only a good cannon shot distance from the coast of the Cerro, from Montevideo almost three miles. The wind was blowing from the south and caused in the bay, varying according to the momentary strength of the wind, a considerable swell which was noticeable, especially as I crossed from the island to the breakwater (molo). I had a launch, bought a short while before for the government, and a few sailors with me. The boat used for the transport of the cannons, which had precisely a square shape, we took in tow. Naturally we advanced only slowly with this load and with the contrary wind drifted considerably towards the northern part of the bay. Suddenly we discovered warships coming towards us under full sail and soon were so close to us that our sentinels clearly heard the enemy caution "zitto zitto" ("Quiet, Quiet") to his men. Without doubt it was the enemy squadron; but speaking softly and doubling our oar strokes we got away without being molested. Our salvation was almost a miracle, although I believe that it must be ascribed to a totally different circumstance. Probably the small ships of the enemy had gone to the island to attack it, so that it had no other means with which to pursue us. That he did not even fire a shot against us is understandable, for he did not wish to attract the attention of our men on the island, whom they wanted to surprise. Hardly had we safely landed on the breakwater when we heard a terrible firing from the island. I sent word immediately to the government and went aboard to prepare our small flotilla for the relief of the island, on which I had left only 60 badly armed men.

At daybreak I set sail with two ships, a yacht and a boat, since the third one was not in condition to fire. Still our valiant countrymen fought with laudable courage although they were not trained soldiers and had not only driven back the enemy, but had also damaged him considerably. Yes, for several days one saw the bodies of the Rosas soldiers floating in the waters of the bay. A small boat which I had sent to the island brought me back the favorable news, and as soon as I was sure of the fate of our men I sent an officer over with a large store of munitions and several men to service the guns. But hardly had these landed when the enemy renewed his fire; our men on the island replied vigorously with their two cannons and I myself, placing my two ships in such a way that the wind blew us towards the enemy, did what I could. But the battle was all too unequal, the enemy disposing of two brigantines and two goelettes, one of which carried six cannons, compared to our two pieces on the island, not even mounted on a platform and fired by not very experienced cannoneers. The sea was not stormy but agitated enough to render the shelling difficult for our ships. In short, everything seemed unfavorable to us and again it appeared as if all hope for victory was lost.

But again God helped! Commodore Pierce,[98] who commanded the English fleet stationed in Montevideo at the time, sent a negotiator to Brown and the latter discontinued the fire soon thereafter. From that moment on, negotiations began; the enemy squadron left the bay and the island remained in our hands. Whatever may have been the motive for the intervention of the commodore, I believe that I may assume that some chivalrous generosity towards an unfortunate but brave people guided the humane son of Albion. Montevideo knew from that moment on that it had a friend and protector in the English commodore.

The affair near the island, the favorable outcome of which was ascribable to luck more than to anything else (although nothing had been omitted that could have been done by us in its defense), heightened the renown and esteem of Republican arms. And in this way, namely through small but fortunate undertakings, our cause aspired again to success, although most people had become despondent. The excellent and patriotic administration under the guidance of Pacheco, the conscientious and skilful execution of the war by General Paz, the fearless attitude of the population commanding respect and purging it of traitors and cowards, the successful arming of the foreign legions, all this led to hope for a successful outcome of our undertaking.

Chapter XXXVI

Further Feats of Arms of the Italian Legion

The Italian Legion, which had materalized in spite of the mockery of the French, soon caused the envy of the best troops: undefeated, it participated in the most difficult undertakings, in the most sanguineous fighting.

Near Tres Cruces, where dare-devil Colonel Neira had broken through the enemy line and fell behind their front, our Legion fought one of those Homeric battles, man against man, pushing the Oribists from their strong positions and retrieving the body of their leader. The losses of the Legion were very considerable in comparison to the small number of combatants, but the accomplished action far from exhausting it, favored its further development; daily it grew in numbers, and its newly engaged recruits fought like veterans. That is how the Italian soldier is, that is how the sons of that despised nation are, when they are imbued with the idea of the great and the beautiful.

Not less important than the engagement of Tres Cruces was the crossing of the Boyada on 24 April 1844. A division of the army had marched from Montevideo under the command of General Paz and had advanced along the northern shore of the bay against the right wing of the enemy as far as Pantanoso, where uniting with the troops posted at the Cerro, it was planned to overwhelm two enemy battalions standing on the swampy shores of the small river Boyada. Through lack of prompt collaboration this operation did not succeed, and we saw ourselves involved in an extremely bitter battle in forging the river-crossing.

Of the three divisions of which our corps consisted, about 7000 strong, the one which formed our rear guard was attacked by the enemy so violently that it could only with great trouble save itself in the extremely difficult river passage. I commanded the division in the center and the general gave me orders to come to the aid of those in trouble. Of course I obeyed, but with heavy heart, for defeat seemed inevitable. Our men fought bravely, but suffered from a lack of munitions and were surrounded by the enemy, who had already taken a fortified position (saladero) beyond our rear guard. The advance guard of the Italian Legion entered the saladero after the enemy column had already occupied it; now began, towards our side, a terrible battle man against man, from which the Italians emerged victorious. The ground was strewn with bodies, but our men were safe and had maintained themselves on the battlefield. Soon after they retreated, covered by a corps of troops which had just arrived. The French Legion, which at the same time was operating in another place, was defeated.

No less glorious for the Republic and for the Italian Legion was the 28th of March. The enemy commanded by General Nuñez, who in the beginning of the siege had gone over to him in a shameful manner, operated against the Cerro and showed such great daring that several times he came up to the defense works of the fortress, threatened to cut the connection with the city and destroyed the lighthouse by incessant fire. General Pacheco ordered several corps transferred to the Cerro, among which was also our Legion. The movement was carried out during the night, and at daybreak the Legion had taken up positions in an old powder tower, half a mile distant from the batteries of the Cerro. Although in ruins this building still had its protective wall and was just large enough to house the Italian Legion, that is, with difficulty. The affair soon became serious; the enemy daringly fell upon us and took the strong position called *quadrado* and was a shot's distance from our powder tower. Several of our men were already wounded, among whom the Colonels Tajes and Estivao, our best officers, when Colonel Caceres who directed the battle, gave the command to attack.

I shall always be proud to have belonged to that brave little group, which I had seen only on the road to victory; but on that day our Italians distinguished themselves quite particularly by their cold blood and courage. It was a question of attacking the enemy on a hill, behind a strong breastwork and protected by a ditch. The space over which we had to run in order to attack was anything but level, so that our undertaking was made considerably more difficult. But on that day the Legion would have braved even the devil himself, marching upon the enemy without firing a shot and without stopping. In a short time the enemy was thrown back to Pantanoso, three miles from the battlefield; Nuñez fell, and many prisoners came into our hands. The other corps also fought with great bravery, and if the above-mentioned movement had only been delayed a bit, so that our right column under Colonel Diaz would have had time to place itself between the river and the enemy, the latter would not have been able to save a single man of his infantry. The success of this feat of arms nevertheless did the greatest honor to the genius of General Pacheco.

Innumerable were the battles in which the Italian Legion participated during the first years of the siege; it never lacked dead and wounded, but nowhere did it show itself unworthy of its reputation. Its bravery was also appreciated. On 30 January 1845 General Rivera wrote me the following:[99]

"Sir! When last year I made a present to the honorable French Legion, which was accepted and of which the newspapers spoke, a present of a quantity of lands, then I hoped chance would bring to my headquarters any officer of the Italian Legion, who would give me the opportunity to fulfill a burning wish of my heart, namely to prove to the Italian Legion the respect which I feel for it because of the important services which it has rendered the Republic in the battle against Buenos-Ayres.

"In order now not to postpone any longer what I consider the fulfillment of a sacred duty, I enclose in this letter and with the greatest pleasure the act of a grant which I make to the brave and glorious Italian Legion as a sincere token of my personal gratitude for the heroic services rendered my country.

"The gift however is not in proportion either to the services or to my wishes; but you, Sir, will, I hope, not refuse to offer it to your comrades in my name and to inform them of my good will and of my thanks towards them, as well as towards you, Sir, who have led the Legion so worthily, and who even before this period have gained such an inalienable right to our gratitude by supporting our Republic.

"I take this opportunity, Colonel, to ask you to accept the assurance of my entire appreciation and my high esteem."

Fructuoso Rivera

The landed property, I must mention, which the patriotic General offered us was not property of the state, but his own inheritance. I answered him:

"Excellentissimo Signore! Colonel Parrodi in the presence of all the officers of the Italian Legion handed me according to your wish the letter which you were kind enough to send me dated 30 January and with this letter a document in which out of your free will you make a present to the Italian Legion of a number of lands in your possession between the Arroyo de las Avenas and the Arroyo Grande, north of the Rio Negro, and in addition a herd of cattle, as well as the haciendas located on this property.

"You say that the present is made by you in gratitude for the services which we have rendered the Republic.

"The Italian officers, after noting the content of the letter and its enclosure, have unanimously declared in the name of the Legion, that when they begged for arms and offered their services to the Republic they in no

79

way expected to receive anything other for it than the honor to participate in the dangers which awaited the children of the country, and who
received them hospitably. In acting thus, they obeyed the voice of their
conscience. While having satisfied what they simply regard as the fulfillment of a duty, they will continue, according to the needs of the siege, to
share the trouble and dangers of the noble population of Montevideo,
but they ask no other prize and no other recompense for their pains.

"I therefore have the honor to communicate to you, your Excellency,
the answer of the Legion with which my feelings and opinions are wholly
in accord.

"Consequently I am returning to you the original of the grant.

"May God grant you a long life."

Joseph Garibaldi

So the Italian Legion continued to serve without recompense. The
only way to procure some money, when it proved absolutely necesary to
buy a piece of clothing, was to do duty for a French or Basque merchant,
for which the latter paid two francs to the substitute.

Chapter XXXVII

The Expedition up the Uruguay River

At India Muerta General Rivera was defeated; consequently he
was banished by the Montevidean Government as being the source of the
country's reverses and fled to Brazil. The defense of the capital however,
was not neglected because of this: on the contrary, the garrison was
strengthened and trained in daily fighting and proved morally superior to
the besiegers. Colonel Correa took over the command of the garrison,
while Pacheco and I remained the soul of the defense. Added to this was
the English-French intervention which gave matters a decidedly favorable turn. Among the operations recommended by the governments and
the admirals of the two friendly nations, the most important was an expedition up the Uruguay, which was entrusted to me.

The national flotilla had recently been increased by several vessels, of
which some were rented, some sequestered and others seized from enemy
merchant fleets visiting the various points of the shore which belonged to
him. In addition two ships of the Argentinian squadron were sequestered

by the Anglo-French and put at the disposal of the Oriental Government, so that the expedition which we undertook up the Uruguay consisted of about 15 ships, the largest being the *Cagancha,* a brigantine of 16 cannon, and the smallest some whalers.

The landing troops consisted of 200 men of the Italian Legion, 200 native soldiers under Colonel Batlle and about 100 cavalrymen, besides two small four-pounders and six artillery horses. It was towards the end of the year 1845 when the expedition left Montevideo. The quickly-won results were brilliant but without avail for the unfortunate population of the Banda Oriental. Our purpose was to occupy the Island of Martín García, the city of Colonia, a few other points and especially the Salto, as a result of which communication with Brazil was reopened.

We first reached Colonia, where the Anglo-French squadron was waiting for us. The taking of the city was easy. Under cover of a superfluous firing I landed with the legionaries. The enemy resisted at first, then soon after dared make a sortie to measure his strength with ours. After us, the allies landed, whose protection I had requested from the admirals; but hardly had we begun the battle and achieved certain advantages, when the allies, I do not know for what reason, retired and forced us to do likewise, since alone we were not equal to the enemy.

Now the enemy decided to evacuate the city, forcing the inhabitants to leave and setting the place afire. The legion under Batlle's command, which had been landed first, pursued the enemy on his retreat, while the allies, who came later, occupied the devastated city. Amidst the rubble and places burned it was of course difficult to maintain strict discipline or avoid looting: the English-French soldiers, in spite of strict orders from their admirals, without further to-do appropriated the property scattered on the streets and in the houses.

Our men followed and only partially were we successful through our intervention to restrict this dreadful state of things. Naturally the main loot consisted of provisions and mattresses which had been forgotten during the evacuation of the city; but however that may be, certainly those excesses could have been avoided if the allied soldiers had set a better example. On purpose now I am insisting upon the details of this event, in order to nullify through a faithful and true account certain insinuations which have emanated from a Mr. Page, at the time commander of a [French] brigantine of war.

His countrymen said that he was a pawn of Guizot[100] sent out to inform him of what happened. I cannot decide whether this Page was a diplomatic spy or not; but this much is sure, that among the population French sympathies were aroused and that on landing in Colonia I was forced to send my men under cover, for the French ship fired upon us without ceasing. Several of our men were wounded by the splinters of rock which were deflected by the shots.

We were then ordered somewhere else to reinstate the authority of the Republic along the coast of Uruguay. The Island of Martín García surrendered without resistance. There I received a number of oxen and some horses.

It was in Colonia that I met for the first time a matrero. He was called Vivorigna[101] and was one of the strangest of men who belonged to this patriotic group. The services of these valiant adventurers were very useful to our expedition.

The matrero is indeed a truly independent man. In that part of South America one of them often rules over an extensive stretch of land with the authority of a chieftain. He does not levy taxes and duties, but he demands and receives from the inhabitants whatever he needs for his wandering life. A good horse is indispensable to him. His arms, which usually consist of a carbine, a pistol, a sword and a knife are his inseparable companions and without which he does not believe he could live. The ox supplies him with everything: the saddle, the *maneas,*[102] or thong, with which he ties up his horse on the pasture, the *bolas* (balls for throwing), indispensable for catching wild horses, the *lazos* or slings, which always hang on the right hip of his horse, and finally the meat which is the only food of the matrero.

When one realizes that the knife is indispensable to him in making these objects, one can imagine how highly he esteems it; also he uses it with a strange ability in wounding and slitting the throats of his enemies.

The matrero is the gaucho of the Rio Grande, that is, the *monarco de la cuchilla* (the monarch of the knife),[103] only freer and more independent than the latter. He only obeys the authorities of the country when the ruling system corresponds with his opinion and his sympathies. Field and forest are his dwelling and the ground his bed. He is easily satisfied. When he enters his house he finds there one who really loves him and shares his hardships and dangers with an endurance and strength of soul which equals his.

Woman, according to me the more perfect creature, seems by nature to be more chivalrous and more ready for adventure than man, and it can only be ascribed to the slavish upbringing to which she is condemned in that country, if examples of feminine heroism are to be found there so rarely.

Vivorigna was the first matrero to join my troops, although he was not the best one. On the east shore of the Inferno Canal between the Island of Martín García and the continent, he commandeered a vessel by merely putting his pistol to the chest of the helmsman and compelling him to take him to the island, where he offered himself to me. Several matreros followed him and they rendered us great services during the last operations of the war. But the man whom I must praise especially, because with the boldness of a matrero he combined the good sense and the cold blood of a good captain, was Juan de la Cruz Ledesma, who in this account will be mentioned repeatedly later.

Juan de la Cruz with his black headdress, his eagle eyes, his noble bearing and fine character was a faithful and untiring companion of the

Uruguay expedition, which I regard as the most brilliant in which I was ever involved. He and Joseph Mundell, equally brave but of more refined manners, will remain unforgettable forever.

While Colonel Batlle entrenched himself with the natives of the garrison in Colonia, we left Martín García, where we had hoisted the Republican banner, left behind a few of our men and moved inland along the river. Anzani directed the vanguard with a few of the smaller vessels and took possession of several merchant ships sailing under the protection of the enemy fleet. Thus we reached the Jaguary, a river flowing into the Rio Negro and the Uruguay.

Here the Rio Negro forms several islands of considerable size, which even though covered with forest and pasture are made almost uninhabitable because of the frequent floods; and still our troops, apart from some wild horses, also found several oxen on them. These islands also gave us the very important advantage of being able to land our horses here and offer them some recovery after the strain of travelling.

On the other side of the islands, formed in the south by the Rio Negro and in the north by the Uruguay, lies the *Rincón de las Gallinas,* a kind of promontory connected with the mainland by an isthmus and which is famous as one of the favorite places of the matreros.

My first care was now to occupy a strong point on the shore of the Rincón with a part of the troops already landed. From here I sent out Vivorigna with Miranda, one of his companions, for reconnoitering. They soon came upon several other matreros who readily joined the expedition and whose example found rapid imitation, so that in short time we were able to form a not inconsiderable cavalry corps. During the course of the same night still another attack on a small enemy detachment was undertaken which had a most happy result. To a certain Gallegos, who had accompanied the troops from Montevideo, this command was entrusted. He surprised the enemy, twenty in number, of whom he made six prisoners and wounded several more. The result of this small affair was that we captured several horses, an acquisition most profitable for us in the present circumstances.

The enemy was trying to send the inhabitants into the interior, to cut off every connection between them and our troops. But this decided many of those unfortunate ones to join us on the larger islands, where they found a cordial reception and a safe refuge. Our soldiers did not neglect to drag along a large number of animals, mainly sheep, for our food.

In the meantime I started to worry about Juan de la Cruz who had left us several days before. From the matreros of the Rincón who were with us at the time I learned that he had, at the head of his troops, fought against several enemy irregular bands, that then he let his men scatter as he yielded to the superiority of the enemy and had fled into the innermost thicket of the forest. He had to abandon even his horse, and using a canoe looked for a hiding place on one of the least frequented islands of the Uruguay. But even there, he was in no way safe from enemy pursuit, especially after the Battle of India Muerta, when there no longer existed a national corps in the country and the enemy could pursue the matreros all the more without being disturbed.

I therefore ordered an old companion of Juan by name of Saldaña to seek out his hiding place, accompanied by a few other matreros and to bring him back. The mission was successful. After a few days of fruitless searching he was found on an island hiding in a tree to which he had tied his canoe, since it was the time of the floods and the island was under water. The spot he occupied was chosen so cleverly that he easily could have fled into the forest if enemies instead of friends had found him out.

The young Italians who took part in that expedition got a taste of the life which they would be called upon to lead if they wanted to see their own country liberated. There was indeed no lack of hardships, difficulties and adventures; still until then we did not have to bemoan any serious mishap. The saving of Juan was for us an important asset: from that day on we had all the matreros of the surrounding district at our disposal and an excellent cavalry, without which little or nothing could have been undertaken in those districts.

The Isla del Biscaino, the largest island of the Uruguay, soon became a small colony populated partly by the families which had escaped the barbarity of the enemy and partly by other refugees from the capital. Then, as soon as we had properly organized and equipped ourselves with the most necessary, we started to penetrate further into the interior and soon reached a place lying on the shore of the Jaguary River by name of Fray Bento, where our ships anchored. About eight miles further up on the other shore in the province of Entre Rios, belonging to the enemy, is the mouth of the River Gualeguaychú and six miles distant from that lies the place of the same name. But in order to undertake an attack in that direction we needed several horses, of which there were excellent ones in that area, as well as cloth to clothe the soldiers. A raid was undertaken with this aim, and in order not to arouse suspicion, I continued my trip up the river. During the night the smaller vessels manned by the Italian legionaries and a detachment of cavalry approached the landing area.

An hacienda was located at the mouth of the river and we knew also that a small warship and several merchant ships were there, all of which had to be overpowered for the attainment of our goal. This was carried out. Our troops succeeded in reaching the house of the commander of Gualeguaychú and to surprise him in his sleep. Soon all the authorities and the National Guard were in our hands, and we posted Republican troops at the strongest points. When this was done the expedition began to muster horses and whatever else we needed most urgently. We also seized some money, which I ordered to be distributed among the soldiers and sailors. A corps of enemy cavalry garrisoned there, but which was absent on our arrival, soon approached and when the sentinels posted by us saw it return, we sent out against it the best of our mounted men. An engagement took place in which the enemy was driven back, and the favorable outcome encouraged the Republicans no little.

The expedition now penetrated further into the interior, as far as Paysandú, without experiencing anything worth mentioning. A considerable enemy occupation was there: the enemy had erected several batteries and had sunk ships in different places of the river to block our passage. But we overcame all obstacles. A few holes in our ships and a few wounded were the only consequences of a heavy cannonade from the enemy batteries.

Here I must mention two officers, one English and one French, who commanded two small ships under their own flags and accompanied me almost during the whole expedition, although they had orders not to fight. Dench, [104] the English lieutenant, remained only a short while with me, but Morier,[105] the French officer who commanded the schooner l'*Eclair,* did not leave me and became dear and valuable to me because of his agreeable personal qualities.

We reached Hervidero, formerly a splendid settlement but now empty and deserted and only enlivened by the raging and seething of the innumerable whirlpools which make the river, studded with reefs, like a cauldron of boiling water. In fact the name Hervidero, from hervir *to boil,* apparently was so-named because of this, and as can be imagined, at this spot passage is extremely dangerous.

On a height overlooking the left bank of the river was situated a very spacious house with a terrace on the roof. All around it were many *ranchos* or barracks with straw roofs which proved that in quiet times the owner possessed a large number of slaves. As I approached the house I found herds of *ganado manso* (tame oxen) wandering about the abandoned quarters as if looking for their banished masters, also a *majada* or herd of sheep of 40,000, while the *ganado cuero* or *alzado,* i.e. the wild cattle, was spread far over the fields.

From these few remarks one can get an idea of those tremendous properties which are called *estancias* in the America of the south. Finally there was also a *saladero* here, that is, a slaughtering house and a place where the meat was salted, and the hides, the fat, in short everything that the slaughtered animals of the country provided, were prepared for export.

Anzani took possession of this settlement and occupied it with troops. When I learned from some of the men sent out by Juan de la Cruz that the previously-mentioned matrero Mundell was to be found at the Arroyo Malo, 30 miles below the waterfall, I decided to go towards him. This Joseph Mundell had come to this country when still a child and had made himself familiar with its inhabitants and their customs. He owned one of the most beautiful estancias of this region and belonged to those privileged ones who seem born to rule. Without any special personal distinction he was still of a strong enterprising nature and of noble mind. Through his generosity he won the hearts of all, ensured their allegiance and toned down their rough habits. He was extremely adventurous. Although he had spent the greatest part of his life in the desert, he had developed his spirit and acquired unusual knowledge. He never took part in politics except if it was a question of a presidential election or similar matter. But when the foreigner under the banner of Oribe invaded the Republican territory, he deemed indifference to be treachery and rushed into the ranks of the defenders.

With his influence it was easy for him to gather several hundred men around him, so that scarcely had this happened, when he notified me that he wanted to join me with his men. Mundell's self-sacrifice easily explained the readiness with which I rushed towards him. The enemy however, made use of my absence and already during the first night made an attack on the Hervidero. I had not yet reached the Arroyo Malo when I heard cannon thunder and musket fire. This upset me no little, although I trusted in the ability of Anzani, to whom I had transferred entire responsibility. This attack on the Hervidero had been so cleverly thought out by the two enemy commanders, General Garzón from Entre Rios and Colonel Lavalleja (originally) from the Oriental state, that in case of success it would have become extremely fatal for us.

Garzón with his 2000 men was to hold the right bank of the river, while Lavalleja had been entrusted with the attack on the Hervidero, and in order that everything should happen simultaneously the enemy had posted two burning ships in the smaller River Juy, which even if not destined to burn the Republican flotilla, at least was to prevent the sailors from assisting our land troops. The courage, the cold blood of Anzani and the braveness of the soldiers however, foiled all attempts of the active enemy.

Garzón accomplished nothing with his continuous musket fire because they fired from too great a distance and because the shore was defended courageously by our flotilla. The burning ships abandoned to the current drifted by our ships at some distance and were destroyed by their fire. In vain Lavalleja pushed his troops against the valiant legionaries barricaded in the dwellings; in fact, the calmness and firm resistance of the latter unnerved them. Anzani had commanded that his people were not to stir and not to fire until the enemy had approached so closely that their clothes could be singed by the shooting. This plan succeeded. Believing the houses to be empty, the enemy approached unsuspectingly and when unexpectedly they were received with a general musket fire, they had no other choice but to flee at once.

After I had arranged with Mundell that he was to come to the waterfall [Salto] only after its occupation by the Republicans, I returned to the Hervidero. At this same time I also learned that Colonel Baez was preparing to join me with his men. Concerning the enemy, his only ship was stationed on the Juy and it went over to us with part of its crew. In short, everything seemed to favor our expedition.

The province of Corrientes was dominated again by Rosas after the Battle of Arroyo Grande; but the admirable resistance of Montevideo, and other influences, continued to keep alive in the people the spirit of independence. Madariaga and the chief leaders of the revolution turned over the command of the army to General Paz of Montevideo and this aged and brave leader soon succeeded in convincing the province [that is, state] of Paraguay of an offensive and defensive alliance and to collect a considerable contingent.

From the Hervidero I sent a *balenera* (a small vessel) on a mission to General Paz; but my delegates, observed and pursued by the enemy, were forced to flee into the forest. The same thing occurred three times until finally a brave Italian officer by name of Giacomo Casella, utilizing a strong tide overcame all obstacles and arrived unharmed in the province of Corrientes.

Favored by the same tide I reached the town of Salto with the flotilla. It was in the hands of Lavalleja, who had driven out the inhabitants after barely three days of fighting. His troop camp was on the left bank of the River Tapebí,[106] 21 miles distant from Salto. We took the town without resistance and got ready to erect some fortifications, since we were exposed to constant attacks from the surrounding land.

One of the main hardships consisted in the lack of meat, for all animals had been driven away. But when Mundell, together with 150 men whom he had collected around him, had fought themselves through an enemy corps and had reached Salto safely, we began a number of foraging expeditions in which we captured enough cattle for the subsistence of our troops. Now with the cavalry of Mundell and Juan de la Cruz we were strong enough to campaign. Some of the enemy's deserters had informed me exactly about his position and the number of his troops and I decided to attack him immediately.

One evening I left Salto with 200 cavalrymen and 100 Italian legionaries with the intention of surprising the enemy before daybreak. Deserters were our guides. Although they knew the country, they still lost their way in the pathless region we were traversing, and as morning dawned we were three miles distant from the camp which we sought. It was perhaps not wise to attack an enemy superior in force and entrenched in his camp, who might at any hour receive reinforcements, which he had asked for; but to turn back would not only have been shameful, but would have reacted disadvantageously upon the spirit of the new troops. Thus I advanced. Soon I reached a height where the enemy had posted advanced guards. On my approach they retreated. From that point I could clearly discern the enemy camp and observed how from all sides detachments were returning to it; they apparently had been sent out during the night to spy upon our movements. I let Mundell, who commanded the vanguard, go ahead with a strong cavalry corps in order to prevent their concentration. The enemy did the same, to delay our marching and to shield his troops. The brave Mundell however succeeded in destroying several detachments, but in the heat of battle he continued his pursuit too far and soon his men saw themselves surrounded by their enemies and in the greatest danger of being separated from the main corps.

My original plan was to unite the Republican fighting forces and then to make a decisive attack, but when I noticed that Mundell's situation allowed no delay I left behind the infantry under Marrocchetti's command and rushed ahead with the cavalry reserve in small detachments. The first echelon advancing under Gallego's command reinforced Mundell's corps, and an attack of Juan de la Cruz drove the enemy back into his camp. Now I ordered the reserve echelons to attack in a compact mass, so that Mundell and his men, who had fought so bravely, could straighten out their ranks again. Soon after our troops in battle order marched upon the enemy camp; the infantry was in the center, with the command not to fire a shot, while Mundell was on the right, Juan on the left, and a small echelon of cavalry formed the reserve.

After the first clash the enemy cavalry posted itself behind the infantry, protected by a row of carts. Still the firmness and perseverance of the Republicans, approaching silently and in closed ranks, intimidated our enemy to such an extent that it offered only slight resistance. The battle was soon over, or rather, it had not been a battle but a complete rout and hasty flight of the enemy towards the Tapebí ford. On arriving there some of the bravest tried to make a final stand, although this was indeed most difficult. They had stopped the Republican cavalry, but at the command "grape shot to the neck" the Republican infantry flung itself into the river with true contempt of death and all resistance was eliminated.

The victory was now complete. The whole infantry and a part of the enemy cavalry was in our hands, as well as all the families of Salto the enemy had dragged away from their dwellings, and finally, also 34 carts heavily loaded with all possible merchandise. We also captured many horses and a brass cannon made long ago by a certain Cenni in Florence. With this same piece they had shot at us from the Hervidero, and since it had been damaged by our fire, it was now waiting for necessary repairs in the enemy camp.

After arranging our men we began the march back. Our march to Salto was a true march of victory; the population poured blessings upon us from the houses whose reoccupation they owed to us. This victory earned for the army a well-deserved renown, since its three divisions had all proved that they could hold the field.

Our agility had been of the greatest use to us, for the enemy, as mentioned before, expected considerable reinforcements and General Urquiza, who shortly before had triumphed at India Muerta, was en route with all his forces to Corrientes to fight against the army of that province. Indeed the next day after our return there, Vergara, who commanded the enemy advance, appeared already in sight of Salto and captured some of our horses which were scattered in the surrounding pasture. Threatened by such a superior enemy we had to try our utmost to offer him resistance.

An entrenched battery laid out by Anzani in the center of the town was in the meantime making surprising progress. Soldiers and citizens worked on it; the houses suitable for defense were occupied and every man was assigned his post. Several cannons were fetched from the vessels; in short, everything was done to equip the battery well. Soon Urquiza, who had assured his friends that he would take the Republican flotilla without delay and cross the Uruguay with their help, presented himself. But this prophecy did not come true, although he did not let us wait long for his attack.

East of Salto, about a cannon shot distant from the first houses, there is a hill which dominates the whole town. The Republicans had not occupied it for lack of fighting forces and Urquiza, as was to be expected, took possession of it with six cannon. At the same time he let his infantry advance with rapid pace on the right flank of the Republicans.

Our battery was equipped with two pieces of artillery, but was lacking in breastworks, as well as in terraces, and the enemy after firing quickly threw himself onto the terrain still unfortified. Our right flank was the weakest, since the enemy could reach it unseen through a hidden gorge. This is indeed what happened. Before we realized it, he broke forth from this hiding-place. The attacked wing yielded and whoever was in the houses fled towards the river. I was at the time with the battery along with a company of Italian legionaries, whom fortunately I had stationed in my vicinity as a reserve. I let them charge the enemy; they did, and carried out the charge with so much bravery that the attackers finally had to take to flight. Discouraged by this, the enemy desisted from further attacks, confining his operations to a moderate cannonade. The amount of his dead greatly surpassed ours; on the other hand, we lost a large part of our wild oxen. Kept in a corral (or enclosure), they took the first opportunity to flee from it and scatter into the surrounding territory.

During the next three days however, Urquiza renewed his attacks, but he found the besieged increasingly better entrenched, for we let no moment of the night pass unused. Five pieces of artillery comprised the battery; the terrace and the breastwork were ready, and the *Santa Barbara* or line of explosions, was also prepared. A proclamation in the meantime was issued; signed by Colonel Baez and me, it proclaimed that anyone leaving his post was punishable by pain of death. In addition small vessels were forbidden to approach the river bank, and those which were already there were obliged to move away. The enemy thus noticed that he could hardly accomplish anything, so consequently blockaded the town closely by land; but even that was of little avail, for we, lords of the river, were able to bring up everything necessary. During the 18 days' siege we were very busy; especially we did not neglect to attack the chain of advanced posts the enemy set up around us, first here, then there, and always we were successful.

Urquiza tired of the affair and, perhaps called by more important business to another part of Uruguay, retreated and crossed the river above Salto. Only the Generals Lamas and Vergara with their divisions and 700 horses remained to continue the siege. Nevertheless from that time on it was impossible for the enemy to enforce the blockade because we made sorties from time to time, capturing sometimes oxen, other times horses, which were particulrly useful to our cavalry, sorely tried by the hardships of the siege.

A peculiar operation was carried out in those days by the Republicans. General Garzón, who had pitched his camp in Concordia, opposite Salto, had marched to Corrientes to unite with Urquiza; in Concordia he left behind a reconnaissance corps of cavalry. Its sentinels could clearly be seen from Salto and we had observed how the *cavalladas,*[107] or herds of horses, of the enemy every morning came to the river bank, probably because they found better pasture there, and returned again at night. A plan was made to capture these animals.

About twenty of our cavalrymen, accompanied by a company of legionaries, stealthily descended to the river bank. Towards noon, when the sun's rays were burning most strongly and the enemy sentinels were resting without suspicion in the shade of their distended *ponchos,* the soldiers, who had taken off their clothes and were armed only with a sword, rushed from their hiding place upon a given signal and threw themselves into the river which at that place was unguarded and only 500 feet wide, while the legionaries quickly stepped into waiting boats. Soon they had all reached the opposite shore, and when the sentinels awoke they heard nothing but the whistle of bullets of their agile attackers and saw nothing but the amphibious centaurs who, on their just-captured horses, were pursuing them along the river bank as far as the nearby heights.

Only South American cavalry is capable of such an undertaking, since man, as well as horse, are excellent swimmers and can cross a mile-wide river without difficulty. They hold on to the mane or the tail of their animals, carrying their arms and baggage in so-called *pelotas,* which are made of a piece of leather (carona)[108] and at the same time are part of the horse's harness. Some of our centaurs remained on the hills to hold the enemy in check, while the others captured the horses scattered on the pasture and drove them into the water and to the opposite shore. Whatever enemy offered resistance, he was tied up and brought to the boats. During this maneuver the legionaries exchanged only a few shots; the number of the enemy did increase, but was not sufficient to chase away our men.

In this manner within a few hours we gained over 100 horses without losing a man. We could watch this whole affair from Salto. The horses of Entre Rios are valuable and generally prized, and this sortie provoked our enemy, not without cause, to renewed attacks.

Vergara's division meanwhile harrassed the town in the most stubborn way. From the testimony of some natives sent to spy upon the enemy's position, it was impossible to surprise him during the day, so the night had to be used for that purpose.

Hence I gave Colonel Baez the command of the cavalry and Anzani that of the infantry. We left Salto at nightfall and headed for the enemy camp which was about eight miles distant. Although the troops were marching very softly and carefully, they were still heard by the enemy sentinels. The attack followed immediately, but unfortunately only the cavalry could take part, for the legionaries, in spite of all efforts, had not reached the battlefield on time. The enemy fought bravely, but upon the call "the infantry" which was sounded at the right time, he broke ranks and fled; he was followed for several miles, but due to darkness little was won, with the exception of a few prisoners and a few horses which we captured.

At dawn several enemy troops became visible on the heights and Colonel Baez remained behind with the cavalry, partly to pursue them, partly to collect a herd of oxen, while the other troops returned to Salto. Just at that time, that is, in the beginning of the year 1846, we received news that General Medina had left Corrientes with a number of refugees from the Oriental state and were headed for Salto. We were expected to protect his march which was all the more difficult since Lamas, upon hearing of Vergara's defeat, had rushed to his aid and both were now preparing with their united troops to blockade our position.

Colonel Baez, who had close relations with Lamas,[109] knew that he would arrive on 8 February, and we therefore decided to meet him with our cavalry. At daybreak on 8 February 1846 we left Salto and headed for the small river San Antonio on the left bank of which the General [Medina] with his army was expected.

The enemy, according to the custom of the land, advanced small cavalry divisions from time to time onto the hills lying on the right, probably with the intention of hindering us in catching horses. Colonel Baez set up a line of marksmen against these enemy troops and engaged them for several hours. The infantry stopped in the tapera of Don Venanzio,[110] a locality lying on the river, and from here we watched the guerrilla fighting led by Colonel Baez, which we observed with the acutest attention and the most vivid interest. But the enemy only tried to hide his real strength through that military play by letting only a small part of his forces advance to deceive his opponents, while withholding his large reserve corps for an opportune moment to advance unexpectedly.

The terrain of this whole district is hilly, permitting the enemy to bring his important forces unnoticed into our immediate vicinity. When I reached the observation point, I was shocked to see that on the west side of a neighboring hill on the far side of San Antonio, where only a few of the enemy had been seen before, a true forest of lances was now shining! Seven squadrons of cavalry with unfurled banners and an infantry corps twice superior to ours formed a terrible battle array only two lengths of shooting distance from us.

This entire might advanced on the double to attack us with drawn bayonets. "Let us retreat" said Baez to me, but since I had convinced myself that this was impossible, I replied: "There is no time, we must fight." Then I rushed to the legionaries and in order to wipe out, or at least alleviate the impression which the appearance of such a mighty enemy might make upon them, I cried out: "Today we must be brave and we shall triumph in spite of our small number!"

At the spot where we took up our positions stood several poles driven into the ground, which had formerly been part of an old building; at each of these posts a legionary was posted. The remainder formed three small divisions and were stationed in a column behind the building. On the right of the infantry stood Baez with the cavalry; the carabineers dismounted, while the lancers remained on horseback. Our whole might comprised 100 cavalrymen and 186 legionaries. The enemy on the other hand had 900 cavalrymen, according to some sources 1200, plus 300 infantry. If the enemy had attacked in columns or in different groups, instead of in an extended line of battle, he could have easily broken our ranks, indeed annihilated us totally, and San Antonio would still today be white with Italian bones. But he was foolish enough, luckily for us, to advance upon us in one line and only when he reached a certain point did he open fire. This moment was decisive. Many of our men succumbed; but also the attackers became confused as their ranks thinned out in face of the Republican fire. Then by throwing ourselves upon the enemy in a compact mass and attacking him with almost mad courage we succeeded in beating him back.

It cannot be denied that there were for us moments of disorder and indecision. Among us we had a number of prisoners who, despairing of any success, looked for a way to flee. But they were prevented from doing this by some of our bravest men, who reanimated the cowards with the cry: "The enemy flees!" which gave them new hope.

From that moment on, as I became engaged with the enemy infantry, I saw nothing more of Baez and his cavalry. But the defeat of the enemy infantry let me hope that all would end well. I employed a quiet moment to arrange my men again. Among the dead, especially among those lying on the spot where the enemy had taken position, we found a large supply of cartridges; also the muskets of the dead men were very welcome to us.

The enemy although unsuccessful in his first atack, repeated it several times; however, this only increased his losses, since I always stood ready with my brave legionaries to reply to his attack. Several times he tried to take up a position close to us; in the end our best marksmen harrassed him so long that he took flight.

The battle had begun at one o'clock noon and lasted eight hours; at nine o'clock preparations for retreat were made. Almost all our officers were wounded. It was a difficult and touchy undertaking to transport them. Some were laid on horses, while others, who could still stand, limped after us supported by two comrades each. The retreat of the soldiers, divided into four groups, offered a beautiful spectacle. They moved in a close column with orders not to fire until they reached the edge of the forest bordering on the River Uruguay.

I had entrusted the wounded to the vanguard, convinced that the enemy would direct his attack on our flanks and rear guard. There was no lack of such attacks; repeatedly the enemy lancers rushed into our ranks, but every one of their attacks was answered with the bayonet, while our soldiers closed up more and more as they successfully reached the forest's edge. Here a halt was made and upon the command "Right face!" and "Fire!" a general volley followed, thinning the ranks of the enemy in such an unexpected manner that he abstained from further pursuits and retreated.

What had tormented us most on that day was the thirst which we had to endure, and it can therefore easily be imagined with what eagerness the soldiers rushed towards the river. A chain of sharpshooters kept up a steady fire to protect the left wing, and in this way we moved along the river until we reached the town.

Anzani was waiting for us at the gate and did not tire in embracing me and my companions. He had never despaired of us, although the undertaking was more than difficult. What troops remained with him he had collected in the fortress, and the invitation made to him during the battle to surrender he had constantly answered with the threat to blow up everything rather than to capitulate. The enemy had repeatedly sent word to him that all Italians were captured or slain. But he never despaired, and I cannot often enough cite the example of this man to my fellow citizens, who despair of Italy. Alas, how few of them resemble Anzani! Still he who despairs is a coward!

We arrived towards midnight in Salto and in spite of the late hour found all the inhabitants still up. They rushed to give all possible help to the wounded. Poor, poor people, who had suffered so deeply from the misfortunes of war; never shall I think of you without being penetrated by a feeling of profoundest thankfulness!

General Servando Gomez, who had surprised us so disagreeably and who had threatened to annihilate us totally, began his retreat on 9 February, leading his division, in a pitiful state and with many wounded, to

Paysandú, leaving the fields of San Antonio strewn with dead. The first day after our return was dedicated to the care of the wounded, where the services of two French physicians were most welcome to us. They were officers on board the French ship l'*Eclair* and with them was a third young physician by name of Desroseaux,[111] who remained for quite some time in contact with the Italian Legion. He fought during the whole campaign as a common soldier and then took care of his wounded companions. The tender efforts of the ladies of Salto also were not lacking to the patients and, as always in such cases, had an extremely beneficial and comforting effect on the sufferers.

The next days were devoted to the collecting and burying of our dead. This battle had been so memorable that I thought we should immortalize it by giving its victims an unusual burial ceremony. Thus I chose a spot on a height from where Salto is overlooked and which had been the scene of several of our successful engagements. There a mass grave was dug for all; then the soldiers shovelled earth upon it until a burial mound arose, which probably is still standing today as a memorial. A cross was planted upon it with the inscription:

Legione Italiana, Marina e Cavalleria Orientale
8 Febbrajo 1846

General Medina was not able to reach Salto without obstacle with his men; he kept the supreme command until the outbreak of the revolution in Montevideo which, begun in favor of Rivera, was a hard blow for the Republican party. The war ceased to be national and was led by miserable factions. At the same time took place the revolution in Corrientes, called forth by Madariaga against General Paz. The same leaders who had freed their country from Rosas' despotic rule and had gained in this battle fame and laurels, now debased themselves, driven by greed, ambition and treacherous intrigues, thereby ruining the cause of their fellow citizens. General Paz was forced to leave the army of Corrientes and go to Brazil. After his departure the province of Paraguay called back its armies from the scene of battle. Madariaga's troops, now reduced and left to their own resources, were totally defeated by Urquiza, and Corrientes fell back into the hands of the dictator of Buenos Ayres once again. In Montevideo things did not go much better. The Italian Legion, rightly esteemed because of its daring and glorious deeds, as usual rotated with the other corps and did sentinel duty in the capital. Anzani remained with it and, although no important battles took place, yet it always was worthy of its reputation. As for me, I became more occupied with the navy by equipping some of the most necessary vessels and by cruising on the River Plata with the schooner *Maypú*.

French intervention meanwhile prevented the outbreak of new hostilities without solving the problem. Several diplomats were sent off to negotiate, but Rosas deceived and even ridiculed them. Nothing was gained but short armistices, creating no other result except that the provisions gathered together with difficulties in Montevideo were eaten up.

France and England changed their agents along with their policies. Men such as Deffaudis and Ouseley as ambassadors, Lainé[112] and Inglefield as admirals, who had become dear to the people because they supported a liberal policy, were removed and into their places stepped men whose policies were bound to bring ruin to the country.

The government, powerless and robbed of all means for resistance, finally saw itself forced to submit to the dictates of the intervening powers. A lamentable situation!

Rivera, who through his partisans had come to power again, knew how to remove everyone who did not gain his favor. The largest number of those who had taken part in the heroic battles for unselfish patriotism were tired of the cleavages and cleared out willingly to make place for Rivera's creatures.

Still I found in Montevideo, that wonderfully changing city, elements of a new army and brought them to Las Vacas on the left bank of the Uruguay. The soldiers of Montevideo are born to win, and this they proved in their first meeting with the enemy. Especially in Mercedes they carried out wonders of bravery. Rivera suffered some defeats and again embarked for Brazil, his position in Montevideo, which he had made the scene of cruel spilling of blood, having become untenable. The contempt and curses of all followed him into his voluntary exile. Soon after his flight the fortunate battle against the troops of Lamas and Vergara took place.

These two divisions had been organized and reinforced after the San Antonio affair, where they fought under Servando Gomez, and now took up positions again near Salto, changing their camps from time to time, but always remaining a few miles distant from us. We did not neglect to harrass the enemy, especially when he went out to capture animals.

I had his position discovered by spies and advanced in the night of 19 May to attack him with 300 cavalrymen and about 100 legionaries. Poor youths! Since then you have been cruelly decimated! I proposed to surprise the enemy before daybreak and indeed we reached our goal at the desired hour. Captain Pablo, an Indian by origin and a brave warrior, seconded me. His infantry was mounted; it marched the whole night and at early dawn came into sight of the enemy forces on the right bank of the Dayman River. The infantry attacked. Victory was easy, for Vergara's troops took to flight and threw themselves into the river, leaving behind arms, horses and a few men, whom we took prisoners. But the triumph was not complete, since it was already bright daylight and our troops had to get back.

95

Only a small stream separated Vergara's camp from that of Lamas, and the latter had at the first alarm occupied a hill from where he could overlook everything, whereby it became easier for the fleeing troops of Vergara to unite with him.

For my part I occupied the camp abandoned by the enemy and, after collecting all usable horses, I began to pursue him, but without result; his men were well mounted, while mine had only *rodomons,*[113] that is, horses captured only a few days before. We had to be content with our half success and tried to make our way to Salto. A cavalry squadron divided into groups marched at the head, the infantry in a column in the center, the remaining cavalry also in a column as the rear guard. Two strong groups of cavalry commanded by Majors Carvallo and Fausto covered the right and the *cavallada* with the horses of the infantry the left flank.

The enemy after having arranged his forces again, which amounted to 500 cavalrymen, and after convincing himself how superior he was to us, began to attack our right flank. I had entrusted to Colonel Celesto Centurion, a very valiant officer, the command of the cavalry and that of the infantry to Carone. To the latter I recommended that he prevent any disorder in his ranks and never to turn back; his only maneuvers were to be sidewise. The infantry was to serve the center as a point of support and also to fill in any gaps. Our troops marched over splendid hills about two miles distant from the Dayman. The grass was in its most complete abundance and the surface of the earth was as wavy as the ocean. Neither tree nor shrub offered an obstacle and over the whole region lay a majestic quiet. A wonderful battleground for the mightiest armies!

We reached a brook which I did not consider wise to cross, for, being small in number, we might easily have become disorderly in crossing. Then only a hill on the right separated us from the enemy, who not far from us, was marching in a parallel direction.

I expected to be attacked on that spot, and so as not to have the advantage of the offensive taken from me, I sent to Colonel Centurion the order for him to attack. His column soon reached the top of the hill and halted. At the same moment an adjutant came rushing to me with the news that the enemy was advancing against us with his whole might in battle order. There was no time to lose. The cavalry of our wing stood on the right; the infantry took a position opposite the right wing of the enemy, while only a mere pistol shot distance separated us from him who was rushing upon us.

I must admit that they had made a movement of which my troops would not have been capable and which proved that they were brave, militarily disciplined and well commanded. Immediately I commanded an attack, but the enemy attacked in groups and thereby paralyzed the effectiveness of our infantry. I did not hesitate and let our cavalry gather close together, so as not to lose the advantage of the impetus of the horses, and indeed they attacked bravely. Several attacks were made on each side and with varied success. It would be difficult to decide which party showed the more courage.

The enemy, superior in number and quality of the cavalry, drove back ours and forced us to try out the strength of our infantry. Soon he began to measure his bayonets with our lances. Then came hand-to-hand fighting. The young Italians performed remarkably, and I am thinking of them and of that twentieth of May with particular joy.

Compact as a bulwark and on the double, they rushed to every point where their help was needed and always drove the attacker to flight. The enemy only fired a few musket shots but they were all aimed and sure. However after several attacks he was in complete disorder, while our troops, supported by the infantry, knew how to rearrange themselves constantly. The engagement lasted for half an hour in this manner and, since no new attack was made, we arranged ourselves in battle order and made a decisive attack. The enemy scattered and fled. Here we used the *bolas,* whose whirling motions in the air offered a very strange spectacle.

The *bola* is one of the most terrible weapons of South American cavalry. It consists of three iron balls covered with leather, fastened to three leather straps, whose ends are tied together in a knot. One of the balls is held in the hand, while the two others are swung overhead in the air until the command for slinging is heard. A horse hit by a *bola* usually falls to the ground and many are captured in this way. The South American cavalry soldier is inferior to none in the whole world and even in defeat he is superior to all in pursuing the enemy. On the field no obstacle bars his way. When a branch of a tree prevents him from advancing sitting, he throws himself back onto the back of his half-wild horse so as to practically vanish into his harness. On reaching a river he throws himself into it while holding his weapon between his teeth and sometimes wounds the fleeing enemy even from the stream. Besides the *bola,* he also carries the *cuchillo* (knife), which he uses with special skill. Woe to the soldier whose horse tires. If it is boleado,[114] that is, hit by the *bola,* he cannot escape the knife of his pursuer. The latter jumps aground, cuts his throat and jumps back again on his horse ready to catch up with another. Often horrifying scenes of this kind occur. I myself was a witness of such a combat which developed between several of our men and one of the enemy soldiers whose horse had been killed. The fallen rider got up and began a desperate fight with the one whose bola had laid him low; but a second, a third and more of our men rushed up, until the unfortunate one saw himself involved with six. I hurried to save him, but unfortunately too late!

The enemy was now totally dispersed and our victory complete. However, because of our lack of good horses, our immediate advantage was not what it might have been. Still we had the satisfaction of knowing that as long as our troops remained in Salto this department was spared the enemy. The battle which we had had to undergo with an experienced enemy, far superior in numbers and equipped with better horses, had been an unequal one in every respect. Nevertheless on that day our cavalry did wonders.

As far as the infantry was concerned, I shall mention only one example which sufficiently shows with what kind of spirit it was imbued. Colonel Carvallo, who distinguished himself in each one of these engagements by extraordinary bravery, had the misfortune to be wounded in the face and notably in strange symmetry on each cheek and in the same spot. The second wound he received in the beginning of the battle of Dayman, and after its end he asked for permission to return to Salto to nurse his wounds. When he passed the city battery and was asked what the fate of the day was, he replied, although he could hardly speak: "The Italian infantry is firmer than your battery."

After the Battle of 20 May nothing of importance happened in the Uruguayan campaign. I, as well as the Italian Legion and the ships of the flotilla, was ordered to Montevideo; the smaller vessels remained in Salto where Commander Artigas,[115] a brave officer who equally distinguished himself on 20 May, took over the supreme command until he was displaced by Blanco, a man of Rivera's side. Thus because of all kinds of errors which were committed in Corrientes and Montevideo, unfortunately Rosas' cause gained, and the people of the Plata gradually fell into a lamentable condition.

The English-French intervention was supervised by disloyal, intriguing men. In the interior one position after another fell into enemy hands. Salto, which had been won so heroically and kept, was taken by assault, and Colonel Blanco,[116] an old and brave soldier, fell with the majority of his men in its defense.

The devotion of the noble oriental people survived only in Montevideo. There gathered together all the men which six years of dangers, heroic deeds and misfortunes had bound together. There they had to erect anew a building which had been shaken to its foundations through bad management. Villagran, a 40 year's veteran, as well as Diaz and Tajes,[117] shamefully banished by Rivera because they wanted to serve their country and not him, and a large number of young officers who also had been dismissed by him, returned to their posts resignedly, but with their consciences bent upon justice; and around them gathered the decided and brave ones to fill the ranks of the defenders.

Americans, Frenchmen and Italians rushed to help the besieged city. From not a single lip fell a word of discouragement. The siege of Montevideo, once it is known in more detail, will count among the most heroic defenses of a people fighting for its independence with sacrifices of all kinds. In sum, it proves what power a nation possesses when it is determined not to bow to the will of a tyrant; and whatever the future fate of the city may be, it deserves the praise and sympathy of the whole world.

END OF VOLUME I

GARIBALDI'S

MEMOIRS

Volume II

GARIBALDI'S

MEMOIRS

from

his manuscript, personal notes and authentic
sources assembled and published

by

ELPIS MELENA

Volume II

With a map of the battle scenes on and near
the La Plata River

Preliminary Remarks by Elpis Melena to Volume II

The first volume of these Memoirs contained the narration of his life up to the year 1848, written down by Garibaldi himself.

The second volume is inferior to the first in that it does not contain a continuation of this autobiography. Garibaldi has not written such a volume yet.

In the second volume Garibaldi appears only once speaking directly: the fourth book *Anita* is written down by himself and communicated to the author.

The remainder of the second volume describes from various sources the fate of that memorable man up to the Italian uprising of the year 1860. But these sources are the most valuable and most reliable ones. The last book is based on the opinion of the author and on verbal communications made by Garibaldi. The description of the siege of Rome and the retreat to San Marino is taken from the best works published on the subject. The rescue of Garibaldi, the third book, is compiled from the notes of Signor Bonnet, who brought about this rescue.

BOOK TWO

GARIBALDI'S RETURN TO EUROPE

THE DEFENSE OF ROME

Chapter I

Garibaldi's Return to Europe:
The Death of Anzani

Garibaldi remained in Montevideo until 1848, appreciated by the inhabitants of the city, highly respected by the authorities, admired and loved by his comrades. His way of living was simple, in fact, rather poor. The following anecdote exemplifies this.

One day an officer called upon him in order to add, in the name of General Pacheco, an oral thanks to the written appreciation already communicated for the manner in which he directed the engagement at Salto. The officer came in the evening to Portón[118] Street, where Garibaldi lived. He entered the dwelling, a small house which could not be locked, and stumbled about the hall in the darkness looking for the door of the living room. In doing this he bumped into a chair and cursed silently to himself.

"O! Wife!" Garibaldi cried inside, "do you not hear that there is someone in the hall? Give some light!"

"And with what can I make light?" answered Anita, "don't you know that we haven't even two sous in the house to buy a candle?"

"That is true," admitted Garibaldi like a philosopher, and getting up and opening the door, called: "This way, this way!" as if to guide the stranger by his voice.

The officer came in, but the darkness was so great that he had to identify himself in order to be recognized by Garibaldi.

"Sir," Garibaldi then apologized, "you must excuse me, for when I made my contract with the Republic of Montevideo, I neglected to ask for a ration of candles and Anita has not enough money to buy a candle. So we shall have to remain in the dark. Fortunately I suppose that you are here not to see me, but to chat with me."

Indeed the officer chatted with Garibaldi, for he could not see him. On the way home he went to General Pacheco and related what had happened to him. The General immediately took 100 patagonians (500 francs) and sent them to Garibaldi.

Garibaldi did not wish to offend his friend Pacheco and took the money. The next day however, he had it distributed among the widows and children of the warriors who fell at Salto.

In 1847 news reached Montevideo of the progress Italy was making under Pope Pius IX. All the world believed that a new era had dawned. So did Garibaldi. Consequently he and Anzani wrote the following letter to the Papal Nuncio:[119]

"Sir,

"From the moment that we received the first news of the raising of Pius IX to the pontificate and of the amnesty which he granted the poor exiles, we have followed with ever growing attention and interest the course of glory and freedom which the head of the church is pursuing. The praise, the echo of which even reaches us from the far shores of the sea, the approval with which Italy welcomes the calling of deputies, the wise concessions which are being made to the press, the institution of a militia, the encouragement which is given to public instruction and to industry, without mentioning many particular regulations which all aim to improve the position of the lower classes and the formation of a new administration, in short, all this has convinced us that finally there has emerged from the lap of our country the man who understands the needs of the century, and who knows how to bow to the requirements of the times according to the ever new, ever immortal teachings of our exalted religion. And even though all this progress had no direct influence on us, we still have followed it from the distance and have accompanied the unanimous public opinion of Italy and of all Christianity with our rejoicing and our wishes. But since we found out a few days ago about the blasphemous attempt in which a fraction, encouraged and supported by foreigners, which still does not tire to tear apart our poor country, wants to overthrow the present order of things, it seems to us that admiration and enthusiasm for the pope would be too weak a tribute, and that we have greater obligations.

"We who are writing to you, dear Sir, are the ones who were always inspired by the same spirit which drove us into exile, taking up arms in Montevideo for a cause which seemed just to us and who gathered together a few hundred people, our countrymen, who had come here because they hoped to find here less agonizing times than in their native country.

"But in the five years of the siege each one of us more than once had to give proofs of resignation and courage. Thanks to providence and to the ancient spirit which still burns in our Italian blood, our Legion has had occasion to excel, and every time that an occasion arose it did not let it escape. Indeed, and I believe I may say this without vanity, on the path of honor it has left behind all other corps which rivalled or tried to emulate it.

"Thus, if at present the arms which have had some practice in carrying weapons are accepted by His Holiness, it is unnecessary to say that we will more gladly than ever devote ourselves to the service of him who has done so much for country and church.

"We should therefore be happy if we can lend a helping hand in Pius IX's work of liberation, that is, we and our comrades for whom we are writing, and we will not consider this work paid for too dearly with our blood.

"If you, dear Sir, believe that our offer might be agreeable to the pontifex, you may lay it at the foot of his throne.

"It is not a youthful pretention that our arms are essential and that they move us to this offer: we know quite well that the throne of St. Peter is based upon foundations which human help can neither shake nor fortify, and that on the other hand the new order has numerous defenders who will know how bravely to beat back the unjust attacks of its enemies. Nevertheless, since the work must be divided among the good and the heavy work be given to the strong, may the honor be granted us to be counted among the latter.

"In the meantime we thank fate for having saved His Holiness from the machinations of the *tristi* and we direct fervent wishes to fate that it give Pius IX many years for the happiness of Christianity and Italy.

"It only remains for us, dear Sir, to ask your pardon for the trouble which we are causing you.

"Yours very respectfully, etc.

"Montevideo, 20 October 1847

G. Garibaldi
F.Anzani."

The letter remained unanswered; from neither the Nuncio nor the Pope was word ever received.

The year 1848 began; exciting news came from Europe, and Garibaldi and Anzani decided to go to Italy with a part of the Legion.

The passage money was raised by subscription among the Italians resident in Montevideo, and Garibaldi embarked with wife, children and 85 companions. Of these however, 29 intimidated by the dangers which according to the whisperings of Garibaldi's enemies were threatening them, left the vessel while it was still lying at anchor. Among those remaining aboard were the bravest members of the Legion,[120] including almost all those who participated in the battle at Salto. Also a negro by name of Aguyar did not want to leave Garibaldi and sailed along to the shores of Ausonia.

In Garibaldi's home town of Nice,[121] Colonel Anzani, Garibaldi's most intimate friend, breathed his last. Anzani was tuberculous, and the emotion which the sight of his native land caused him seems to have overwhelmed him.

Garibaldi left his wife and three children, Menotti, Teresa and Riciotti, in Nice and then went with his followers to the battlefield in Lombardy to offer their services to Charles Albert, King of Sardinia.

Chapter II

The Fighting in Lombardy

On 29 June Garibaldi reached Genoa and went directly to the camp of Charles Albert to offer him his services. The King received him with frosty politeness; he said that he could do nothing without the consent of his ministers, so advised him to go to Turin and there await the decision of the Minister of War.

Garibaldi went to Turin and called upon Minister of War Ricci. But the reputation that he openly took up the cause of the Republicans had already preceded him, and the Minister refused his offer with an empty pretext. Instead he advised him to go to besieged Venice, there to take over the command of some vessels and try to harm the Austrians at sea as much as possible. There he, the hero of the La Plata River, would be in his right place.

Garibaldi's prompt reply was: "I am a bird of freedom and not for a cage," then turned his back on the minister.

Soon after Garibaldi received an invitation from the provisional government of Milan to come to Lombardy and there organize a corps of volunteers. After arriving there he was given the title *General,* but that was about all. The government badly supported the great plans which he immediately unfolded. It furnished him neither uniforms nor guns, so that he was forced to procure them himself. In spite of this, within a short time he organized two battalions of volunteers, mostly young men from the best-known families of Milan and Vicenza. Most of them were able to buy arms for themselves; from the coats seized from Austrian soldiers, blouses were made which served as uniforms. Medici, a comrade-in-arms of Garibaldi from Montevideo, commanded one of the two battalions, Garibaldi the other, which he called the *Anzani Battalion.*

When the group was ready it marched to Bergamo singing patriotic songs. There they found Mazzini, who also seized a musket and joined the corps. A regiment from Bergamo with two cannon belonging to the National Guard joined them too.

By that time, in the middle of July 1848, Charles Albert's star had already begun to set. The battle at Vicenza had taken place in the beginning of July and had resulted in the capitulation of Durando. On 12 July the king took the offensive against Radetzki, pointing his army against the famous Austrian quadrangle of forts. He fought bravely but unsuccessfully on the hills of Somma-Campagna and near Custozza (23-25 July). Then followed the massacres near Goito and Volta, and finally, the complete dissolution of the Piedmontese Army.

It was in those days full of confusion and mourning that Garibaldi's Legion marched forth, and only too soon did it feel the effects of those discouraging conditions. Scarcely had Garibaldi entered Bergamo when an order from Milan compelled him to return on the double. On the way, in Monza, he found out that Milan had capitulated too and that an Austrian cavalry corps had been dispatched to pursue the Legion.

At once he ordered a retreat, turning towards Como. Among his men however, who in Bergamo had reached 5000, demoralization set in during the strenuous march. In Como the greater part ran away and fled over the Swiss border; only 500 remained with him. But Garibaldi even now did not give up the thought of further resistance, hoping rather to organize a true people's war along the slopes of the Alps. Proclaimed commander-in-chief of the Italian People's Army by his faithful troops, he tried in Camerlata to reorganize the remnants of his corps by requesting all leaders of volunteer corps still fighting and scattered in Lombardy against Austria, namely Manara, Griffini, Durando (the brother of the Roman General who had capitulated near Vicenza), Apice, etc., to get in contact with him.

The requests however had no result and desertions continued. Nevertheless Colonel Medici succeeded in finding in the region a few hundred more volunteers so that the corps came to 800 men again. Even before this, Garibaldi, determined to go into Piedmont, judged his handful of men sufficient to throw against the Austrians, so at least not to leave the region without fighting. On 12 August he delivered the well known proclamation in which he proclaimed Charles Albert a traitor and invited the Italians to trust in themselves and to persist in their opposition. Then he marched to Arona, confiscating there two steamers and several small sailing vessels with which his corps crossed over to the other side of Lake Maggiore to Luino (16 August).

Garibaldi now fell ill; he was suffering from intermittent fever and an attack tortured his iron body just upon his arrival in Luino. Immediately he took quarters in an inn which stood isolated on the edge of the village and with the intention of getting a few hours of sleep, threw himself upon a bed, leaving Colonel Medici to make the necessary arrangements for security.

But hardly had he rested half an hour, when the cry was heard: "The Austrians! The Austrians!" The General staggered from his bed, surveyed the territory from his window and, seeing no less than a detachment of 1000 to 1200 enemy troops approaching on the highway, gave commands. He divided his group into two parts: one with about 400 men strong was to offer resistance to the Austrians on the highway, while the rest was to take up positions on the side, partly to prevent by-passing and partly to come into the fighting on their own at the right moment.

The Austrian attack was not expected, still Garibaldi's column took the offensive. It hurled itself upon the enemy with determination; but it encountered strong resistance and did not advance. Then the leader, mounted on horseback and in the thickest rain of bullets near the inn, called up the column stationed on the side and made another attack with the total of his forces. The far superior enemy was defeated; the Austrians retreated in confusion, leaving 100 dead and wounded on the battlefield and 80 prisoners in the hands of the victor. Colonel Medici pursued the fleeing enemy but could not reach him.

The next day Garibaldi led his corps to Varese. There an Austrian spy was brought forward and shot, but not without revealing first that three Austrian corps were approaching, one towards Como, the next towards Varese and the third towards Luino. The Garibaldians abandoned Varese. Apparently the Austrians planned to throw themselves between Garibaldi and Lugano and thus to cut off all possibility of escape, be it towards Piedmont, be it towards Switzerland. Garibaldi turned back to Luino and unhindered reached first Arcisate and then Viggia. In the village of Ligurno Colonel Medici, who was leading the vanguard, was overtaken by the Austrian General Aspre and was separated from Garibaldi. Medici with about 100 men, favored to be sure, by an excellent position set up on Mount San Masseo, offered opposition to 5000 Austrians for more than four hours. His men first used up all their ammunition and then crossed over onto Swiss soil. General Aspre in his order of the day boasted of having won a bitter battle against the whole army of Garibaldi, as well as having beaten it into complete disintegration.

Notwithstanding this development Garibaldi continued his march to Luino. En route however, he learned that the place was already occupied by the Austrians. His retreat to Switzerland was now extremely endangered. In front of him in Luino stood Austrians, behind him the corps of Aspre. He still had 500 men and decided to turn right towards Morazzone.[122] Hardly had he arrived there and placed his troops as safely as possible from an attack, when he saw himself surrounded by 5000 Austrians.

The next morning the Austrians attacked; but they were not to win laurels against this leader. They were turned back with bloody heads by the handful of braves. In vain they renewed their attack and the fighting went on the whole day. But still the Italians did not give way. Even a highly biased reporter of this war, the Austrian General Schönhals, could not refrain from praising the opponent, whom he despised, in this manner: "They offered fairly brave resistance."[123]

After nightfall Garibaldi called together the whole of his devoted corps which remained, formed them into closed ranks, and they threw themselves upon the enemy with the bayonet to force a passage. Bloody fighting ensued and a path was made; then once behind the Austrian lines, an hour from Morazzone, he dissolved the corps and urged each man to get away as best he could into Swiss territory. He himself, disguised as a peasant, successfully escaped to Lugano via Luino and across the lake.

This encounter near Morazzone, this daring unafraid resistance against superior forces more than ten times greater made Garibaldi's name popular all over Italy. Towards this man who never wanted to put his sword into its sheath until everything was tried, towards him all the hopes of his fellow countrymen were directed.

Chapter III

Garibaldi Fights for the Roman Republic: The 30th of April

The war in Lombardy was at an end; near Morazzone its last shots were fired. Garibaldi returned to Piedmont and from there went to Genoa. Here he remained only a short while, for a deputation of Sicilians came to him inviting him to go to Sicily and there devote his efforts to the cause of the revolution. Garibaldi was not disinclined; he collected 500 men and went to Leghorn with them. But here he learned of the dangerous state of affairs in Rome, gave up the expedition to Sicily and rushed with his men to the Marches.

The Roman state was in a critical position at the time. The population was full of enthusiasm for the changes being effected. Rossi[124] was murdered on 15 November 1848, the Pope fled to Gaeta, a provisional government was appointed and agitation for the calling of a constituent assembly had begun.

Garibaldi quickly collected a considerable group of volunteers in Bologna and Ravenna and then went to Rome to place himself at the disposal of the provisional government. But in the government there were at the time conflicting elements; alongside of the confirmed republicans, there were those who had the majority and who still thought of a conciliation with the Pope. Garibaldi and his corps were more feared than thought of as a help; in fact, he and his volunteers were almost considered as a band of bandits, so much so that an attempt was made to get rid of him expediently by attempting to persuade him to go to Venice. The outcome was that Garibaldi's services were not exactly declined, yet not knowing what to do with him, they assigned him first in one place, then in another for quarters. Thus he stayed for a while in Macerata, then in Tolentino, Spoleto and finally in Rieti.

In the meantime in Rome the decision was eventually taken to call a constituent assembly. On 27 December 1848 the decree was ready. An excommunication from the Pope in Gaeta followed immediately after. The elections took place amidst tremendous excitement; 200,000 electors participated and on 5 February 1849 the Roman National Assembly held its first session in the Palazzo della Cancelleria in Rome.

Garibaldi, elected deputy from Macerata, went to Rome to take his seat. But his parliamentary activity was not to be of long duration. Pompeo Campello, the new Minister of War, in spite of seemingly unsurmountable difficulties, was not deterred from working on the reorganization of the army. Disregarding ridiculous insinuations, he did not hesitate in taking Garibaldi's Legion into his pay. Also, with the commission to increase his followers as much as possible and to protect the eastern borders of the state against the king of Naples, Garibaldi was sent to the Neapolitan border and only returned to Rome on 26 April 1849 when the French landed near Civita-Vecchia.

In Rome for a moment there were different opinions on how to behave towards the French. In the Constituent Assembly, which had declared itself permanent upon receiving the first news of the landing of the French, some demanded that the gates of Rome should be opened to the French and that they should be received as friends. Others demanded firm resistance, and this opinion prevailed. Hence the following decree was proclaimed:

"In the name of God and the people! The National Assembly places the honor of the Republic into the hands of the Triumvirs and orders them to drive out force with force."

On the evening of the day on which this decision was taken and posted on the street corners, there rang through the streets of Rome the cry:

"Garibaldi! Garibaldi!"

And indeed soon thereupon he entered the city at the head of his Legion. The enthusiasm with which he was received can hardly be described. An unending throng marched in front of him, others accompanied the Legion, while all gave vent to their enthusiasm in the lively manner of a southern people. They shouted to him, threw their hats into the air, waved banderoles briskly and congratulated each other on having within the city walls the only man who could save the Republic.

The enemy advanced quickly. On 28 April his vanguard was in Paolo, on the 29th in Castel-Guido, about five hours from Rome.

Oudinot, the commanding General of the French Army, sent ahead his brother, Captain Oudinot, and an adjutant officer with 15 horsemen to scout. The horsemen came as far as the place where the old and new Via Aurelia meet, that is to say, an hour outside of Rome, without meeting an obstacle. There he met the Roman advance post.

"What do you want?" the Roman officer shouted to the Frenchmen.

"To ride to Rome!" was the reply.

"That is not possible," replied the Roman.

"We speak in the name of the French Republic!" spoke out Captain Oudinot.

"And we in the name of the Roman Republic!" retorted the other, "so back, gentlemen!"

"And if we do not want to turn back?"

"Then we will make you turn back!"

"With what?"

"With force."

Upon this answer the Frenchman ordered fire and he himself discharged his pistol against the enemy post.

"Fire!" the Roman shouted a moment later; one of the enemy riders fell. The rest rushed back. That was the beginning of the siege of Rome. Early in the morning of 30 April the general march sounded to call together the National Guard and announce to the Romans the coming battle.

The Roman troops were divided into four brigades of which Garibaldi commanded the first. It consisted of the Italian Legion, a battalion of students, that of the finanzieri,[125] the reduci[126] and some other small divisions, a total of about 2300 men. It took up the whole position which extends outside the city walls from Porta Portese to Porta San Pancrazio.

All signs pointed to the fact that the enemy, whose forces ran to 8000 infantrymen, two squadrons of cavalry and 12 field pieces and was divided into two columns, was planning a simultaneous attack on the gates Angelica and Cavalleggieri. He had one of his columns advance along the Villa Pamfili and towards eleven a.m. already had occupied two villas from which he directed a lively artillery and musket fire into Porta Cavalleggieri.

In the meanwhile Garibaldi, under protection of several heavy siege cannon, let his left wing advance towards the enemy through Porta San Pancrazio and his stronger right wing through Porta Cavalleggieri. A murderous and persistent fighting began, rich in deeds of personal bravery and heroic courage, and proved that present-day Italians know how to show themselves worthy of the ancient glory of their ancestors. Garibaldi stood still on horseback in the thickest hail of bullets, without moving, like an iron statue of the God of War. His example fired the courage of the Romans.

During this engagement the French made several other attacks on the gardens of the Vatican and on the whole line of Porta Cavalleggieri, but the Republican troops withstood their attacks with the bravery and cold blood of proven veterans, so that the enemy retreated at all points after great but fruitless efforts and without making a new attempt to advance. This battle, which entitled the Romans to the most promising hopes, lasted not less than seven hours, without counting the small skirmishes which continued until the evening.

If it had depended on Garibaldi, the French Army would not only have been beaten, but annihilated.[127]

Towards evening he wrote from the battlefield to the newly appointed Minister of War Avezzana: "Send me fresh troops and I assure you that not a single Frenchman will reach the ships again in Civita Vecchia." It is said that it was Mazzini who opposed the execution of the plan to attack and destroy the beaten French on their retreat. On the one hand he did not want to mortally offend France, and on the other, he feared that the young Roman soldiers might not be equal to the enemy, who although beaten was brave in the open field.

The losses of the French on that day amounted to 18 to 20 officers, 600 men dead and wounded, and nearly 500 prisoners. On the side of the Romans only 300 men were "hors de combat."

Garibaldi however did not receive fresh troops from the Minister of War, but at least, the permission to pursue the enemy with his Legion. The next day, the first of May at dawn, he started. He divided his Legion of about 1200 men into two columns, one under Colonel Masina, which marched through Porta Cavalleggieri, and the other he himself led through Porta San Pancrazio. The 60 lancers of his Legion were reinforced by a squadron of dragoons.

The General's intention was to attack the French in their camp, and he probably expected that once the battle had begun, they would rush to his aid from Rome. But when he reached the camp he found it deserted. Instead he heard gunfire in the direction of Castel Guido, where Masina had gone, and quickly hastened towards it. Masina had reached the rearguard of the French and attacked it. Garibaldi had scarcely arrived on the scene of battle when he threw himself upon the flank of the French Army and occupied an overlooking height. Now, as he was about to throw himself again upon the enemy, a French officer rode up and asked to negotiate with him.

The officer identified himself as an envoy of Oudinot and was sent to negotiate an armistice, and also, to convince himself that the Roman people truly had a Republican government and that it wished to defend its rights. At the same time he offered to free the priest Hugo Bassi*, who had been made prisoner the day before.

Simultaneously with Garibaldi's discussion with the envoy, the command came from Rome that he and his Legion return to that city. The afternoon of the first of May Garibaldi arrived in the capital, leading with him the envoy.

At night the whole city was illuminated. No disorder disturbed the general rejoicing and with thundering *evvivas* Garibaldi and his staff were welcomed in the streets of Rome. From now on he meant everything to them. Yes, it can be said that on this day Garibaldi's career of glory began.

This leader, little known until now, crowned with modest laurels of transatlantic guerrilla warfare, from now on became the hero of the day, the idol of the people. Anyone who has ever seen him, and especially who saw him now, will understand his popularity. His appearance is imposing, despite his medium stature. His face is sunburned; his features, half hidden by a reddish beard, are full of expression and of classical regularity, and his deep seated dark brown eyes express intelligence coupled with mildness and strength of character. He sat firmly in the saddle of his horse and rode as if he were born there. His chestnut brown hair flowed out from a pointed small-brimmed hat with full black ostrich feathers. Above the red blouse fluttered his white American cloak. His staff also wore the red blouse, and later the entire Legion was clothed in this color. Behind him rode his equerry, the negro Aguyar who had followed him from America. He was wrapped in a black coat and held a long lance with a red flag. All Garibaldi's men wore pistols and fine daggers in their belts; none lacked the big American riding whip of buffalo hide.

Chapter IV

The Battle Near Palestrina

The retreat of the French to Civita Vecchia and the armistice which followed upon this first engagement gave the Republicans a welcomed respite and opportunity to turn their attention towards the King

---

*Hugo Bassi had rushed among the fighters during the battle unarmed but unafraid, encouraging the fighters, helping the wounded, comforting the dying. In doing this he was wounded and captured.

of Naples, whose important forces were already near Velletri, Palestrina and Albano.

Garibaldi asked for permission to be allowed to advance against the Neapolitan Army and it was granted. For this expedition a special brigade was formed from Garibaldi's Legion, the Battalion of Bersaglieri under Colonel Manara*, composed of a troop of Lombards under Colonel Medici, the finanzieri, the emigrati,[128] the universitarii (studenti) and two squadrons of dragoons, a total of nearly 3000 men.

At nightfall on 4 May Garibaldi marched out of Porta del Popolo at the head of his brigade and reached Tivoli the following morning; on the 6th he occupied Palestrina and thus took up positions between the Apennines and the right wing of the Neapolitan Army.

Palestrina is situated at the foot of a steep height on the peak of which is located Castel San Pietro, and three sides of the town are surrounded by walls, even though damaged. The brigade had an almost unattackable position here. During the next days Garibaldi sent out large and small bodies of scouts to keep the Bourbons in check and to harrass them; and indeed he succeeded, for these wasp-like stings finally obliged the enemy to undertake a definite move.

The Neapolitan Army comprised a total of 18 to 20,000 men and under the command of General Nunziante stood on and near the Via Appia, which leads from Rome via Terracina to Naples. The main force was concentrated near Velletri, while detachments had reached beyond Albano headed towards Rome. A larger detachment of about 5000 men had pushed ahead to Valmontone to cover the right flank of the main army advancing along the mountains. Garibaldi had to deal with this detachment. However he did not dare attack this force in its protected position in Valmontone, but he did succeed in so tempting it that it attacked and was beaten.

On the morning of 9 May Garibaldi was informed that the enemy had left Valmontone. The Republican leader, accompanied by only one officer, rode out to scout them. When he saw the enemy and convinced himself of his strength, he returned and took the necessary measures with calm and wisdom. Col. Manara was to command the left wing, the walls and gates, while the buildings next to the gates were put into a state of siege; two companies, followed by a third as a reserve, were ordered to march against the enemy army.

The battle then began. The Neapolitans received the advancing companies with rifle fire and grape shot, but the bersaglieri and legionaries did not even hesitate; they formed themselves into chains of sharp-

---

*This Battalion of Bersaglieri formed in Lombardy had fought bravely in the war between Charles Albert and Radetzki, had hurled itself into the Apennines after the Battle of Novara, and had reached Rome just in time to take part in the victorious encounter against the French on 30 April.

shooters and pushed on. For hours they fought in the isolated hilly terrain in front of the town. Garibaldi sent several companies of reinforcements and had tired ones relieved. By three o'clock in the afternoon the right wing of the enemy had been thrown far back, his cannons silenced and the victorious left wing of the Romans threw itself upon the enemy center.

Here and on the right flank, however, the battle came to a standstill, and the Neapolitans persistently defended a few houses on the slope of the mountain which they had seized, even attempting to scale the city walls. But turned back from the wall by the *studenti*, which Garibaldi himself led against the enemy, they were forced to yield to the effective onrush of the legionaries and the bersaglieri. With fixed bayonet the latter threw the Neapolitans out of the houses; the flight became general, and only the falling darkness ended the pursuit.

The Neapolitans, seized with panic and still fearing to be pursued, put the torch to everything, houses, huts, etc. which they came upon during their retreat, in order to block the roads. They camped at a distance of five miles from Palestrina, and Garibaldi, after having strongly occupied this small town, took up positions not far from La Vittoria, exactly where two thousand years ago Pyrrhus with his victorious elephants had pitched his camp.

The ultimate gains of this victory however were not so great. Garibaldi's brigade had 50 dead and 100 wounded, the Neapolitans about the double amount and in addition lost 50 prisoners and three cannon. But all the more important were the immediate advantages. The via Valmontone to the southern towns which used to supply Rome with wine, oil and grain was reopened. The Neapolitans from now on could not undertake a march on Rome without getting rid of the dangerous enemy on his sides. Finally the defeat demoralized the enemy and raised the courage and confidence of the Romans. Barely 3000 Garibaldians had put to complete flight a Neapolitan corps almost twice superior.

But already on the tenth Garibaldi received the command to return to Rome and on the morning of the eleventh he marched with his brigade through Porta Santa Maria Maggiore into the city and along the Colosseum to Campo Vaccino. In the ancient forum Commander-in-chief Avezzana, surrounded by thousands, received the victorious column arrayed in a single file and stretching its wings from the Colosseum to the Capitol.

The general rejoicing, the veneration for Garibaldi and the warm reception accorded all who had fought at Palestrina were indescribable. As during the night of 30 April, similarly on this evening the city was festively illuminated.

Chapter V

The Battle of Velletri

In the meantime Oudinot had again approached Rome from Civita Vecchia, to which he had retired after the 30th of April; here he quartered his troops in a camp near Castell di Guido on the road from Civita-Vecchia to Rome, waiting partly for the outcome of the negotiations which had begun, and partly for reinforcements.

Immediately after its return from Palestrina Garibaldi's brigade was spread about Rome and its surroundings. Then on 16 May the government decided to profit from the armistice concluded with Oudinot to possibly get rid of the Neapolitans entirely, who although not terrible, still were bothersome neighbors.

The command of this expedition should without doubt have been given to the victor of Palestrina, but the wisdom of the Ministry of War gave it to General Roselli; Garibaldi was given command of one of the three brigades of the division.

However on the evening of 16 May the corps, practically the complete army of the Republic, left the city through Porta San Giovanni. They were 8000 in number, including about 700 cavalrymen with 4 cannon. Colonel Masi commanded the first brigade consisting of four battalions, Manara's bersaglieri and altogether 2400 men. The second brigade was led by General Galletti and comprised five battalions of line troops, one battalion of carabinieri, 300 horsemen and two cannon, or a total of 3600 men. The third brigade was Garibaldi's which consisted of his own Legion divided into three cohorts: 1500 men, the 300-man-band of Colonel Medici, 200 emigrati, and 60 lancers with two cannon, a total of 2000 men.

The division was already under way when it was noticed that Manara's battalion was missing. It was found out that the high command had neglected to notify the Colonel; his battalion was called up quickly. Such bad evidence spoke against the wisdom of the commander; and such was to occur repeatedly.

After a strenuous march at night the division, Garibaldi and his brigade forming the vanguard, reached Zagarolo[129] in the morning on 17 May, remained there until the evening of the 18th, then continued on to Valmontone. Now the marching was carried out very cautiously since it was known that the Neapolitans, among whom was the king, stood near Velletri and that in Valmontone they probably would meet enemy detachments. By nightfall the Roman Army reached a narrow passage which begins two hours before Valmontone and extends directly to it. Here it bivouacked for the night, the vanguard in and around Valmontone, which the Neapolitans had abandoned.

The next morning Garibaldi started early with his brigade, following the road to Velletri, towards which the enemy was retreating. This road, six or seven miles long, goes over undulating terrain which greatly favored the resistance of the enemy, for the parallel waves one behind the other were cut through vertically by the road. Every height was a new position for the Neapolitan rear guard and one after the other had to be taken by Garibaldi's troops. Small shrubbery, underbrush and vineyards along the road strengthened further these small positions, besides limiting the masses of men, the horsemen and the cannons to the single, even though wide, road.

Now we come to the battle itself. Garibaldi knows no hesitation, no doubts! On the contrary, instead of relenting in his thrust, with double force he rushes the weak cohorts and the few horsemen under Masina towards the enemy. He exposes himself to the heaviest fire, gets shot in the hand and a grazing shot in the foot, his white cloak is pierced by bullets, and still nobody learns of his wounds until the evening, when he permits the doctor, and only him, to dress them. So little did they bother him and so little did they hinder him in directing the battle! Little by little the General engaged his whole infantry on the right and left of the road and kept only a small reserve, his lancers and the two cannon with him on the road. As soon as the fighting relented at the wings, the cannon on the road went into action firing a few grapeshot as the lancers with great bravery hacked the enemy infantry incessantly. In this spirited manner the enemy was kept in an uninterrupted retreat, which however, cost this daring squadron a third of its men and horses.*

The enemy rear guard, so relentlessly thrown out of one position after another, fled to Velletri under the cannon of its main forces. This town of 12,000 inhabitants is surrounded by walls and situated on a hill. A 3 to 400-foot-wide small valley divides this hill on the side towards Albano and Valmontone from other mountains about equally high.

As Garibaldi drew quite close to the town, he sent out a scouting unit to provoke the enemy to the offensive; but this did not seem to succeed, so daringly Garibaldi assumed the attack himself. On the heights, on the flat tops of the hills, in the valley and on the highway a murderous battle developed.

In these decisive moments the incapacity of General Roselli almost deprived the Romans of victory. For some days already those troops

---

*This passage is taken from the excellent book of Gustav v. Hoffstetter *Garibaldi in Rom*, a book upon which the following description is based.

which had taken part in the earlier expedition to Palestrina now noticed to their disadvantage from the poor food supply that Garibaldi was no longer taking care of them; also some understanding officers shook their heads over the confusion in the general staff and the resulting disorder during the march. Roselli indeed proved negligent in supporting the leader of the vanguard. Garibaldi demanded the immediate moving up of the division; instead he received the answer: *"The troops have not yet been arranged."* For three hours the vanguard fought, while the rest of the division merely entertained preparatory orders.

But even though the aid arrived late, there was still time to give the battle a favorable turn. The Commander-in-chief with the main part of the Roman Army joined those already fighting below the hill of the Cappuccini. Thus reinforced, the Romans attacked the fortified position of Velletri. It was a marvelous competition of daring and bravery between generals, officers and soldiers who, inspired with indescribable enthusiasm, pressed against the enemy disregarding death. It is certain that if night had not fallen, the eagerness of the Republicans could have overcome that same evening all the difficulties of the terrain and the resistance of the defense.

With the early dawn of 20 May the Roman Army went forth to make a new attack on Velletri, but a strong group of scouts which had been sent out found the city walls cleared of the enemy and all positions abandoned. The wings of the night had hidden the flight of the cowardly Neapolitans! The king himself, with the Swiss regiments and a few other divisions, a total of 5 to 6000 men, had already left the town the day before, during the battle.

The losses of the Republicans amounted to 200 men dead and wounded and thirty horses. How great it was on the side of the Neapolitans is not recorded, although the inhabitants of Velletri assured the victors that many wagons of dead and wounded had been taken away.

The flight of the Neapolitan Army relentlessly went towards the frontier.

On the 21st Garibaldi started a diversion to that Neapolitan frontier, since those regions were still in possession of the troops of General Zucchi. Along the mountain road leading from Ceprano into Neapolitan territory he came to Frosinone via Aragni and Ferentino, where on the 24th in the evening he entered amidst an enormous crowd and shouts of joy of the inhabitants and stayed at the magnificent papal palace. Upon a rumor that two regiments of Swiss were approaching from San Germano and Ponte-Corvo he sent various divisions to Ceprano and Arce, but this rumor proved unfounded, and Zucchi with his carabinieri in fact fled to the castle of Arce at the approach of the Republicans and from there escaped along mountain paths. In Arce, which already lies in Neapolitan territory, the vanguard sent off by Garibaldi was hailed with the cry: *"Capitulazione, buoni amici, bravi Romani!"*

But it seems that Garibaldi undertook his coup on his own and had crossed the Neapolitan border only to have the pleasure of stabling his horses in a Neapolitan town, for already at dusk of the same day the return march was begun. At the same time he received orders from Rome and had to rush to Frosinone again. In Ceprano he left behind a battalion of Masi and the lancers, and on the evening of 1 June he reached Rome from Anagni with his staff.

Chapter VI

The Defense of Rome

Here in the meantime things had come to a head, and on the evening of the second at all street corners one could read a proclamation signed by Oudinot, according to which the French general would begin the attack on the morning of the fourth.

When Garibaldi returned to Rome with his brigade on 1 June uncertainty still reigned concerning the outcome of the negotiations being made with the French. The sending off of a corps of troops to defend the Legations and the Marches against the invasion of the Austrians was still under consideration. But soon enough the treachery of the French Republic was to be disclosed.

On 2 June appeared an announcement in Rome that an armistice had been concluded with the French, subject to 14 days' notice. But on the very same evening, a poster at the street corner announced that the attack of the French Army was to be expected for the fourth of June.

The first announcement was based on the agreement between the Roman government and the French negotiator, Mr. de Lesseps, the second on a communication from the French Commander Oudinot to General Roselli. This letter declared:

"General! The orders of my government are positive; they command me to move into Rome as soon as possible. I have denounced to the Roman government the armistice which I had granted at the request of Mr. de Lesseps. I have sent the written instruction to our advance posts that both armies would be within their rights to begin hostilities. Only in order to give your countrymen, who might wish to leave Rome the possibility to do so without disturbance, do I postpone the attack of the place until at least Monday morning.''

> The Commander-in-Chief of the Army
> Corps of the Mediterranean
>
> Oudinot, Duke of Reggio.

According to this letter it was expected that the third would still be peaceful; consequently everyone went to bed quietly the evening of the second. But even before dawn an unexpected thunder of cannon announced the treachery of the French and their perfidious attack on Villa Pamfili. What was taking place follows:

In Villa Pamfili two companies of bersaglieri were quartered. They were carefree and expected no attack. Soon after midnight a French column approached. The Roman guard hailed them. *"Viva l'Italia!"* was their answer. The sentinel took the columns for Romans and gave no alarm. In the meantime the French moved up, cut down the guard, penetrated the villa and killed some of the occupants while taking the remainder prisoner.

A few who were lucky enough to escape, alarmed two companies posted nearer the city. These received in good order the quickly encroaching enemy but succumbed to superior force, giving up, after a stubborn resistance, the villas Valentini and Corsini.

Avezzana, until then commander-in-chief in Rome, had become Minister of War, and Roselli took command of the defense of the city. At the first shots he gave orders to Garibaldi to go to the threatened point; the latter rushed from Porta San Pancrazio at the head of his Legion in order to meet up with the treacherous enemy who had immediately intrenched himself firmly in the villas Corsini and Valentini.

A great moment had arrived. The two mentioned villas became the scene of a battle such as history perhaps has only few to record. In the buildings, behind every wall and battlement the French were most daringly attacked, since every soldier had become a hero. Twice the Legion penetrated the enemy's positions, each time with Garibaldi at the head restoring order. His hat and cloak were pierced by bullets, but fortunately he himself was spared. His staff suffered terribly, while his Italian Legion was decimated in a furious battle against a force almost four times superior in size. Only the leader's iron fortitude and staunch courage held together the remnants until the expected aid arrived.

The following faithful translation of Garibald's order of the day for the third of June may be of interest to the reader:

"From the gate of San Pancrazio a road leads directly to the Villa Vascello, a distance of about 250 paces. Here it divides into two branches, the principal one leading to Civita-Vecchia descends on the right; the smaller on the left, which extends along the garden wall of Villa Corsini, is 300 paces further distant from the Vascello. The Villa Vascello is a large and massive building of three stories, surrounded by gardens and walls. The Villa Corsini*, placed on the highest part of the ground, commands all the neighborhood. It is surrounded by gardens and high walls. The position of the Villa is very strong, and the more so because one wishing to attack it without showing any preparation of approach beforehand, by passing through the gate at the foot of the garden, would be exposed to the concentrated fire which the enemy, defended and covered by the hedges and vases, or from within the Villa itself, would direct towards the point of entry, located where the walls meet at an acute angle.

"The terrain of the Villa Corsini is also very favorable to the enemy; it slants downward, and being scattered with groves and crossed by deep streets, he can concentrate his reserves in security from our fire, such as when our cannon obliged him to abandon the house.

"The first attack made by the Italian Legion was against the Villa Corsini, abandoned by our troops because surprised, betrayed and overpowered by the great number of the enemy. The attack was made with the bayonet without firing a single shot. The Legion sustained for about three quarters of an hour the whole weight of the enemy; then Manara arrived with his bersaglieri. They threw themselves into the garden and vigorously attacked the enemy right under the walls of the Villa. Our losses were great, but from that moment the houses on the left were ours.

"The enemy stopped advancing and the Vascello, strongly occupied, poured on him a murderous fire of grape shot. Our brave artillerymen soon also disturbed the enemy in Villa Corsini. The Manara Bersaglieri from the houses on the left, joined by the Italian Legion from the Vascello, drove the French Tirailleurs from the garden and hedges. The enemy was no longer able, even though reinforced and protected by two pieces of artillery, to take from our troops the positions held with so much valor. Our artillery fired upon the Villa Corsini so vigorously that the enemy was finally compelled to retreat, after setting it afire.

"In the meantime our cannon in the right bastion, reinforced by our advancing bersaglieri, also drove the enemy out of Villa Valentini. He then occupied numerous small adjacent houses, from which he made a heavy but useless fire.

"Two companies of the Manara Bersaglieri were then sent to the left, towards the French camp, advancing a considerable distance in order to annoy the enemy hidden in the vineyards. A very severe conflict ensued and continued all day, always to our advantage as we succeeded a second time in driving him beyond Villa Corsini.

"Towards evening several companies of the Third Regiment of the line were sent to reinforce our troops in the Vascello; simultaneously the Medici Legion was ordered to relieve the Manara Bersaglieri.

---

*Because of its location it is also called the *Villa dei Quattro Venti*.

125

"Our cannon fire, masterfully directed by the brave Lieutenant Colonel L. Calandrelli, reduced Villa Corsini almost to rubble. The enemy was beaten at all points. Our troops, and especially the Manara Bersaglieri and the Italian Legion, again and again charged the enemy breast to breast.

"The first company of the Manara Bersaglieri threw itself into Villa Giraud and made many French prisoners. The Italian Legion several times advanced up to Villa Valentini.

"As night fell the battlefield was ours. The French admired our valor and our troops had only one desire, namely to resume on the next day the battle which had been so courageously begun.

"The commissioned and noncommissioned officers whom I wish to honor, because they fell as martyrs and brave patriots, are the following: Colonels Masina, Daverio and Pollini, Major Ramorino, Adjutant-Major Peralta, Lieutenants Bonnet, Cavallerio and Grassi, Captain Dandolo and David, sub-lieutenants Scarani, Tarete and Cazzaniga.

The Division Commander
G. Garibaldi."

The losses on that day were great and irreplaceable. Altogether a small division of barely 4000 men was subject to Garibaldi's command; it lost 1000 men, among whom 100 officers. During the night more than 180 wounded officers were brought to the different hospitals some of whom had fought in front of Gate San Pancrazio and some on the other side of the city which had been attacked at the same time.

Oudinot himself admitted in his report on the happenings of 3 June that little by little he had led to battle 20,000 men. Against these, 6000 Romans, 4000 under Garibaldi at Gate Pancrazio and 2000 at Monte Mario had offered successful resistance.

The glory of that heated day belonged to the hero of La Plata. Hoffstetter says of him: "He stands unique in the bloody combat for lost positions. What greatness of soul, what unyielding endurance, even when almost all his friends lie on the ground! It is not stubbornness, nor ignoble ambition that inspires him to sustain these great sacrifices; he feels the full significance of the fighting; at any price he must regain Corsini. Without Garibaldi Rome would not have fallen so nobly. In the evening of this furious day everyone sought rest and recuperation, but not he. The whole night his white cloak was visible here and there. Everywhere he armed and prepared for the next attack, while no one had thought at that time of a regular siege of the city."

At the same time that the combat in front of Porta San Pancrazio which has just been described was taking place, the French had crossed

Ponte Molle from Monte Mario and had established a bridgehead on the left bank of the Tiber River. From here on as far as the Basilica San Paolo everything was uncontestedly in the hands of the French, and however glorious the combat of the third of June had been for Italian arms, it could not prevent the fall of the city; it was merely a question of time.

Chapter VII

Continuation

The improvised Roman Army performed wonders and the enthusiasm of the people on the barricades was without limits; but the bravery and enthusiasm had to yield to the slow but sure advance of an army which possessed inexhaustible war materiel and all resources of science at its disposal.

At daybreak of the fifth of June the Republicans noticed that during the course of the night the enemy had erected considerable siege-works and, with their batteries at Testanio, Sant'Alessio and at Bastion No. 6, they opened a vigorous fire, to which the French replied, although not with equal energy.

The 6th, 7th and 8th of June were uninterrupted days of battle, during which the French corps of engineers dug approach trenches and thus drew ever closer to the city. On the 9th the indefatigable Garibaldi marched out of Porta San Pancrazio and attacked the enemy strongly entrenched in his positions. The combat lasted one hour, disturbed the siege preparations of the enemy and at least convinced him how difficult the march into Rome would be if the city had a regular army.

On the 12th the Republicans again fought a heated engagement when the enemy tried to disturb their trench-digging in the garden of Villa Corsini. The Colonel of the Roman engineer corps let a battalion take to their arms and in one column charge an enemy bastion. The first spurt brought the Romans into the enemy fortifications, but the fire of the French killed the chief of the battalion, several other officers and 25 men and forced the assaulters to retreat. Garibaldi in person rushed over, ordered the fighting stopped, dissipated the confusion and immediately sent the commander of the engineers to Castel Sant'Angelo under strict arrest.

The next morning a mortar battery and three new batteries of cannon were to direct a murderous fire against the city, but before it started a bearer of Oudinot's truce flag came to Rome with a proclamation to the Constituent Assembly, which read as follows:

"We do not come to bring you war, we come to strengthen your order and freedom. The intentions of our government have been misunderstood. We have led the siege-works as far as your ramparts. Until now we only desired to reply to the fire of your batteries from time to time. Now we are at the point where the necessity of war must bring terrible misfortune. Avert this from a city which is filled with so many glorious memories. If you insist on driving us back, the responsibility of inevitable disaster will be solely yours.

The General en Chef: Oudinot, duc de Reggio.''

The Constituent Assembly unanimously rejected this request for capitulation, and it was not long thereafter that a very vivid cannonade began again between the French and Roman batteries which, be it said in honor of the Italian artillerymen, continued for seven days. Only on the 21st did the French succeed in setting up their breach cannon.

The epoch which followed offered most impressive scenes of the patriot no less than of the warrior to the painter and the poet, for everyone seemed to compete in heroism and devotion to the fatherland, beginning with the incomparable Garibaldi, who stimulated the whole population with his example, down to the youths and not excepting the gentler sex. When it is realized that within 24 hours 180 bombs fell into one bastion alone, one can get a slight idea of the tenacity with which the French bombarded.

"Already on the first day of the bombardment," reports a participating eyewitness, "our people began collecting enemy cannon balls, which we piled up one at a time at headquarters in order to be able to help out our artillery in case of need. The soldiers were not impressed by the renewed cannonading; in fact they worked and cooked as cheerfully as before behind the rampart through which at every moment splinters and cannon balls penetrated. The General, who wanted to observe at close quarters the effect of the enemy battery and visited the bastions several times, was always greeted with enthusiastic *evvivas*. The most trigger-happy ones pushed towards the embrasures to harrass the French cannoneers. The setting sun of 13 July illuminated a picture which must remain unforgettable to a soldier's soul. From the pavilion of Villa Savorelli, where headquarters were pitched, a magnificent spectacle was unfolding. Some 40 large cannon thundered from the most beautiful gardens, adorned by the fullest splendor of their greenery, while brief pauses were filled by the rattle of muskets. At our feet the animated life of our own camp was heightened by the swelling music from two regimental bands around which our soldiers danced with exuberant joy. Outside, the dark heaps of earth freshly dug up by the enemy, and behind them the tents of the French camp, were gilded by the last rays of the setting sun. Peace proudly reigned in Rome, and she had faith in her sons!''

Even more stirring is the account of another warrior, who participated in the combat which took place the following day in between Ponte Molle and Monte Mario:

"The French put the torch to the straw heaps lying along the river bank, believing that they might be of use to our bersaglieri, who were being harrassed. For the same reason we on our side put fire to the small houses close to Ponte Molle, and I shall never see such an imposing spectacle again as this spreading fire at night, whose flames and smoke mingled with those of the cannon and the muskets. The shouts of the fighting men, the wailing of the wounded, the crackling of the burning materials and the thunder of the artillery combined to make a truly gruesome scene. I imagined the shades of the old Romans as they opened their graves, roused from the slumber of death, stretched towards us from afar their fleshless arms, and called to us: 'Free our fatherland and drive the barbarians out forever beyond the mountains and the seas.' Then I threw myself into the fray blindly, spurred on by a single wish, to be allowed to die on this ground where the bones of the Scipios and Fabians rest."

It was in this combat of the 14th of June that the good-looking young canteen worker Orsola, from Spoleto, showed exceptional heroism and reached the bridgehead of Ponte Molle before all the others. Like this young woman, the twelve-year-old Gasparo from Anagni excelled on a bastion not far from Garibaldi's headquarters. This boy instead of doing his little tasks deserted every morning to the rampart, asked for a rifle from the soldiers, who all liked him, then fired at the French cannoneers with great skill. When an officer wanted to chase him away from the wall saying "you are still much too small," he retaliated with the shout: "The General is not tall either." Garibaldi supposedly gave a hearty laugh when this reply was told him.

On the 18th an armistice of one day was agreed upon, in order to bury the dead.

The fate of Rome was to be decided at Porta San Pancrazio. On the morning of the 20th the second parallel (line) of the besiegers was completed, and on the evening of the 21st three breach batteries placed close to each other became operative. The night of the 21st to the 22nd brought great losses to the Republicans. Whether there was treachery, as some maintained, is difficult to decide. It is a fact that the French most unexpectedly mounted the breach and took several bastions and that the Roman battalion fled panic-stricken to Villa Casimato. Before daybreak the generals held council, Avezzana and Roselli having rushed to the spot. They decided in cooperation with Garibaldi to storm the lost bastions and to drive out the enemy from them. All preparations to that end were made, and the plan of attack was laid. An additional regiment which did not belong to Garibaldi's division was put at his disposal. But it was a risky and dangerous undertaking. Several superior officers found the difficulties so great that in all seriousness they felt that they had to advise against the execution of the plan. And on this occasion Garibaldi proved that he was not unamenable to well-founded objections. It was Hoffstetter and Colonel Manara who went to see him. The former reports the counterdecision in the following manner:

"The General maintained his decision. But my conviction that the attempt was a desperate one became ever stronger and the danger seemed so threatening to me that I decided to make a second attempt with the General. I spoke in a tone of deepest conviction. He scarcely seemed to hear me as he looked fixedly towards the breaches which had been so shamefully lost, those same places which were still ours only a few hours before. Finally, long after I had ceased speaking, he suddenly said: 'Very well, we will not attack, but if I still had my men of the third of June one would not have convinced me.' "

Oudinot, now master of the bastions, established himself on a part of Rome's walls and from this point he dominated the city and the Italian camp. Everyone understood that as soon as he had concentrated sufficient artillery there, Rome would have to capitulate and the Republic would be irrevocably lost. In spite of this the Roman artillery did not diminish its efforts, as proved by the following account of a French eyewitness: "More than 800 cannon shots," writes Officer Delmas, "were fired in the course of a few hours against our columns and our approach trenches. The fire of the Roman artillery was incredibly lively and the shots followed upon each other with the rapidity of running fire. The terrain occupied by our troops was literally illuminated by the enemy caseshot and cannon fire."

During the course of the 25th, 26th and 27th of June this persistent bombardment did in fact annihilate the French batteries set up during the night on the central ramparts and the occupied bastions. But in the morning of the 28th seven French batteries opened a murderous fire in unison. Indescribable and terrifying beyond all measure was that whizzing of innumerable missiles, to which were added hundreds of bombs catapulted by the enemy mortars simultaneously. The cannon of the Republicans were practically stifled and the Villa Savorelli, Garibaldi's headquarters, was reduced to a heap of rubble.

The Roman people behaved admirably during these days of supreme ordeal. Driven out of their burning dwellings old people, children and mothers with their infants at the breast wandered in the lanes in the depth of the night and under a rain of murderous missiles. The din of war and heart-rending lamentations echoed in the streets. But not one voice was heard which spoke of capitulation. Only one shout drowned out all the others: "Ecco un Pio Nono, ecco la benedizione del Papa, ecco le bombe cristianissime!"* which was heard all around whenever a bullet came

---

*"Here is your Pius IX, here is his Papal benediction, here are the most Christian bombs!"

whizzing by or a grenade exploded. Who will ever be able to wipe out from the memory of the Roman people the gruesome remembrance of these nights?

Had the French, who had proclaimed themselves a short time ago the protectors of every republic, not been induced by ambition to break their word in a most shameful way, they would have heard a voice from that heap of stone and rubble, calling to them: "Halt your triumphal chariot, oh France, for the invisible spirit of the ancient Roman Republic is fighting here. You desecrate the tombs of the Scipios and Brutuses; do you not see, oh deluded one, that this handful of braves is holding high the banner of future Italy at your side, and that with their blood they have written on those stones the name of a people which today takes its place in the council of nations. No human power is able to annihilate its name, it is written with indelible letters that *'Italia sarà'.*"

On the morning of the 29th the French batteries renewed the bombardment, possibly with even greater vehemence, and all Rome shook under the infernal firing. The Italian artillerymen who heroically died at their cannon were silently replaced by line soldiers. The entire National Guard was under arms, and even those wounded who could get around left the hospitals to rejoin their corps.

Nor was there any lack of heroic women who exposed themselves to the enemy artillery on the city walls during these hours of peril. Anita Garibaldi, the Brasilian heroine, hastened from Nizza to share the fate of her dear husband.

As long as a cannon was still standing upright, the Republicans tenaciously replied to the enemy's fire, but by the evening of the 29th almost all their batteries were smashed and the breach of the bastion at Porta San Pancrazio was wide and practicable. At ten o'clock at night nature's anger seemed to unite with that of man, or was it perhaps heaven's just indignation at such a terrible blood bath? The rolling of thunder mingled with the din of the cannon and the lightning flashing through the sky joined the luminous parabolas of the hissing bombs.

It was the holiday of Saint Paul and Peter, and even though the two armies were fighting each other for life and death and the city resembled a vast battlefield covered with a forest of barricades, still on that evening, according to the custom of the church, everything was illuminated, including the cupola of St. Peter's.

The *eternal city* seen from Monte Pincio offered a unique spectacle. A broad valley studded with churches and palaces through which the Tiber meandered spread out at the feet of the spectator. On the left the capitol, on whose tower the Republican flag was flying, was surrounded by thousands of torches. On the right was the sombre Monte Mario, with papal and French flags intermingled. Below Michelangelo's Pantheon, bathed in a sea of light, with as a frame the Janiculum and the whole line of San Pancrazio, blazed in a very different fire, the deadly fire of cannon and muskets!

At midnight the clouds parted in the sky and on earth also a pause set in. But it was a deceptive quiet because most unexpectedly before two o'clock the most terrifying din of battle was heard again. Two feint attacks were made at Porta San Paolo and at the same time at Porta del Popolo in order to distract the attention of the Republicans from Porta San Pancrazio where the decisive attack was being made. Garibaldi's headquarters was moved back to Villa Spada. When first startled, everyone took up arms with lightening speed, but imagine their consternation when they saw the French outside the gate of Villa Spada! The shouts of joy of the infilitrating victors in ever increasing numbers, the thundering of artillery and the bursting of grenades in the deep of night created an indescribable scene. There were no limits to confusion and helplessness.

It was then that Garibaldi bared his saber and beginning a war hymn threw himself alone against the invading enemy. The bravest of his men followed him, spurred on by such a high-minded example and thrilled by this voice which had always led them to victory. Like a stream the remaining men followed their heroic leader. Seven times the enemy broke into Villa Spada, and seven times he was repelled. The walls in the meantime collapsed, penetrated as they were by coarse missiles; dead and wounded lay in all the rooms. During the night Garibaldi surpassed his own reputation. He and his braves glorified the defeat by deeds of heroism worthy of the ancient republic. Four hundred bodies covered the battlefield when the sun went down, and the daylight which fell on the Republic for the last time, also lit up for the last time the faces which mourned in death. The brave Colonel Manara, the twenty-year-old youth Morosini, the Achilles of the Republican Army, Garibaldi's moor and many other braves perished here. The sad survivors of the Italian Legion still stormed against the enemy with the cry *Viva la Repubblica!* As night fell, the Italians remained masters of Villa Spada; the battle continued on, when the news arrived: "The Municipio wishes to capitulate."

Rome had fallen! The Triumvirate was dissolved and the Chamber had laconically decreed that: *The Constituent Assembly abandons a defense which has become impossible and remains at its post. 1 July 1849.*

The bloodiest, as well as the most glorious, combat of the Republic had been fought and the Assembly, as did the ancient senators of Rome, awaited in permanent session the new Brennus and the new Gauls. The National Guard quietly carried out its duty: every official was at his station and not a post was abandoned. The people on the other hand were either busy with the construction of barricades on the left bank of the Tiber, or rushed aimlessly and as if demented through the streets of the city.

After many useless negotiations between the Municipio and the French General the Assembly declared that the Republic had yielded only to force. The troops were then ordered to their quarters and the city opened its gates.

But *one* man did not wish to yield to the power of circumstance, and this man was Garibaldi. This iron soul, whom fate could indeed bend but not break, decided instead of laying down his arms before the proud victor, to take to the mountains and there to make his way with his saber through four enemy armies.[130] To any one who wished to follow him, he confessed frankly that he could promise nothing but hunger, thirst, danger and combat.

BOOK THREE

GARIBALDI ON THE RETREAT FROM ROME

Chapter I

Garibaldi's March to San Marino

The tenacious resistance which Rome offered during the thirty-day siege is an honor to the inhabitants of that city and to its brave leader, who was the soul of that resistance. It was an heroic combat of a mostly untrained people's army against an army much superior in numbers and in military training. Against Oudinot's besieging army of 34,000 men, well supplied with all necessary equipment, Rome was able to oppose for its defense only 14,800 regular troops and volunteers and 8 to 10,000 men of the National Guard. How these defenders fought behind improvised siege works is attested most impressively by their total losses. When the city capitulated, 300 officers and 4000 noncommissioned officers and soldiers were dead or seriously wounded, not to mention the lightly wounded.

But an even greater honor than his tenacious resistance on the walls of Rome merits that brave leader Garibaldi for his daring march by which he withdrew from the shipwreck of the Republic, avoided capitulation to a treacherous enemy, while posing the last questions to fate — namely, whether the liberation of Italy could still succeed and whether he could preserve himself, unconquered, for that memorable day in the future.

Already during the siege there had not always been complete unanimity between Garibaldi and the Ministry of War, nor with the government of Rome, concerning the measures to be adopted. When it became clear that Rome must fall, the General made a proposal to the Triumvirate carrying on the government to leave Rome and, if necessary, go to Naples to organize a people's war, and then to return to Rome with reinforced power. A daring proposal, to be sure, worthy of that unshakeable fighter for Italy, and not completely without prospect of success. At that time more than 10 to 15,000 determined soldiers were still available and these might have sufficed to defeat the Neapolitan Army, to make the Kingdom of the Two Sicilies rebel and to prepare a reliable focus of revolution there. It was doubtful whether the French would pursue them there; it was even more questionable whether the Austrians stationed in the Legations would do so, and if they did pursue, at least time was gained; the Republican Army would have been strengthened enough to count again on the success of its arms and on the fluctuations of European politics. Unfortunately the government did not consider this plan, preferring instead to negotiate with the French. For a moment Garibaldi now considered laying down his command. The objections of his officers, and probably also the dropping of the negotiations on the part of the government, convinced him to stay.

When the defense of the city was abandoned by decree of the Constituent Assembly, Garibaldi made a last attempt to induce the Triumvirs to move the government away from Rome and to take measures for the withdrawal of all troops. But again this attempt failed, for among the army officers and influential civilians complete hopelessness prevailed, while the Triumvirate was no longer in a position to support the General's suggestions effectively. The only thing which the latter obtained was written plenary powers from the Constituent Assembly made out in Garibaldi's and Roselli's names, whereby the two were named commanders-in-chief of all Italian troops and empowered to do anything deemed useful for the enslaved fatherland, to make requisitions of all kinds, etc., and to be accountable to no one but to the people.

On the second of July the French made arrangements to move into Rome. At the same time Garibaldi with his Legion began his retreat to the left bank of the Tiber. Preparations to this end had been made quietly on the previous day. The General exhorted other troop units to join him although he in no way hid from them, nor from his legionaries, that his undertaking was dangerous and desperate. "To him who wishes to follow me," he said, "I offer hardships, hunger, thirst and all the perils of war."

At six in the evening the Legion stood ready to march from Porta San Giovanni on the eastern side of Rome, waiting only for those who had promised to join it. Two hours passed, but no reinforcements came. Almost all the officers who had promised to march with it, beginning with Roselli, stayed away; scarcely a handful of men arrived from the various corps. However, a large crowd of people, among them many National Guardsmen, surrounded the Legion; later they accompanied it for a distance, wished it good luck, then bid it farewell.

It was dusk already, after the two-hour wait, when the detachment set off. Garibaldi in person rode in front alongside his heroic wife and the well-known and brave Ciceruacchio, Angelo Brunetti,[131] the Roman people's orator; close behind them rode a vanguard of 30 cavalrymen. Some distance behind these followed a company of infantry, then the baggage and the main part of the column, that is, the cavalry with one single cannon, the infantry and finally the rearguard consisting of both riflemen and cavalry. Altogether there were 2500 infantrymen and 400 cavalry. The war treasure contained just enough paper money to pay the troops for four weeks and to buy food.

The Legion marched throughout the night without interruption, from ten at night until seven in the morning. It was a question of reaching the mountains quickly in order to gain on any French units that might be following it, then to deceive them as to the adopted route. All safety precautions were observed during the march: commands were whispered only, no one was allowed to smoke. A halt was made in Tivoli, where the corps was reorganized and the remainder of the day was devoted to rest. Towards evening Garibaldi broke camp and with his whole column pursued the road towards the south in order to spread the idea that he was turning towards Neapolitan territory. Instead after one and a half hours of marching, he deviated sideways across the fields, skirted Tivoli and pursued a northerly direction.

And thus the march continued for a while undisturbed; they had indeed succeeded in spreading a completely false idea concerning their direction. Garibaldi's wife rode ahead on a splendid grey horse, an Amazon in dark green dress and Calabrian hat adorned with an ostrich plume, followed by two mounted youths from Bologna who acted as her pages. The General himself, now with the vanguard, now with the rearguard, took constant care in watching over the provisions and the safety of his group. In camp he was the last to lie down on the modest resting place selected by Anita. No one but he, with the possible exception of his chief of staff, Major von Hoffstetter, knew the next destination. Garibaldi knew how to obtain reliable information concerning the enemies' positions, while deceiving them by sending detachments here and there so as to impart false suppositions concerning the direction of his marches to the deputations from towns and villages that reached him. Usually they made two marches per day, one in the morning from two to ten o'clock, the other in the evening from five to eight o'clock. They camped near a spring and requisitioned bread, wine and meat, as well as feed for their horses, from the nearest localities. All the time Garibaldi observed a very strict discipline; he who stole or plundered was threatened with death, and more than one marauder was shot. The soldiers loved the General, although they also feared him; they knew that if necessary, he would have them shot without even taking the cigar out of his mouth.

On the 8th of July the corps arrived in Terni unmolested. Here it was joined by a legion of 600 men under the command of Colonel Forbes, an Englishman. The strength of Garibaldi's column, which had already suffered by desertions, thus rose to 3000 men again, among whom 450 cavalry. But from Terni on, the danger also rose with every step. East of Terni, not far from Spoleto, Austrian advance guards were stationed. In the southwest the French were approaching from Civita Castellana. In the northeast, in and around Perugia, further Austrian units were stationed, which were getting ready to bar the way through the mountain passes against the Romans, apparently en route to the Adriatic Sea. At the same time from here on the hardships of the march increased. As delightful as this part of the Apennines may seem to the eye of the peaceful unmolested wanderer, with its hills covered with brush and boulders, the steep ravines and narrow valleys are a laborious and exhausting trek for a pursued army.

As far as Todi Garibaldi followed a straight northerly direction, then he suddenly swerved to the left moving westerly towards Orvieto, and then further on towards Cetona in Tuscany, thus extricating himself from the Austrians in superbly skillful marches.

It was probably here that Garibaldi was finally convinced that he could no longer think of a continuation of the war, nor of a new insurrection of Italy, but that it was only a question of reaching the Adriatic seacoast in order to embark his Legion. Everywhere on his march he found patriots who gave him help, the masses showing sympathy for the brave defender of Rome, but who nevertheless opposed strongly any new attempts of resistance.

On the 18th of July the Legion camped near Sarteano, where its leader had a characteristic coup carried out. It was commonly known that the blackcoats upon hearing of Garibaldi's approach organized armed resistance in the nearby town of Chiusi and its surroundings. The General therefore sent a detachment of infantry and cavalry from Sarteano to a Capuchin monastery near Chiusi to capture the inmates and bring them back as prisoners. On the morning of the 19th the priests arrived, some 24 in number, panting and covered with perspiration since they were unused to marching and most of them were very obese. Quite docilely and with impassive faces, they listened to the stern words of the General. Among other things, he told them: "You have fanned the flame of civil war; you call yourself *Ministri di Dio* but you are Ministri del Diavolo!" Finally he informed them that they would have to go with them as hostages until two prisoners, who had been captured by the garrison of Chiusi, were returned to him with their arms and horses. One of them was sent to Chiusi with these demands, the others were turned over to the camp patrol. But a few days later Garibaldi let the Capuchins go, for their imprisonment made a visibly bad impression on the people, who not knowing the cause of the priests' captivity viewed them with reverence as they were marched off piously with hands folded in prayer.

If he wished to gain the east coast, it was now a question of leaping from the sub-Apennine chain over to the great Apennine Mountains. Well informed about the position of the Austrian units, Garibaldi led his Legion in slow marches from Cetona to Torrita. Here he suddenly turned northeast and in a forced march through the plain reached the small town of Fiorentino; then passing by Arezzo the course was eastward in crisscross marches through the center of Austrian detachments, some of whom were completely ignorant of the proximity of the feared enemy, while others were actually repulsed in daring advance guard actions.

On the 27th of July the Legion, still some 2000 men strong, reached the ridge of the great Apennines. The baggage was carried by mules,

Garibaldi having taken care soon after retreating from Rome to replace the wagons and carts with draft animals. On the east flank of the mountains they followed the course of the Metaurus River. On the 28th of July it seemed that the corps would finally meet its fate. News came that the Austrians stood near Sant'Angelo in Vado, where the valley of the Metaurus, hitherto narrow now widened into a basin of 1000 paces in width and 2000 in length. In fact, it was evident that the eastern part of the valley was occupied by several Austrian rifle companies in well protected positions. Thus for the Legion to march forward down the Metaurus Valley became practically impossible, while in the meantime in their rear coming from Arezzo other Austrian troops were closing in on them. Nothing but a desperate combat and an honorable death seemed to await them now.

Fortunately it was discovered that the Austrians had neglected to occupy a small sidepath which leads northward over a branch of the mountain range from the Metaurus Valley into that of the Foglia. This was the route the column followed. En route however, they renewed their provisions in the small town of Sant'Angelo, encountered Austrians victoriously and then safely reached the Foglia Valley.

From here on Garibaldi turned to northeast again leading the Legion directly towards the territory of the Republic of San Marino. They skirmished continuously with the Austrians but managed to reach the frontier. Here they lined up their remaining 1800 men in a valley still in Papal territory and rode to the city of Marino to ask the government for permission to retreat into their territory.

The government not only granted this request, but also promised to take over the provisioning of the Legion. As the General returned to his troops he heard shooting. "Despite the dangerous stony paths," a person in the General's escort recounts, "we raced *ventre a terre* towards our men. But the latter were fleeing panic-stricken towards the road to Rimini through the ravine at the foot of the rock of San Marino, pursued by several Austrian rifle companies. As we arrived at the slope we perceived the General's wife throwing herself alone against the fugitives with drawn riding whip and demanding a halt. No one of her escort had had the courage to follow her. Soon the General reached her and led the column up to the city, raging with anger at this cowardly flight."

. Next to San Marino the troops pitched camp. Here Garibaldi decided to dismiss his men. The latest proof that they were not completely reliable under fire may have precipitated this decision. But more probably he was influenced by the reasoning that a single man on his own could more easily escape than all the men amassed in a group.

To the government of San Marino he declared his willingness to lay down arms, if the Austrians promised to let the men return quietly to their homes; and with this declaration the government sent an agent to the commander of the nearest Austrian corps.

To his Legion Garibaldi released the following order of the day:

"We have reached the soil which grants us refuge and we owe our generous hosts our best behavior. Thus we will earn the respect which is being paid to us, persecuted and unfortunate as we are. From this moment on I release my companions from every obligation and permit their return to private life, but I remind them that Italy must not remain humiliated, and that it is better to die than to live as slaves of the foreigner."

On the evening of the first of August an agreement was reached with the Austrians. Its main points were:

1. General Garibaldi was to hand over his weapons, munitions and horses to the Republic of San Marino, which in turn would pass them on to the Austrians.
2. The officers and men were to be escorted to their homes. At the same time complete amnesty was guaranteed to them.
3. Garibaldi upon his word of honor to leave Italy would receive a pass for America or England.
4. The Austrians were permitted to camp on the territory of the Republic of San Marino.
5. Garibaldi with his corps would remain quietly at ease in San Marino.
6. This agreement was to be completely validated only after its ratification by the commander in Bologna.

When the government of San Marino submitted this agreement to Garibaldi for signature, he signified his acceptance except for two points: first, that concerning his person. He said that he had undertaken negotiations not for himself but for his soldiers only, and secondly, that he could not give his word of honor to leave Italy, but would act according to his feelings. Neither could he agree that his officers and men were to be transported home; instead he asked that they be permitted to withdraw freely.

Towards the end of that first of August, Garibaldi assembled his officers, explained the situation and bid them farewell, then asked them to inform their men of his proposed departure, so that those who believed themselves heavily compromised could join him.

At nightfall Garibaldi mounted his horse and left the camp accompanied by his wife, who because of illness could barely remain on horseback, and Ciceruacchio. In a thicket about one mile distant from the city he waited for those who might wish to join him. Little by little some 200 arrived, amongst them 100 cavalry, mostly officers, and the others on foot. This troop then slipped silently and rapidly into the night and in single file on footpaths along the edge of the mountain range passed the Austrian patrols undetected and headed northward.

How Garibaldi fared later during the night we do not know. The troop disintegrated, only about two-thirds remaining with their leader, while the remainder disbanded and disappeared completely.

Chapter II

The Flight: The Death of Anita

This chapter is based upon papers which Signore Bonnet, Garibaldi's savior, turned over to the author. It is he who is speaking in the following pages.

Garibaldi successfully embarked with his group in twelve small vessels, locally called *bragozzi,*[132] in Cesenatico, a small harbor town on the Adriatic Sea not far from Rimini. Besides Anita, the inseparable companion of his life, and 150 remaining faithful followers, he led away with him a captured brigadier of the Papal Carabinieri and a few soldiers, since he did not want the latter to harm certain inhabitants of the locality who had compromised themselves by helping him during his perilous embarcation.

When all sails were hoisted and the General had surrendered his small flotilla to the turbulent sea, he had the course set for Venice. Previously when Garibaldi on Italian soil and with a considerable army of volunteers was protecting the banner of a newly founded republic from the persecutions by France, Spain, Austria and Naples, the leaders of the Austrian-Papal troops had taken the severest measures in the province of Romagna. They disarmed innocent communities, proclaimed martial law, requisitioned all vessels, blocked the harbor entrances with some of them while dismantling others with the purpose of rendering them unusable; at times they even considered whether they should burn them.

With the approach of Garibaldi, the hero, the more that was heard of him, the more fanatically the foreign despots behaved; gripped by fear, they had many harmless citizens arrested. Unfortunately the population had sunk to a state of lamentable demoralization and only few seemed ready to expose themselves by patriotic actions to the tyrannical wrath of the foreign commanders, which cruel as it might be, was however still more bearable than that of our native despots.

143

In the meanwhile the excitement increased daily and on the second of August it was conveyed to the Austrian officer in command of the town of Comacchio* that he should be on his guard, for it was already learned that Garibaldi had left San Marino. This news was sufficient to cause the greatest confusion in the garrison there. The captain, at the head of his company of Croats and accompanied by all the carabinieri and customs officers that he could muster in a hurry, rushed to occupy the harbor of Magnavacca. However he was soon informed by a courier that it was too late; Garibaldi had already embarked at Cesenatico.

I was determined to spy on the movements of the Croats and followed them without delay to Magnavacca, which is only four miles distant from Comacchio.

Very soon it was rumored that twelve bragozzi were visible on the open sea, apparently steering for Venice. But a few sailors who had been under arrest in the small port for the last month climbed up the lighthouse immediately and, equipped with field glasses, they declared that the boats were almost completely empty and probably following the route to Venice which Garibaldi had chosen. Furthermore they had already in the early morning seen several vessels sailing by in the same direction and, (this was perhaps wishful thinking on their part), according to them, Garibaldi must have reached Venice long ago.

Somewhat relieved I returned to Comacchio, even though I had not obtained complete certainty as to Garibaldi's fate. Unable to sleep I spent the whole night in torture and restlessness. At daybreak a cannon shot startled me; immediately I surmised the terrible truth. I jumped out of bed and rushed to the window. A second cannon shot followed which confirmed my ominous presentiment. Each of my movements had the speed of lightning. Getting dressed and rushing to the stable was a matter of an instant. My mare, usually so unruly that even the most skillful person had difficulty in harnessing her so that I myself had never tried, was meek as a lamb this time and, as if she had understood whose salvation was at stake, let me harness and hitch her to the biroccino** without delay.

The sun was just arising from its purple bed as I reached Magnavacca. Cannon shots still resounded. However, the soldiers had not yet been ordered to move. I mingled with them and without asking questions learned that the shots heard were those of an Austrian brig which had sighted the bragozzi last evening, had overtaken them and now was pursuing them. This notwithstanding, it was still rumored that the vessels were almost empty and that not one of them had landed anywhere on the coast.

---

*Comacchio is located north of Cesenatico, a few miles distant from the coast on a small river at whose mouth lies Porta di Magnavacca.

**A high two-wheeled vehicle very common in Romagna, to which the Romagnoles usually hitch excellent horses and cover tremendous distances with incredible speed.

Of course I did not challenge this opinion, but I myself was firmly convinced that the pursued boats sheltered none other than Garibaldi and his followers, which indeed was confirmed all too soon. In fact soon after it was reported that the brig had overpowered a bragozzo containing red-clad men, from which it was deduced that the remaining ones could not be far away. Strangely enough this news spread fear and terror among the garrison. The captain himself lost all presence of mind and was at a loss at what to do; before long disorder prevailed.

In the midst of this general confusion a little Chiosotto* approached me and whispered: "They have landed five miles from here." Nothing could hold me back. I jumped on my biroccino and just as I was signalling to a young man of my acquaintance that he should accompany me, the Croat captain hurried towards me with the question: "Where are you going?"

"To the forest," I replied nonchalantly.

"I myself should get to Comacchio without delay," reported the Austrian, bewildered by fear and excitement. But not paying attention to this hint, I shouted back in the presence of all that urgent business called me away at once and that I could not lose a moment; and in great haste I started in the direction indicated to me by the Chiosotto. Halfway, on a piece of land which belonged to me, I left my vehicle, for it was easier to plunge on foot through the sand dunes which dominate this shore. After covering a short distance I came upon a group of men gathered on one of the sand dunes. I rushed towards them and recognized some twenty of our country folks observing the small sea encounter from here.

Tenaciously the Austrian brig, as well as two armed boats, pursued the small boats which contained Garibaldi's men, three of which had already landed.

The peasants (who would believe it!) were beside themselves with rage because of their own cowardice which prevented them from plundering the stranded bragozzi. The crews had abandoned them and sought shelter in scattered huts and houses nearby. But the enemy fire, which had obliged the sailors to abandon all their belongings on board, now prevented the rapacious peasants from taking possession of their loot.

Within minutes they recognized me and, encouraged by my urging, readied themselves to follow me. We were only a gunshot's range from the bragozzi when I noticed coming towards me between two sand dunes a man whose red dress revealed him to be one of Garibaldi's soldiers. To my question, "Where is the General?" he replied with tearful eyes that Garibaldi had to wade through water and marshes carrying his very ill wife on his shoulders, and that his most valuable documents, the little money which he possessed and all his remaining belongings had re-

---

*This is how the Romagnoles call the inhabitants[133] of the harbor town of Chioggia, situated not far from Venice.

145

mained on board. This soldier, who was from Urbino, pointed out to me Garibaldi's vessel.

Immediately I ordered the peasants to approach this vessel and to break open its lockers. They achieved their objective rapidly, but there ensued considerable confusion; instead of bringing me the valuable objects I desired, they spent their time rescuing things which I deemed unimportant. Also it was difficult for me to communicate with them, since they had to wade way out into the water for a considerable distance. As I began to get impatient at the waste of time, they made me understand from afar that they lacked the necessary tools with which to break open the lockers. Notwithstanding this I still did my best in urging them on and to minimize their objections. Consequently by following my instructions they soon broke open the door of the forward cabin; however, it contained nothing but provisions and the ship's gear. We were just getting ready to proceed similarly with the rear cabin, when a cannon ball from the enemy brig, which had approached in the meantime, hit the ground right next to me. The explosion and the whizzing of the shot at close range terrified the peasants and provoked such a scene of desperation, that I would be ashamed to describe it. With lightning speed the peasants went ashore, without heeding my commands, threats and entreaties. Two further cannon shots from the brig, coupled with the approach of a bark manned by ten Austrians, put an end to their remaining courage. They scattered like mad and in the confusion of their flight their loot disappeared with them.

Now that my hope for saving the documents and money from the bragozzi was shattered, there was nothing more for me to do in this very dangerous spot. I mounted my horse and tried to find some trace of the General, who was exposed to indescribable misfortune and great peril. But in vain I scoured the nearest surroundings in all directions; in vain I tried to sound out every soldier I met about Garibaldi's fate. Some replied that they knew nothing, while others directed me to places I had already searched.

Helpless and despairing I climbed a hill from which I hoped to spot one or the other of the red-clad fugitives; I hurried towards each one who appeared, but in all of them I encountered the same resistance and the same mistrust as to my intentions.

Finally I reached some Lombards, whom I likewise entreated to give me information concerning the whereabouts of the General; I assured them that my only thought was to rescue him and that if he died it would be their responsibility, unless they helped me. This time I was luckier. The sincerity of my intentions must have been apparent from my eyes, for after giving me a searching look, the Lombards pointed to a certain spot and said: "Very well then, go this way." I followed their directions and close at hand I soon discovered four persons, two of whom were supporting a woman dragging herself along with slow steps and great difficulty. I would have gone towards the group immediately, if the presence of a young man whom I could not get rid of had not made me fearful of greeting the General by name. Pretending not to know him I approached slowly, but as soon as our glances met I realized that Garibaldi did not intend to remain incognito; in an instant he rushed forward and calling me by name embraced me.

He anticipated his deepest gratitude intimating that he was counting on me as his only hope; but I will not repeat his words here, although they would rightfully fill any man with pride.

Inspired by Garibaldi's confidence in me and more than ever touched by his desperate situation I decided to do everything in my power to save him, even at the cost of my life. The spouse of the fugitive hero especially required care. Garibaldi and a man from Comacchio, a well-known vagabond who inspired me with little confidence, held her up by the arms, dragging her along. Consumed by a deadly fever and tortured by acute pain in the chest, the unfortunate woman complained incessantly. She dragged herself in her bare feet and scanty white gown. I did my best to encourage her by promising a safe refuge where she would recover; in the meantime I entreated her to remain calm. But in vain; the usually indomitable amazon was completely crushed physically and morally. To the Comacchiese I pointed out the house of one of my friends, to which he should take Garibaldi, his wife and Leggiero, the only one of his followers who accompanied him, while I tried under various pretences to get rid of the remaining attendants who were burdensome and more or less suspect.

On arriving in my friend's lodging I had the suffering woman put to bed, ordered some wholesome beef broth with egg yolk for her, then begged her to cease worrying and to rest. Garibaldi and I sat down on an overturned cart in the shade of a rustic straw roof where we refreshed our parched lips with a delicious watermelon. In the solitude of this pleasant forest I was privileged to converse at length with the sorely afflicted warrior; we talked of the misfortunes which we had endured together and in devoted commemoration we recalled the deeds of those valiant ones who died on the walls of Rome, victims of their love for the fatherland and their own heroic bravery!

While we were speaking freely, Leggiero surprised us with the unpleasant news that the small amount of money which Garibaldi's spouse had carried on her person could no longer be found; we could not ascertain whether it had been taken from her on this farm or already during the landing. Verily, where else could something like this have occurred if not amongst a population such as this, bowed down and demoralized by long tyranny and rule of the priests? Eyewitnesses of the bitter lot of the harassed and pursued patriot, they appeared to lend him a helping hand, while secretly they were bent upon theft and treason! The young man who accompanied me did his very best to find the author of this vile deed, but without result.

147

This event served to make me more distrustful and more circumspect. Thus I could not avoid asking the General whether the Papal brigadier whom he had embarked with him in Cesenatico had also landed. All the time I thought it probable that since the brigadier held hostile opinions he would not fail to inform the government of all that had taken place. In fact when Garibaldi replied in the affirmative I was seized with such anxiety and fear that I could no longer remain there.

"I must leave you for the time being and hurry to Comacchio to look after some most urgent matters," I said to the General, taking his hand. "Be of good cheer and entrust yourself wholly to my care."

"Will I see you again?" asked Garibaldi.

"Will you see me again?" I replied. "Nothing will keep me from being back soon with you. General, I am not wealthy, but in case of need I can count on one hundred, even two hundred scudi; permit me to put them at your disposal."

"I thank you, my friend," he replied and led me to the bed of his wife, reassuring me that in spite of the theft, she was still in possession of a few gold pieces which would be sufficient for their needs for the time being. I could not make my offer more pressing, for I felt that it would annoy him. Nevertheless my presence seemed to do some good to his suffering wife; she whispered to me some moving words of thanks and reluctantly let me go. Her condition, by the way, had deteriorated greatly and the poor woman was enduring cruel pain. Still I found it unwise for the fugitives to prolong their stay in this house. I therefore made all arrangements that they should look for another refuge as soon as the condition of the sick woman permitted it.

No place could have been more suitable for this purpose than my brother-in-law's property, situated in a remote hidden valley and whose house I recalled was inhabited by my relative's brother and his wife; they would spare no effort to provide Garibaldi and his spouse with shelter and care.

As for Garibaldi's hosts and the guides to whom I had to entrust the moving, I used both threats and entreaties to convince them of the necessity of observing the utmost caution and secrecy, instructing them on how they should act if an inquiry or search were to take place.

After a warm farewell to Garibaldi I jumped into my biroccino and rode to Comacchio at the fastest speed of which a horse is capable. I handed the vehicle over to my companion and unhesitatingly mingled with the crowd assembled in the main square, among whom were some sbirri* and vagabonds. Soon I recognized the Papal brigadier mentioned previously; disguised as a soldier, he still seemed to attract everyone's attention. Fear and terror were visible on his altered features as he narrated to an attentive audience how audaciously Garibaldi had embarked in Cesenatico, adding a mass of lies and vileness which is unnecessary to

---

*Plain-clothes agents of the sheriff.

repeat here. Of course I had to wait until the carabinieri and the brigadier left, since I was seeking ways and means of getting Garibaldi out of danger and into safety. Rapidly I looked for persons who might be useful to me in reaching this aim. After long consultations with a few trusted persons I had taken into my confidence, I decided to take along two *guardiani dei valli**, accompanied by a reliable foreman (*capo*), who would carry out my plan of abduction conscientiously and with secrecy. In fact I had no difficulty in finding the right man quickly, instructing him to select two of his most capable *guardiani*, because it was question of saving a person very dear to me.

This accomplished, and when the men had engaged a well-armed punt, I indicated to the *capo guardiano* the exact place where he could find Garibaldi; here, amongst Garibaldi's disbanded legionaries, he would find my brother Raimondo, solely for whom I pretended to be concerned. The capo and his men would have convinced even the most disbelieving person with their assurances. They then embarked in good spirits and promised to reach the destined spot in less than two hours.

Hardly had my emissaries left when the Croats[134] arrived with many carabinieri from Magnavacca. They made a short halt in the city square and shortly after received the order to embark via the shortest route through the Valli di Comacchio for the spot where Garibaldi had supposedly landed. In addition they received strict instructions to search the surrounding countryside closely, in order to pick up the trail of the fugitives and to pursue them.

My predicament can well be imagined! Under these circumstances I myself should not be seen on the waters of the swamps since the carabinieri, to whom I was well known, would naturally have become suspicious if they had met me there. Hence there was no other course left to me except to look around for a fresh horse with which to reach my destination by land. But even to procure a horse was difficult, and only after a long unsuccessful search was I able to persuade a friend to lend me his horse for this purpose; he was however, willing to accompany me, and God knows how many by-ways we traversed at a gallop in order to escape from the Croats. These had already landed, and in broken Italian spoke of nothing but *fusilare*[135] and *bastonare*.[136] A few curious loafers standing harmlessly by a tavern were immediately surrounded and terrified as they were ordered about at gun point.

After much roaming around I encountered a peasant who introduced himself to me as an emissary of the woman who inhabited the house of my brother-in-law, which I had destined as the second refuge for Gari-

---

*The swamps surrounding Comacchio are called *valli*, and today they are just as famous for their fisheries as they were at the time of Ariosto and Tasso. The way in which fish strayed into these swamps from the sea and were prevented from retreating seaward was described long ago by these two poets. The men employed in these fisheries are called *guardiani*.

baldi and to which he had actually moved during my drive to Comacchio. It appeared that the woman, perhaps made suspicious by some of Garibaldi's words, had become convinced that he could be nobody but Garibaldi himself and in her deadly fright, which was quite understandable, she begged me by means of this peasant to hurry towards her without delay. I did and found her, as well as the other inhabitants of the house, frightfully excited. All of them wanted to flee so as not to be shot, as they insisted the Croats would do at once, if Garibaldi was discovered among them.

I pacified the woman as best I could, told her that my friend was not the General but one of his officers, and ordered the peasants to observe order, secrecy and obedience. Thereupon I asked my friend, whom I mentioned previously, to take up a position between the house and the place where I was planning to have Garibaldi embark, in order to forestall any possible liaison between the peasants and the boatsmen.

Only when this had been arranged did I go to see my persecuted friends in the upper story of the house. I found the spouse of the General in a pitiful condition; she was tortured by spasmodic pains, the labor pains of a premature confinement. Garibaldi was in the room next door, dozing. The peace of mind which is a quality of great men had not deserted the General even in this hour of affliction. The very sight of this peacefully sleeping man was a powerful sedative for me too, and, taking him as a model, the most desperate undertaking appeared to me now easy and transitory. Unwillingly I tore him from his restful slumber which hid the stark reality from him, because the imperious necessity of the moment required it.

"I am ready," uttered Garibaldi upon awakening.

"General," I replied, "everything is arranged for the flight, but I must not withhold from you that your Anita is a considerable obstacle to your rescue. Her condition requires great nursing care, so that it is unthinkable that she should share the dangers of the flight with you any longer. Entrust her to me without hesitation. I will take her to my house, where she will be nursed and cared for with love and devotion. Even if her identity becomes known, this does not worry me. You must therefore follow my advice, which moreover is the only feasible course."

Garibaldi in no way disapproved of my proposal and communicated it to his wife. She seemed to agree with it at first, but a moment later declared that she would not be separated from her husband at any cost. In order to support her desire, she even pretended to feel a little better, and our dissuading arguments remained fruitless.

I had some refreshments served to the General, as the master of the house joined us, and since I had made his acquaintance previously as the colonel of our National Guard, and because Garibaldi had also met him in Ravenna, we did not lack topics of conversation and common recollections.

Our quiet conversation however was interrupted by the approach of my friend whom I just mentioned and whom I had posted as a guard. He brought the bad news that the guardiani, suspecting that the man who was to be transported by them was not my brother, but Garibaldi, had declared that they did not want to lend a hand for such a service. I rushed to the spot and soon realized that only by taking a very firm stand would my orders be carried out.

"Whoever my protégé may be," I had them understand, "you must take him to the appointed place without delay, and woe to you if you do not carry out my orders to the letter. Verily, you should deem yourselves fortunate to be selected for such a service! Furthermore you know very well that I have promised you a generous recompense." Then I added pointing to Leggiero, Garibaldi's companion: "This man is determined and desperate, so be on your guard, for in a critical situation he would be capable of anything. Besides, not to him alone, but to all of Italy, you are responsible for your behavior."

My frank words seemed to have the desired effect. The men subsequently declared themselves willing to do whatever I wished, and it seemed that I had removed all their objections. I therefore returned to the General, asked him to exchange his utterly ragged clothes for mine, gave him the pass of my brother Gaetano who was killed in Rome, and urged him to start on his way immediately. I had his wife, who had by now lost all use of her limbs, carried to the punt lying on a mattress and supported by cushions. In spite of these precautions the suffering woman uttered heart-rending moans at the slightest movement.

To get to Venice by a direct route was at this time absolutely impossible; all approaches to the frontier were strongly guarded by the Austrians. Only by resorting to a ruse did I succeed in opening the way for the fugitives in one direction. I had the rumor circulated that Garibaldi with his wife had crossed the Po at Volano and had been seen near Maffenzatica in the company of a well armed escort.

As often happens in such cases, this rumor was confirmed by many as a fact and nobody thought of questioning it. All the Austrians present in the vicinity rushed after the supposed fugitives in the direction indicated, some on foot, others by wagon, horseback or boat. Thus the retreat into the interior of Romagna became feasible for us. It was in this direction that I expected to guide Garibaldi and his group and first in my mind was the Guiccioli farmhouse, which was well known to me and which I indicated to the General as the goal of his next stop.

Yet I had to be back in Comacchio before daybreak in order not to arouse any suspicion, so I bid my friends farewell as soon as it started to get light. It was not with tearful eyes, but with a sorrowful and tormented heart that I parted from the high-minded man whom I loved with so much devotion and admiration, for it was to me alone that he had entrusted himself. Alas, how few were they who assisted me with abnegation in this hour of need!

151

Unfortunately I sprained my foot during the hardships of yesterday. While I was active I thought the damage unimportant; but after sitting for some time in the biroccino I felt severe pain; in fact, upon arriving in Comacchio I was not able to put my foot on the ground. I had to be carried home, where I called a doctor. But since by evening I felt no improvement and because I had many things to do in town and surroundings, I entreated one of my friends to come over and go to Ravenna for me in order to hand a few important letters to my correspondent there. He refused. Fear of the Austrains seemed to have suppressed all other feelings. I spent a sleepless night in search of other means.

It was barely light when the door of my room opened and I saw a woman wrapped in a shawl enter, whom I recognized right away as my brother's wife.

"Get up in a hurry!" she called to me. "There is no time to lose. The capo guardiano who had the order to accompany Garibaldi's punt has returned and says that the guardiani on reaching Paviero refused to go ahead because they were afraid of being shot."

I was beside myself with anxiety and jumped out of bed, hastily cut up a boot into which I forced my sprained foot as best I could and left the room leaning on a cane. The thought that my whole plan was in danger of being wrecked by the cowardice of the capo guardiano made me furious and God knows how I would have received the traitor if he had crossed my path at that moment!

I remembered a certain Michele to whom I had never spoken before, but who used to greet me in a friendly manner and whose honest face always filled me with confidence. I went to see him. "Michele," I said, "I need your help, but before I tell you what it concerns I must know whether you are willing to help me?"

"Do you think that I am capable of helping you?" asked Michele.

"Absolutely."

"Very well then, for you I will do anything," was his frank answer.

I thereupon gave him the necessary instructions and informed him of the treacherous behavior of the guardiani. "I am fearful," I added, "that since they are afraid, they will disclose to the authorities the hiding place of the fugitives. To prevent this you must try to remove them from there by any means, by any pretext and as rapidly as possible."

Michele promised. "Do not worry; your wishes will be carried out promptly, even if it were Garibaldi in person who was to be saved!"

We parted with this encouraging promise. For my part I left for the fattoria* Guiccioli which I mentioned above. From the friend who accompanied me I borrowed a horse and (equally important) a *lasciapassare* made out by the police in his name, then before nightfall I reached the farmhouse located about thirteen miles away. I was surprised and relieved that Garibaldi had not yet arrived. The tenant farmer also

---

*A tenant farmer's house.

was not at home but in Ravenna, a fact which made my stratagem much easier to carry out. I informed the tenant farmer's wife that within a few hours a gentleman with his spouse and a friend would arrive in the fattoria, a person who would bring with him such unlimited authorization from the farm owner that, if need be, he would be empowered to put the torch to the whole property. Thus, so as not to incur the displeasure of her master, she should receive the foreigners with great courtesy and provide them with food and, above all, keep their presence, which would be of short duration, a deep secret.

The woman promised to observe all my instructions to the letter and without tarrying further I started in the direction of Ravenna. But I had scarcely reached the forest when I met a throng of Croats hurrying towards Comacchio in biroccini and vehicles of all types. I was stopped by them and presented to their captain.

"Have you got your passport?" he inquired, and upon my affirmative answer, he added: "Where are you going?"

"To Ravenna."

"And where is this devil?" my inquisitor continued.

"What devil?" I asked shrugging my shoulders.

"Where is this devil?" he repeated, raising his voice threateningly; and because I kept silent, he motioned to an old sergeant to act as interpreter.

"Where is this red devil?" the sergeant began, looking me straight in the eye.

"Garibaldi?" I proffered without embarrassment. "Oh, he has been taken prisoner by your brig along with some of his men."

The captain's face beamed with pleasure when he heard this; he wrote a few words in my friend's passport and as the sergeant handed the passport back to me, he said: "You are duty bound to go to our major in Ravenna to give him this information and for this you will receive a tip of a few scudi from him." And with these words he dismissed me and went on his way.

"For Heaven's sake, what are you doing?" remarked my friend with concern as soon as the captain had left. "Suppose the Croat wrote into the pass that you have informed him of the capture of Garibaldi!"

"But am I not the one who holds that document?" I added smilingly.

Soon we reached Ravenna and left our vehicle outside the gate in order to enter the city as unconcerned strollers. I asked my friend to feed the horse well, to keep it ready for my use later at the Square dell'Aquila and to observe the strictest secrecy with everyone.

In Ravenna I was acquainted with a certain Montanari, who formerly was my major in Lombardy and of whom I always thought highly as an honest, incorruptible and patriotic citizen. I went to see him. I spoke to him very frankly and told him briefly all I had been through in the last few days. He reproached me for my audacity which, according to him, could easily cost me my life. I intimated to him that this was of no concern to me; however, this attitude did not help me. He insisted that it was impossible to do anything for Garibaldi, and only after I had painted in vivid colors the tragic circumstances which had driven the hero from the walls of Rome as far as the shores of the Adriatic, did I succeed in winning over Montanari to my purpose. He promised me his aid in making possible Garibaldi's trip to Tuscany and Piedmont.

In the meantime the confusion among the Austrians in Ravenna increased with every moment. Alarming rumors had spread. The city gates were closed; it was now impossible either to depart or to enter, which made the execution of our plans much more difficult. Nevertheless, encouraged by the fact that the Croat captain had written only one word in my friend's passport, that is, the name of the commander of the city, I decided to go to see him and perhaps obtain his permission to leave Ravenna. In fact I had known him previously, for it was he who had come to Comacchio with his battalion and two pieces of heavy artillery to take down the Republican banner there.

I greeted him respectfully and handed him the passport, but he appeared quite occupied and little inclined to listen to me. When he heard however that I came from Comacchio and recognized his captain's handwriting, he asked smilingly:

"Well, what's new in Comacchio?"

"Garibaldi was on his way to Venice when he was overtaken and defeated by an Austrian brig," I replied, "and many of his bragozzi were captured. Some say that he himself was captured, others affirm that he landed with a small number of his followers. In any case the Austrians are on his trail and I myself have seen several of his men arrested. That is all I can report. In any case, I have come to Ravenna strictly for my own affairs."

"And when are you returning to Comacchio?" the commander asked.

"Immediately" I replied. "If you will be so kind as to issue me a permit for this purpose, since my affairs are urgent." Instead the commander very gently informed me that for the time being he could not grant my request. "But perhaps tomorrow," he added. "Come back tomorrow, I want to give you some letters to take to our captain."

"This is probably the tip in question," I thought to myself. "I am lucky that I was not arrested."

Throughout the night nothing was heard except the sound of drums, musical bands and the marching off of the Croats ordered to Comacchio. In all this clamor I succeeded in sneaking out of the city unobserved. The horse which was waiting for me carried me in a rapid gallop to the fattoria Guiccioli.

The tenant farmer had come home in the meantime and I found him greatly alarmed. He spoke of his number being up, since Garibaldi and his followers had been seen in the vicinity of his lodging and that all sorts of rumors had been spread concerning this.

From all I learned I was forced to conclude that lack of courage and understanding had caused many time-consuming incidents. The immediate victim of these was Garibaldi's wife. Closer to death than to life the unfortunate woman was brought from the punt to the fattoria Guiccioli in a biroccino. There she was put to bed; she asked for some fresh water and soon afterwards died in the arms of her husband. My first question was whether she had been buried.

"Certainly," the farmer replied. "Poor Anita had scarcely breathed her last when the Austrians surrounded the house, and only through a lucky break was the General able to escape. His last wish was that I should bury his spouse until a more propitious moment would permit him to fetch her earthly remains."

Since my staying at the fattoria any longer could be of no further use to my protégé, but could only be of harm to myself, it was now a question of thinking of my own safety and of starting on the return trip to Comacchio. During my rapid ride there I constantly encountered Austrian and Italian troop units. In my home town I found nothing but confusion and discontent. Everyone was surprised at the way in which Garibaldi had been able to get away. Both the Germans[137] and the Italians (be it said to their shame) had only one aim and that was to take revenge on the person who had facilitated his flight. That their attention was directed towards me needs hardly be mentioned.

It did not take long for me to be arrested. I was chained hand and foot, and the guards who took me into custody were instructed to shoot me at the slightest provocation. Such precautions could only elicit a smile from me, and I gave my word of honor to my guardians not to escape. My conscience attested that I had acted from a sincere and noble motive and, considering that I had reached my aim, it seemed to me a triumph to die for such a sacred cause. My fellow citizens, among whom I formerly had influence and enjoyed an honorable reputation, now saw me go through the streets bound in chains and surrounded by a troop of barbarians. I have never denied my principles. Proudly I shouted: *"Evviva l'Italia!"* but my words found no echo.

Some of my friends did their best to win Judge Lovatelli over to my side, but he made it known publicly that there was no hope of saving me, since my death sentence had been decided irrevocably in Bologna by the Commander there. In fact the newspapers had reported my execution as having already taken place, and the Croat captain in Comacchio did not fail to make known his satisfaction concerning this, in order to instill anguish and fear into many of my fellow citizens who held the same opinions as I.

By error I was left for quite some time in the jail of Ravenna, where they had taken me from Comacchio, and I owe my life exclusively to this circumstance, for the Austrian commander, General Gorzkowski, who at all times distinguished himself by his hatred and cruelty towards the friends of Italy, left Bologna just at this time. When I was finally transferred there, I learned from an Austrian court official by name of Pichler, who had pleaded for me in vain with General Gorzkowski, that the order for my execution would have been carried out irrevocably if General Strassoldo, a man of more humane character, had not taken over as commander-in-chief.

Thus I was saved! I wish to God that my example would encourage all fearful persons to disregard every danger when a sacred and just cause is at stake!

BOOK FOUR

ANITA

(From Garibaldi's Notes)

Anita Garibaldi

This incomparable woman was born of honorable parents in Morinhos, a settlement on the left bank of the Tubarão River in the lagoon district of Santa Catarina. In her early years she led the life of a young maiden filled with an exuberant imagination but well protected by family tradition from any mundane influences to her gentle womanliness. The fabulous events of her life began with the incursion made by the Republican Army commanded by General Canabarro which penetrated from Rio Grande into the province of Santa Catarina. I commanded a detachment of this army and it was at this time that fate tossed Anita into the stormy course I followed, to be torn away from me only by death itself.

Being in possession of the lagoon and part of the province of Santa Catarina, I united with General Canabarro in order to arm some vessels and to proceed with them to the Brazilian coast to harrass Imperial commerce. I had three small ships each armed with one gun on a pivot and was steering towards the north. Anita was with me. As we arrived off Santos I met with an Imperial corvette which pursued me for two days.

On the second day I reached the Island of Abrigo, where two enemy commercial vessels fell into our hands. In continuing our raid we seized some more merchant ships and returned to the lagoon after an absence of eight days.

Off the Island of Santa Catarina I encountered a guardship; at the time I commanded the goelette *Rio Pardo* and, in addition, I had with me the *Seival,* "lo Hoop," commanded by the Italian Lorenzo N. The goelette *Cassapava,* led by the North American John Griggs, had been separated from us during a very dark night. The combat which we had to undertake with the guardship was only of short duration and of little damage to us, thanks to the heavy seas. As a result we lost several prizes, their commanders becoming so terrified by the superiority of the enemy forces, that some of them struck the flag while others headed for the coast. Only one prize, commanded by the worthy Ignazio Bilbao, was saved; he cast anchor in the harbor of Imbituba, where the *Seival* also arrived, but with its cannon smashed and a leak sustained during the combat. We sailed into Imbituba harbor with a northeast wind, but because the wind changed during the night and started to blow from the south, it became impossible for us to reach the lagoon.

Forced to lie to at Imbituba, we were obliged to expect an attack by the Imperial forces stationed on the island. In such expectation we lugged ashore the cannon of the *Seival*, dragged it to a peninsula in the eastern part of the bay and there mounted a flying battery.

It was just about daybreak when we discovered three Imperial vessels sailing towards us. With the *Rio Pardo* anchored at the far end of the bay, we prepared for combat. The enemy did not cast anchor, but remained under sail during the whole encounter. The only armed vessel which we possessed remained at anchor without moving, protected by our small battery. The combat was bloody and soon we had to take to our rifles and carbines, for I now realized that the enemy wanted to board us. In fact he made repeated preparations to this effect. In any case, we were quite ready to receive him.

The combat was waged with unequal forces. Still we were determined not to give in, even if we should have to yield ultimately to superior might. We would bring honor to the Republican banner, the same which we had been the first to hoist on the Empire's shores.

It was during this encounter that the American heroine showed the courage and fearlessness of her soul for the first time. Brusquely refusing my request to go ashore where she could watch the fighting without danger to herself, she drew her saber and encouraged the men by her example. The fighting, even though it was among forces of little importance, was hard and fierce. The wind blew gently from the depth of the bay and permitted the sailing enemy to shell us as much and as heavily as he wished while tacking. The deck of our small vessel was filled with corpses and wounded. Anita, always at her post, was occupied with providing the men with munitions being handed her from below and with spurring them on with words and gestures, when suddenly a cannon blast laid her low among three dead bodies on the deck. I rushed towards her to pick up my dear one, but how great was my astonishment to see her get up unharmed. With that passionate disregard of danger, which she always showed in critical situations, she shouted to me: "Don't you see those cowards hiding in the cabin?" Then, even more effectively by action than by words, she convinced the miserable ones who had sought refuge because of fear, to come out of hiding.

Towards evening we were liberated from the enemy because of the death of the commander of the enemy goelette *La bella Americana* and because of other damages inflicted on the Imperial forces. Manuel Rodríguez, a Catalan officer whose post was ashore at the cannon, did his duty well and had offered considerable resistance to the enemy. That night we had to devote entirely to reaching the lagoon; otherwise we would have had to confront new and stronger enemies the following day. Because of the loss and wounding of so many of our comrades, the exhaustion of the survivors and lamentable condition of the battered *Rio Pardo*, we succeeded only with great difficulty in getting the cannon on board again and in reaching the lagoon, despite the enemy's pursuit.

The good fortune of the Republic of Rio Grande had reached its zenith and was to diminish from now on. The glorious encounter which the *Rio Pardo* had just fought, the incursion into the province of Santa Catarina and other advantages gained in various campaigns had made the Republicans so powerful that they were becoming extremely dangerous to their enemies. The Imperial forces, confined to the two localities of Porto Alegre and Rio Grande, were unable to contain them after having lost almost 7000 excellent troops.

The commanders of our troops however, instead of taking advantage of their gains, consumed their time in personal quarrels, while the government, weak as it was already because of the slight respect in which it was held by the military leaders, remained powerless. More than that, treason, which is the son of venality, was being hatched in the very heart of one of our military commanders. It was not improbable that the expedition of Santa Catarina had been undertaken with insufficient means because of reciprocal jealousy. Instead, in such a mountainous region covered with forests, exceptional means should have been taken. Furthermore, the slight respect which the warlike and chivalrous Riograndense showed towards the unwarlike and peaceful Catarinense made the latter feel more like defeated enemies rather than as allies.

The jealousy even increased with the approach of the enemy division commanded by Andrea. A few days after our return to the lagoon we had to abandon all the positions we had won and, pursued by the enemy by land as well as by sea, we assembled our small fighting forces on the southern shore. The same populations which had greeted us a few months ago as liberators now called us tyrants and rendered our retreat much more difficult by their harassment.

For the Republicans an encounter was in the offing which was to become noteworthy for the inequality of forces involved and for the limited space in which it took place. We had with great efforts managed to bring the horses and infantry to the right shore and I had climbed the peak of the promontory of Morro da Barra in order to observe the movements of the enemy fleet of about twenty-two warships, when I noticed that the latter were getting ready to force the entrance of the lagoon. I notified General Canabarro immediately, but he hesitated so in sending the infantry that the enemy suffered considerably less damage than could have been inflicted. A small battery located at the foot of the promontory of Morro da Barra had very little effect. On the other hand, the full fury of the enemy was directed towards the three small ships which I commanded and were stationed along the right shore at the entrance of the lagoon.

On this day Anita was again the magnificent heroine of the combat. The enemy vessels driven by a northeasterly wind and a favorable tide approached under sail with great rapidity. I barely had time to hurry down the slope of Morro da Barra and jump into my dinghy, as the first cannon shots were already being exchanged. The majority of our crew was occupied in transporting our troops, while only a few individuals were on board ship. The men left behind had already been thinking of fleeing ashore, frightened by the superiority of the enemy, but the sight and voice of the amazon, who resembled the spirit of war on that day, prevented them from doing so.

Anita unloosened the grappling irons and distributed them, then turned her attention to the cannons and by the time I got aboard she had already fired the first shot. Three poorly armed, and even more poorly manned, vessels had little impact against the numerous and well-equipped enemy ships. Moreover, favored by the elements, they approached with incredible speed. At the beginning of the encounter Enrique, the commander of the *Itaparisa,* had his chest shattered by case-shot. John Griggs, the commander of the *Cassapava*, after some brave fighting, was torn into two pieces by a cannon shot; in the suddenness of death his bust remained intact with a living expression upon his face. Only one other officer was a casualty, and he was just wounded.

Anita demonstrated incredible courage and cool-headedness. When our cannon had been wrecked by enemy fire, she reached for a musket and fired as long as the enemy remained in sight; not once did she seek the protection of a bulkhead, nor bend down to be less exposed to danger. When General Canabarro gave the command to burn the vessels and retreat, she refused until all the munition had been salvaged.

It must be noted that due to the narrowness of the waterway through which the enemy passed, the disembarkation of the Republicans took place at a distance of not more than 150 paces, so that it was a miracle that they were not hit by enemy shells. Once our ships were consumed by the flames the remaining part of our crew was incorporated into the land division and our retreat began towards las Torres on the frontier between the province of Rio Grande and Santa Catarina.

In conjunction with the enemy Division Andrea, the Division Acunha was also approaching from the province of São Paulo, pursuing its way along the mountain chain in the direction of Cima da Serra. The people of Serra asked General Canabarro for aid and he organized an expedition commanded by Colonel Teixeira to help them. The fleet was to form part of this expedition.

Teixeira, united with the men of Serra commanded by Colonel Aranha, defeated Acunha so successfully that he completely destroyed the enemy division, part of which fell into our hands.

Anita, on horseback, was a spectator of this encounter. I commanded the infantry composed partly of sailors and partly of the remains of a fourth battalion, some 120 men in all, assembled in the lagoon. This victory brought the three districts of Lages, Vaccaria and Cima da Serra under Republican control again. A few days later we marched into Lages triumphantly.

The Imperial incursion had in the meantime instilled new confidence into their forces in Misiones, and the Imperial commander, Colonel Mello, had increased his corps in this province to about 500 men. Our General Bento Manuel, who had been designated to fight against Mello, but had not done so, was content merely in pushing him towards Colonel Fortinhos, who had advanced with his troops in order to observe Mello's retreat.

Our position and our strength should have enabled us not only to oppose Mello's withdrawal but even to annihilate his corps. But fate did not permit it. Colonel Teixeira, uncertain whether the enemy would come through Vaccaria or by Coritibani, divided his fighting forces into two army units. He sent Aranha along the first road with the good cavalry, while he himself marched towards Coritibani with the infantry and the remainder of the cavalry, which consisted mostly of prisoners who had fallen into our hands in Santa Vittoria. This was the direction the enemy chose; we met him, and in spite of the bravery of Teixeira and the infantry, our cavalry was completely wiped out. Of our men only 73 remained, after seeing themselves surrounded in open country by 500 enemy cavalrymen. On this day Anita was to experience very great reverses in the fortunes of war. Resigning herself unwillingly to the role of mere spectator, she did nevertheless hasten the transport of the munitions, afraid that her fighting companions might run out of them at the decisive hour; the uninterrupted firing which the infantry was obliged to maintain caused her to surmise this. In so doing she drew closer to the principal scene of fighting and as an enemy troop of cavalrymen pursued some fugitives, they overtook her and fell upon the guardians of the baggage train. Anita could have hastened the pace of her horse and quickly distanced herself from her pursuers, but her soul seemed impervious to fear. Only when the enemy had surrounded her and escape seemed impossible did she spur on her horse and lunged forward. For an instant she thought that her agility had saved her, but when a bullet singed her hair, and a moment later a second bullet struck her horse to the ground, all thought of flight became impossible. She surrendered and was dragged into the enemy camp as a prisoner. However she was no less admirable in misfortune than in danger. When brought before the officers of the general staff, all of whom were amazed at her courage though not high-minded enough to suppress sneers, Anita rejected with dignified pride every word and gesture on their part which revealed insolence and contempt for the Republican party. She did receive permission however, which she requested urgently to search the scene of action for her husband whom she believed dead, in order to bury him. For a long time her eyes scanned the bloody spectacle offered by the battlefield and, dreading to find the one whom she sought, she turned over those individual corpses more than once in whose features she seemed to recognize a resemblance to her beloved husband; but in vain.

In the meantime I had left the battlefield with a handful of old companions and, repulsing every attack of the enemy with desperate courage, we attempted to reach the area of a *capón* (a group of trees). The worthy Teixeira, after performing extraordinary feats of valor with his cavalry, joined us with one of his adjutants.

From the moment that Anita had ascertained that her husband was not among the dead, her one thought was of flight. Taking advantage of the victory celebration of her drunken guardians, she reached a peasant's hut undetected and an unknown woman gave her shelter. There she had to spend only a few more hours of this fateful day, but these seemed like so many years to her! At nightfall Anita dared leave and disappeared into the forest. Only one who has seen the immense forests which cover the *Serra do Espinasso* and who is acquainted with their colossal tacuari*, those true pillars of this magnificent temple of nature, can conceive of the difficulties which this courageous Brazilian woman had to overcome on her flight from Coritibani to Lages over a distance of 60 miles. The few inhabitants of this region, moreover, were hostile to the Republicans and had taken up arms since the last Republican defeat in order to ambush the fugitives in the most dangerous passes. Hence was it due to her lucky star or rather to the courage with which she bravely faced all difficulties? I do not know; but those waylayers fled before her! Indeed they fled with the anguished cry that they were "being pursued by a supernatural being." And so it was a superhuman sight to behold this courageous woman mounted on a fiery horse, obtained somewhere from a peasant and galloping in a tempestuous night amidst flashes of lightning and precipitous, rocky ground! Four of these cowardly waylayers posted on guard at the ford of the River Canovas fled in terror and Anita made use of their flight to reach the bank of the river. But its waters were swollen by the rains and the mountain torrents could not be crossed in a canoe, as was usually done; still this fearless woman threw herself bravely into the seething waters and, holding fast to her horse's tail and encouraging it to swim across, she reached the opposite shore in safety. A cup of coffee in Lages was the only nourishment taken by Anita in four days, until she joined the corps of Aranha in Vaccaria.

Teixeira and I with 73 companions arrived at Lages, where Anita joined me after a separation of eight days. Nothing of much importance occurred to Anita after that time, except continued dangers caused by the war, in which the sole food to be had was dried meat, and her bed was her saddle. Nevertheless misfortunes and dangers of every kind never for a moment overcame her courage.

At the Battle of Taquari Anita disdained the proposal made to her by General Bento Gonçalvez to retire from the scene of danger. The Re-

---

*Rush or reed-like plants.

publican Army, weakened by various bloody engagements, was obliged to retire from the siege of the capital, making a long and toilsome retreat across the mountains. Naturally Anita formed part of this retreat and experienced all the fatigue and privations that can easily be imagined. To appreciate the sufferings of a troop with no other means of transport but a few mules for its ammunition, it is necessary to have some idea of that part of Brazil, its mountains and forests. The lasso, so very useful on the plains covered with grazing animals, is wholly useless in these jungles inhabited by wild beasts. A few head of cattle tagged along on ropes and constituted the sole provisions of the Republicans. Unfortunately in the thicket of Las Antas, where we remained nine days without being able to find our way out into open country because the incessant rain had swollen the rivers, a great part of the troops remained confined between two tributaries and destitute of provisions of any kind. Famine made its greatest havoc among the children of the natives who accompanied the army.

Scenes unheard of before occurred among those unfortunate but courageous people. Anita wonderfully escaped with her first-born son, then only three months old. I had reserved the last horse for her, all the others having been destroyed, and in crossing the rivers and the most dangerous passes I carried my poor child. Anita got out of the forest before me and with bewildered eyes began to seek some means of preserving its life. Accidentally, and much to her joy, she discovered a party of soldiers who had made a little fire and were assembled around it. They immediately opened a place for her, for they knew her, and one of them named Manzio took the child, which appeared to be dying, and wrapped it in his warm poncho. It soon revived, and I noticed a tear trickle down its mother's cheek. From that moment on she was restored to her usual state of mind, for the life of the affectionate mother hung on that of her infant.

After this the Republican Army reached San Gabriel and I asked for permission to return to Montevideo. Anita, superior in the trials and dangers of war, was also admirable in domestic life. She assisted and consoled me in adverse fortune and in the trying circumstances which we endured when we first took up residence in the capital of the Republic of Uruguay. During all the time I remained in its service she left the city seldom, took no part in the military operations and devoted herself entirely to the care of her family.

The news of the first reforms in Italy in 1848 excited in the minds of the Italian exiles in South America the wish to cross the ocean and aid the cause of their country. Anita and our little family set off as the precursors of the expedition and arrived at Genoa in the early stage of the revolution; a dawning of liberty there promised to our oppressed nation that national existance desired for so many centuries.

From the time of her arrival in Europe she lived in Nice; it was at the time of the Salasco truce. My first absence was borne by her with patience; but not so the second. Hearing that I was sick in Genoa, she immediately went there, then with me she travelled to Florence.

She made a second short trip to Rieti and then the third and most mournful one to Rome, which she entered incognito, passing through our French enemies with the pretext that she had to care for me since I was wounded. When the venerable city was forced to capitulate before the yoke of the perfidious Louis Napoleon, now turned Papal mercenary, I decided to try my fortune outside of Rome and Anita chose to share with me the dangers of the undertaking. I objected, but in vain were all my remonstrances, just as was my entreaty that she should bear in mind that she was pregnant. Was it that I no longer desired having her with me, endeavoring to leave her behind under various pretexts? She asked me whether I doubted her courage! Had I not had proofs enough of this? Oh, that delightful life in camp; the magnificent cavalcades and the combats so delightful to her! And as for fatigue, privations and mishaps, what were they to one whose happiness is in her heart?

Anita! You identified yourself in feeling with Italy and were happy in the hope that its people would be redeemed. She herself would not go armed; she would not be spotted with blood, but her intrepid countenance would animate and cause to blush even a coward. And truly, under the walls of Rome and beyond them, hundreds of brave men fell and lay mutilated on beds of grief; some even tore the bandages from their wounds so that they would die and no longer be eyewitnesses to our burning shame. Yet fortunately, we had to deal with an enemy who was but a weakling.

Oh Anita! a land of slavery contains for the time being your precious remains. Italy will make your grave free; but who can restore to your children their incomparable mother?

As we retreated from Rome to San Marino she already showed symptoms of a dangerous disease and I insisted that she should remain there. But all was in vain! The incredible dangers did not diminish her resolution to go with us.

At Cesenatico, where we labored all night to effect the departure of the boats designed to transport the troops to Venice, Anita, leaning against a rock, sadly contemplated our wearisome toil. We embarked, but the time she spent on board was one of continued suffering. She landed exhausted on the beach of Mesola and hardly was able to walk. In vain she flattered herself by saying that the land would restore her to health. The land; it had nothing to give her but a grave.

People of Ravenna! You are proud to possess the bones of Dante, the most celebrated of Italians. At the time you reverently preserved them we did not realize the true greatness of your noble undertaking; we did not think of the glory you had brought upon our city! Receive also the bones of the American heroine, the martyr who died for the liberation of Italy and place them near those of the great poet, under his protection, where they will slumber until the day of the resurrection. By so doing, you will be doing a pious deed. Every Italian who knew her, every friend of our country, will praise you fervently. Her orphaned children and I will implore the benediction of God upon you, and your name will be glorified by the eternal gratitude not only of all Italy, but also of the new world, birthplace of Anita and of her children.

For the time being, oh soil of the people of Ravenna, press lightly on the bones of the brave daughter of America!

2. Caprera: pencil sketch from Melena's volume
Garibaldi: Mittheilungen aus seinem Leben

BOOK FIVE

A BRIEF SKETCH OF
GARIBALDI'S FATE
FROM THE TIME OF
HIS WIFE'S DEATH
IN 1849 UNTIL HIS
SETTLING ON THE
ISLAND OF CAPRERA
IN 1855

If one has followed Garibaldi's fate and is familiar with the manifold dangers, often almost phenomenal, which have beset him from early youth, one recognizes clearly that a special providence has watched over the existence of this man. The thirty-five days of flight which followed upon the death of the brave Anita, and of which to the best of my knowledge there is no historical account,[138] forms without doubt one of the most memorable episodes of his life. Sometimes the valorous fugitive disguised as a Romagnole had to make his way through crowds of Austrians searching for him, sometimes he had to share bed and board with uncouth Croats, sometimes he had to quench his hunger and thirst with wild berries from hedges and shrubs until he stepped upon his native soil and could enjoy liberty, his life no longer being in danger!

But wherever he disclosed his identity during this adventurous flight, some hearts were always opened to him, full of compassion, goodwill and hospitality. When he left the fattoria Guiccioli accompanied by Leggiero, the only follower remaining with him, and sought refuge in the small locality of San Alberto* three miles away, it was a poor cobbler who offered him his modest shelter.

From San Alberto the General went to Ravenna, where a friend hid him in his house; but Garibaldi was afraid to compromise him, since there was a big reward on his head and the infuriated Austrians did not slacken in their search. Thus Garibaldi fled to Forlì and from there to Modigliana under the protection of a few devoted Romagnoles.

When Garibaldi gave me an account of this flight, he dwelled with special pleasure upon the ingenious method by which his protectors conveyed him from place to place. This was possible only at night and by means of a biroccino. As soon as night had fallen, Garibaldi, Leggiero and a trustworthy Romagnole mounted such a vehicle. At a prearranged

---

*When ten years later I came through San Alberto with the General and was a witness of the fanatical ovation he received there, the poor cobbler lay at death's door. He had already received extreme unction and the viaticum. But when the rejoicing of the populace announced Garibaldi's triumphal march, he attempted to leave his deathbed to greet the hero of Varese and Como. Garibaldi found this out in time and hurried to see his former benefactor who, as I learned later, was so overjoyed by this visit that he recovered.

spot the Romagnole halted and struck a spark with his flint; if the reply came from the depth of a certain thicket by a similar sign, they unhesitatingly drove on to the next prearranged point; but if there was no answer, it meant that there was danger of falling into the hands of the Austrians. In that case the fugitives dismounted and entrusted themselves to another Romagnole who silently led them out of reach of the enemy to another vehicle waiting for them. In Modigliana it was a young priest who led the General as far as Filigare on the Tuscan border. His name was Giovanni Verità and rarely have I heard Garibaldi speak with more admiration of a person than he did of this young priest. He described him as a prototype of manly strength and beauty, praised his skill as a hunter and spoke enthusiastically of his noble-mindedness, as well as of his devotion to his aged mother.

At Firenzuola Garibaldi crossed the Apennines and in a tavern on the military road between La Futa and Prato, where he was forced to remain for a while, he came in such close contact with a detachment of Austrians that it seems incredible that he could escape their suspicion.

Steeped in thought, Garibaldi was sitting at a table leaning on his elbows and hiding his face in his hands, when the detachment suddenly entered the tavern, surrounded him and bothered him with questions concerning the "red devil," whom they sought. For fully three quarters of an hour he had to endure the intrusion of these men; naturally he did not let them have a good look at his face, for if he had, it would have cost him his life, despite his Romagnole costume. The classical features of his face are unmistakable to anyone who has seen them once.

From Prato, Garibaldi arrived at Follonica after passing through Empoli, Volterra, Pomarana[139] and Massa. Here he remained a few days and then embarked for Elba. On the island however, he was exposed to great danger, and, after a stay of twelve hours, he headed towards the continental shore in a small open boat with the intent of reaching Sardinian territory by skirting the coast. He had not yet arrived off Livorno when his fragile vessel was noticed by an English ship sailing by; the captain, a goodhearted seaman, took him aboard and put him ashore in Porto Venere.

After five weeks of exceedingly dangerous wandering, Garibaldi found himself on his native soil at last where he hoped to reach his home town without further difficulty. But he had barely stepped into Chiavari when he was arrested and led to Genoa as a prisoner of state. Here General La Marmora first gave orders to hide him in a remote room of the governmental palace; later Garibaldi was brought aboard the frigate of war *Carlo Felice*, then lying in the harbor, and given the opportunity of choosing a country of exile, for he could not remain in Sardinia. Confronted by this inescapable necessity he only expressed the wish to be allowed to visit his children in Nice for twenty-four hours.

This was granted him; so he was re-embarked on the *San Giorgio* and taken to his home town. After the one day's stay with his family, the same steamer brought him back to Genoa where he was quartered aboard the frigate of war again. Garibaldi praised very highly the cooperation and the courtesy of her commander, whose name if I am not mistaken was Zara, as well as that of all her officers.

For his place of exile he had chosen Tunis. But after the steamer *Tripoli,* charged specifically with this mission, delivered him there, the Bey of Tunis refused Garibaldi the right to land. The Bey was guided by French influence at the time. The *Tripoli* now awaited further instructions from Turin and in the meantime put in at the Island of La Maddalena, not far from the northern coast of Sardinia.

For about one month Garibaldi lived there unmolested in the house of a certain Pietro Susini, but Falchi, the commander of the island at the time, wrote to the government that it was dangerous to have him so close to Sardinia. As a result, another frigate of war, the *Colombo* commanded by Captain Demoro, was sent from Genoa with orders to transport Garibaldi to Gibraltar.

The Governor of Gibraltar permitted him to disembark, but when he had landed he let him know that he would have to leave the city within six days. The unfortunate Garibaldi, who was being exiled for the fourth time from one country to another, had no choice except to entrust himself to the more hospitable sea in a small boat.

He reached Tangier safely, and without knowing the Sardinian Consul resident there, he went to see him immediately. He was received by Mr. Carpeneto* with such warmth and sincere sympathy that he stayed at his house for fully six months, that is, until April 1850.

From here Garibaldi went to Liverpool, where he was seized for the first time with those violent rheumatic pains which were often to afflict him later. In June he embarked for the United States where he remained for one year in New York, for the first half in the city to recover his health, and for the second half on Staten Island, where he sought and found an occupation in the candle factory of his friend and countryman Meucci.[141]

It was during the evenings following upon his arduous day's work that Garibaldi wrote down his autobiography, which forms the first part of this book. On his arrival in New York he refused all the honors of a public reception.[142] Instead he encouraged his exiled countrymen to take up any calling, even a modest one, in preference to receiving help from strangers. But his active mind could not possibly be content with the occupation he pursued at his friend's house, so that when some Americans asked him to take charge of a merchant ship, and when his friend Carpeneto[143] came from Italy to join him, the two men undertook a voyage together to Central America.

---

*At the General's house on Caprera in 1857 I made the acquaintance of this elderly gracious Genoan and two years later in Modena and Bologna I met him again. Carpeneto had lost his position as consul because of his sympathy for the exiled Garibaldi.[140]

First he sailed to Nicaragua, then to Granada and Panama where, however, he became ill with fever and came so near to death that he had to give up the command of his ship. After his recovery he travelled to Lima aboard an English steamer, arriving at the end of 1851. Here he parted with his friend Carpeneto. In January 1852 he took over the command of the *Carmen*, a merchant vessel belonging to a Genoan by name of de Negri. Garibaldi made many extensive trips with this ship and earned a modest living by transporting goods. One of his voyages even led him by the Sandwich Islands as far as Canton, returning to Lima via Australia in early 1853. From here he sailed to Valparaiso, thence to Boston and New York with a supercargo. In the latter city he finally left the *Carmen* and took charge of the ship *Commonwealth*. New contracts soon brought him to England, and after a short stay in Newcastle and London, he returned to Genoa in May of 1854.

Here Garibaldi's Odyssean travels came to an end. The Sardinian Government had become less suspicious and made no objections to his settling in his own country. The General spent a year with his children in Nice in total retirement, except for making a few coastal voyages to Marseille as captain of the *Salvatore*. By now he was weary of a roaming life and decided to settle at Cape Testa, a locality not far from Santa Teresa on the northernmost point of Sardinia. Consequently he embarked on the *St. Georges* destined for Porto Torres.

During the crossing of the Bocche di Bonifacio a violent storm suddently arose. One of the workmen whom Garibaldi was taking with him was washed overboard. It became impossible to reach Porto Torres, so the endangered *St. Georges* took refuge in the safe waters of the Island of Maddalena, even then only after extreme difficulty.

This event modified Garibaldi's plan. He remained on Maddalena for some time, and before returning to the continent he gave power of attorney to someone to buy for him on the neighboring Island of Caprera a considerable piece of land completely uncultivated. He settled there in May of 1855 and his first shelter on this inhospitable mass of granite, as he told me himself, consisted of a sail spread out like a tent.*

Later when he built a rather stately dwelling, considering the circumstances, in South American style, he had his oldest son Menotti and his daughter Teresa with a housekeeper join him from Nice, so that they might share with him his rural occupations and his insular seclusion from the world. In the year 1856 in Portsmouth [England] he bought a cutter named *Emma* for six hundred pounds sterling in which he later sailed in cargo trade from his island to the mainland. In January 1857 he loaded this vessel heavily with building materials for the new *molo* (dock) of the Island of Maddalena and had reached the Punta della Moneta safely,

---

*Garibaldi's family life and occupations on Caprera I have described in detail in *Ein Ausflug nach der Insel Maddalena* (An Excursion to the Island of Caprera; see the Introduction by the Editor.)

when the ship caught fire between the island of Santo Stefano and Maddalena. Much lime was on board at the time and it was useless to even try to extinguish the fire. Fortunately this happened in broad daylight so that Garibaldi and his small crew were able to save themselves. Since the *Emma* and its cargo were insured, the loss for its owner was slight. Only, being deprived of his ship, from that time on Garibaldi devoted himself to the cultivation of his property on Caprera and to the company of his children. Towards the end of February 1859 he was called by the Sardinian Government to Turin and appointed chief of the volunteers, a corps to gain him new laurels and distinguish itself as the *Cacciatori delle Alpi*.

Verily, a new eminent life was dawning for the warrior who had not been heard of for a long time. Now Garibaldi's greatest destiny was to manifest itself. How he added victory upon victory and heroic deed upon heroic deed in the Italian war of liberation; how, surrounded by an almost supernatural spell, he carried the tricolor victoriously from the Alps to Mount Etna, surpassing the expectations of the bravest and eclipsing the most valorous deeds in history; all this I will perhaps be privileged to narrate in another volume.

BOOK SIX

THE PINETA
TEN YEARS LATER

(An Episode from the
Life of Elpis Melena)

3. Elpis Melena (Marie Espérance von Schwartz)
photograph in the Museo del Risorgimento in Milan, Italy

4. *Elpis Melena*
pencil sketch from
the Leipziger Illustrierte Zeitung February 1862
Staatsarchiv, Hamburg

Garibaldi! Qu'est ce que c'est que Garibaldi?
C'est un homme, rien de plus. Mais un homme
dans toute la sublime signification du mot. Un
homme de la liberté; un homme de l'humanité.
Vir, dirait son compatriote Virgile.

Victor Hugo

Ten years after Garibaldi roamed the surroundings of Ravenna as a hounded fugitive, I found myself on the way to Ravenna accompanied by Menotti and Teresa Garibaldi and the D[eidery], a couple from Nice. The rumor that the "famiglia del prode Generale" was due to arrive seemed to have preceded us; as we reached the suburbs innumerable curious citizens rushed to the windows and out of their dwellings to catch a glimpse of the lovely Teresa and her Herculean brother. With noisy clatter our poor carriage horses gathered up the last spark of their sinking strength to make a grand entrance into the palazzo square and draw themselves up below the high archway of this fine building. A dense crowd encircled our carriage.

The General came down the flight of steps to greet us and led us to our rooms with a most cordial welcome. I was overjoyed to find him looking so well. All trace of his last serious illness had vanished from his noble face. The obvious satisfaction with his recently won victories, as well as the dawning fortune which he seemed to foresee for his beloved country, cast a glow on his classical features which greatly embellished them; in fact, the veteran warrior seemed ten years younger than when I had seen him in Turin only a few months before.

Hardly had we shaken off the coat of dust accumulated during our long day's journey, when we were called to dinner. We traversed a row of richly decorated drawing rooms; the General introduced us to some of the dignitaries of Ravenna, then to H.E. the Marchese Rora, who had been sent from Turin to Ravenna by the Piedmontese Government as Superintendent and *Delegato politico*. He received us with cordial hospitality and true benevolence. We had been at dinner less than an hour when the *evvivas* of the crowd assembled below became so tempestuous that Marchese Rora induced Garibaldi to gratify the people by appearing on the balcony.

181

"The cheers you hear," he said to the General, "come from a warm-hearted people. These Romagnoles are forthright; they are not simulators, and they truly mean what they are demonstrating."

The Marchese had to repeat these words several times before he could overcome Garibaldi's reticence. At last he stepped out on the balcony and delivered one of his short powerful speeches which go straight to the heart. Not the slightest sound was heard as his melodious voice resounded in the square and he thanked the people for all their sympathy and manifestations of affection. The air seemed to stand still; the banners hung downward and the attentive multitude seemed hardly to breathe lest it disrupt the rapt silence.

Only one who has followed, as I have, the life of this valiant warrior in all his misfortunes, sacrifices and afflictions; only he knows, as I do, the virtuous qualities which adorn his private life and also knows the fine role which the valorous Romagnoles played during the stormiest period of his existence; only he, I repeat, can appreciate the feelings which overwhelmed me, as I at his side witnessed this spectacle; it was an unforgettable evening.

As soon as Garibaldi had concluded and the first outburst of enthusiastic acclamation had quieted down, he withdrew from the window. But Signora D[eidery], Teresa and I remained on the balcony a little longer, since such scenes were not as familiar to us as to him who had inspired them.

Night had fallen and the whole square glowed in festive illumination. The reflection of the flaming torches produced constantly changing light effects upon the tricolors, on the bunting and on the various parades which made their way through the massive crowd; the joyful sounds of the musical bands, which were almost drowned out from time to time by the thundering *evvivas* and newly coined titles for the "amato figlio del popolo"; and above all, the dark blue sky with its myriad of stars peacefully twinkling seemed to consecrate the homage paid to the Italian hero. This was indeed an impressive sight and even the most indifferent spectator was moved by the thought that such tribute was being paid to virtue, personal bravery and noble-mindedness.

Even today Ravenna, the former capital of the western empire, then the seat of the Greek and Lombardic kings and the metropolis of the Greek exarchs, is still rich in monuments which attest to its glorious history. It would seem that few other cities, except Rome, can boast of such churches, palaces, museums and mausoleums. The bones of the children of Theodosius repose within its walls. And Dante's ashes rest here among the stately funeral monuments of the exarchs and patriarchs. Today this venerable city, however, formerly situated on the Adriatic Sea,[144] would merely be grieving over the decay of its former greatness if nature had not bestowed upon it a treasure whose majestic grandeur will outlive any human monument. Who has not heard of Ravenna's far-famed *pineta*? It is Italy's oldest, most beautiful and most memorable forest. In the old days Dante and Boccaccio celebrated it, and the praise of its splendors resounded in the poems of Byron and Dryden. In ancient times this forest supplied the wood to build the ships of Rome, and the banner of powerful Venice flew from masts which it furnished. And now the forest can add to its classical annals the most moving drama of our time, since it was here that the valorous Garibaldi sought refuge from the Austrians in 1849 during his retreat from Rome. For days and days in this labyrinth of underbrush the exiled hero strayed from farmhouse to farmhouse, from hut to hut, from thicket to thicket, at times separated from a band of furious Croats only by a single shrub! Then, alas, here occurred the most tragic event of his life: the death of his adored Anita! Still it was here also that he experienced the heroic sacrifice and deep devotion of which the uncorrupted and incorruptible Romagnoles are capable.

An excursion to the pineta was included in the program which the General had planned for our entertainment, so that one fine morning at eight o'clock we started out. Garibaldi, Signora D[eidery], Teresa and I occupied the first carriage; the reminder of the party followed in another equipage, while at the end of the entourage followed three biroccini to facilitate our passage through the most difficult areas of the forest.

The weather was splendid; an autumnal breath of air tempered the ardor of the sun's rays. Our horses quickly assumed a rapid trot and within a quarter of an hour we reached the edge of the Roman pine forest. From Ravenna it extends along the Adriatic coast for 35 miles in a northerly direction, covering a flat sandy surface one to three miles wide. A continuous series of delightful clearings and paths interrupts the uniform twilight of this giant grove on whose wall-like greenery climbing plants of all kinds spread out their multi-colored flowers and ripe berries. Wild cherry, apple and pear trees heavily weighed down with fruit, garlands of wild vines similarly burdened with their juicy grapes, shrubs of barberry, blackberry and wild roses, in short, everything seems to be gathered here to pay homage to the queen of the forest — the Roman pine — which reaches in majestic grandeur towards Heaven, as it offers a safe refuge in its graceful branches to the feathered inhabitants of this magnificent solitude, not to mention providing the Italians with a plentiful supply of *pignoli*.[145]

In spite of the vivid emotion which the sight of the pineta most certainly recalled to his mind, the General was in a very good humor on this morning and most communicative. He began by giving us some details concerning his most recent campaign; he described it as "una campagna magnifica," first of all because the dangers to which he and his followers were exposed could be regarded as slight compared to its successful result, and then also because during the whole course of the war he had not once been obliged to reproach his soldiers or to punish them.

He spoke most highly of the Romagnoles and assured us that of all the cities of Romagna, Ravenna had always distinguished itself by a complete absence of caste spirit, as well as by the uprightness and concord of its citizens. Garibaldi named many persons who had assisted him with great devotion during his hour of need in 1849; with visible satisfaction he dwelled upon the self-denial of a certain Bonnet* of Comacchio, who had saved him from the clutches of the Austrians at the risk of his own life.

While such feelings of gratitude towards the valorous Romagnoles filled the heart of the General, they in turn had not forgotten the man for whom they had so readily exposed themselves to the greatest dangers in the past. As the news of his excursion to the pineta spread, they flocked there and before long the usually deserted paths of the forest became animated. And the further we penetrated into the forest, the more often the General was obliged to halt in order to permit further homage to be bestowed on him.

What magnificent types of manly beauty these Romagnoles are! Strength, energy and uprightness radiate from all their features. Some of them were speechless with emotion at the sight of their hero, the "treasure of their heart." They clutched his hand passionately and gazed upon him fixedly with their deep black eyes which spoke more eloquently than any words.

After a thirteen-mile drive through the interior of the forest we came out into the clear again; our carriage made a sharp turn and stopped in front of a farmhouse, where we alighted, and soon I discovered that we were at the fattoria of the Marchese Guiccioli. Here we were shown into a modest room which was no less than the place of refuge where Anita Garibaldi breathed her last in the arms of her grieving husband — Anita, the woman of unlimited heroism who followed her beloved husband until death!

I will not dwell on all the manifestations of joy with which the farmer and his family received the famous hero after an absence of ten long years of vicissitudes; I only wish to mention that in this isolated cottage at the furthest end of the forest we found a table laden with all imaginable delicacies. But of all the exquisite offerings of this banquet, indeed the most savoury was the cordiality and hospitality with which they were proffered.

There were eighteen guests at the table and every few minutes this or that worthy Romagnole stepped into the room to drink to the General's health, or to recall an adventure or a danger he had shared with him during the escape in 1849. Soon the room was jammed full and its exit

---

*This friend of the General also participated in the day's celebration. Garibaldi introduced me to him, and I am indebted to him for the interesting documentation which I have used in an earlier chapter of this book.

barred by a dense wall of heads; the hallway was also crowded with excited, jubilant Romagnoles, while from far and near joyful *evvivas* were heard incessantly, since hundreds, if not thousands, had hastened to attend the celebration of this memorable day.

At the end of the dinner Officer T. of the Engineers gave a short but meaningful speech in which he enumerated Garibaldi's heroic deeds, terminating with a toast to the honored guest, who in turn replied in the following manner:

"You have just recounted the story of my life and now it is my turn to tell you how proud and happy I am to be again among you worthy people, of whose courage and devotion I have had such living proof. I repeat to you, that until the last moment of my life I shall be devoted to my country with body and soul. For fourteen years I served the cause of liberty abroad without compensation, what would I not do for the country of my birth? Events are progressing favorably, but much remains to be done. The day has come when Italy will regain her complete independence; this time it shall be accomplished and the banner of liberty must wave from the Alps to Sicily. Fate has given us the man we needed to unify us. We must rally around Victor Emmanuel to drive out the foreigner from our native land; we will no longer endure his yoke. Once the foreigner has withdrawn and lets us enjoy our own possessions in peace, then we will greet him as a friend; but as long as he wants to subjugate us under his rule, he can expect nothing from us except artillery fire. Only through unity and strength can we gain our freedom. Believe me, if we are strong, no one will dare attack us. Above all, we must be soldiers. Our whole nation must form one single army, and if family obligations retain some at home, let them remain there as soldiers with their musket in their hands. Fifteen days are sufficient to make an Italian into a brave soldier; his pay will not consist of an embroidered uniform. Look at the Zouaves![146] In their simple, comfortable dress they prove to be the best soldiers in the world. I recall that during one of my South American campaigns I found myself in a vast plain without possibilities of being provisioned either from the interior of the country or from the seaports blockaded by the enemy. The herds of the plain were our only source of supplies. Their meat was our food and their skins protected us from the noon heat, just as they did against the coolness of the night. Yet I assure you that our soldiers, armed only with muskets, performed wonders of bravery. We were the terror of the Imperial forces and put the enemy to flight by the thousands. But we need arms, my friends, and I suggest that Italy should open a subscription for a million muskets, so that we are no longer lacking in these. Just consider the number of injustices we have to avenge! Just consider the number of years passed in servitude! Remember the shameful death to which were condemned Ciceruacchio[147] and his sons, Ugo Bassi[148] and Antonio Elia! Perhaps you do not remember this last martyr of Italian liberty, so let me recount to you an heroic episode of his life.

185

"Antonio Elia was a simple sailor from Ancona. When he had barely reached his twentieth year, the ship on which he was sailing was seized by one of those Turkish galleys which were molesting the Adriatic coast at the time. The Turks manned the captured vessel with ten of their sailors and one officer, while incarcerating all the captured crew in the hold of the ship, except for Elia, whom they retained on deck at their service. A strong scirocco[149] and the unusual darkness which accompanied it gave Antonio Elia the idea of liberating himself and his companions. He went to the bow of the ship and seized an axe. Armed with this weapon he returned to the stern of the ship where he had left the chief of the pirates. On reaching the spot where he surmised the pirate to be, he swung his axe at him; but the stroke missed and the axe remained stuck in the deck. As he struggled to pull out the weapon, the pirate chieftain, frightened by the noise and suspecting trouble, drew his yatagan[150] and inflicted a heavy wound on Elia's left shoulder. The latter felt his warm blood flowing copiously, and freeing his axe once more, desperately raised it against his opponent. The pirate was felled to the deck lifeless. Now encouraged by this success Elia rushed at the crew as if endowed with supernatural strength and slew them all but two or three, who jumped overboard with terrifying howls and drowned.

"This Antonio Elia, a veritable lion in bravery, fell into the hands of the Austrians in 1849, and because he refused to escape secretly in a dangerous moment, was executed, leaving behind a wife and children."

The General carried on for some time in this manner, speaking not as an orator who astounds his public by eloquence and carries it away, but as the military commander, the leader and adored friend of the people, who converses candidly and intimately with his devoted followers.

But the performance of a sacred duty of love was yet in store for the General. Regretfully we took leave of our generous hosts and climbed into our carriage. The number of vehicles which had joined ours by now in order to accompany Garibaldi had risen to fifty. We travelled about a mile, then the carriage halted in front of an isolated small chapel where a waiting priest asked us to enter the modest House of God. Soon I and my companions found out the reason for this invitation; we were lead into a small room profusely decorated with freshly picked flowers and wreaths immediately next to the altar. In the room lay a coffin draped in black. This coffin contained the ashes of the unforgettable Anita Garibaldi! With many a tear we placed the wreaths on the coffin while recalling glorious, yet heart-rending memories. A pause ensued which will remain forever engraved in my mind; the solemn stillness was broken only by sobs. Then a mass for the dead one was said.

The next morning we set out for Bologna in the company of the General. Our journey was punctuated by a chain of homages which almost bordered on frenzy. The culminating point was reached in Lugo and Medicina. Horses were quite superfluous; the people, led by the notables of the localities, often unhitched our horses and pulled the carriage through sideways and elevations with constant jubilant shouts of joy. This naturally prolonged our route and was obviously intended to show the idol of the people how much he was loved. As a result, this triumphal procession took no less than seventeen hours for us to reach Bologna, as waves of people delirious with joy rang bells, thundered cannon, showered flowers and ribbons amidst the magic illumination of Venetian lanterns.

A Poem Written
by Garibaldi[151]

Non fra pomposi ed aurei
  Vaghi giardin simmetrici,
Non sotto immensi aerei
  Archi e portenti artefici;
  Ma tra l'ombrose selve
  Piacesi il mio pensier.

Non quando il ciel sereno
  E dei zeffiri il lambito
  All'ente fausto in seno
  Diffonde un dolce palpito;
  Ma quando rugge il nembo
  E scuote l'orbe inter.

Non quando Teti argentei
  I flutti suoi mi estolle,
  Non quando ardenti agli ignei
  Monti il bitume bolle;
  Ma tempestose l'onde
  Sconquassano il crater.

E che m'importa il gaudio
  E dei popoli la pace?
  Che m'importa del Sabaudo
  Il prosperar mendace?
  E del Samnito immemore
  Il codardo giacer?

E che m'importa Italia,
  I lirici concenti,
  Se di Germania e Gallia
  I bellici stromenti
  Nel sen di quell'imbelle
  L'onta fan rimbombar?

Io la vorrei deserta,
I suoi palagi infranti
Ed io de l'Alpi all'erta,
Le sue città fumanti
Scorgere e con sardonico
Sorriso contemplar.

Pria che vederla trepida
Sotto il baston d'un vandalo,
Già prostituta e squallida
Delle nazioni scandalo,
Il suo destin superbo
Stolida rinnegar!

5. Holograph letter from Garibaldi to Elpis Melena
dated Caprera, 28 November 1857

6. Holograph letter from Elpis Melena to Garibaldi
dated Rome, 24 January 1858

ANNEX
by
Elpis Melena

THE WARS OF THE SOUTH AMERICAN REPUBLICS

An explanation of Book One
of Garibaldi's Memoirs

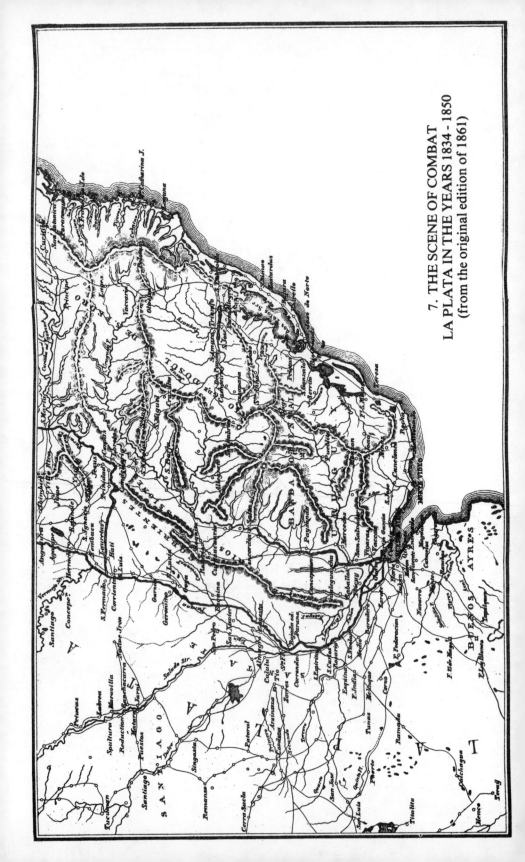

7. THE SCENE OF COMBAT
LA PLATA IN THE YEARS 1834 - 1850
(from the original edition of 1861)

The Wars of the South American Republics

Garibaldi's Autobiography gives only an incomplete and approximate picture of the conflicts which occurred in the forties of this [19th] century between the republics of La Plata and the Brazilian Empire, as well as among the republics themselves. Indeed sometimes Garibaldi assumes knowledge of the situation on the part of the reader, and sometimes he merely intersperses some aphorismic remarks. It is clear that Garibaldi's main purpose was to describe his own experiences, his personal part in the general fate of these states, and thus the reader of the Memoirs finds no answer to the constantly recurring question of how the parties in general reacted to each other. In brief we can say that the episodes narrated by the Italian hero at times lack coherence. The pages which follow endeavor to fill in some of these gaps.

First, in order to gain insight into the conflicting interests of the quarrelsome parties in South America, it is necessary to turn back to the beginning of that century. The Napoleonic wars which shook the foundations of prevailing systems in Europe fifty to sixty years before had their effect in South America as well, even if belatedly. Spain and Portugal, the two usurpers of the immense territory of the southern half of the American hemisphere, became deeply involved in the general turmoil. On the one hand arose British greed for these productive and promising colonies; and on the other hand was the desire for independence on the part of the South American populations themselves.

Fortunately this English lust for conquest was soon halted, partly by the inhabitants' rightful desire for liberty and partly by the altered constellation of European politics. England had considered the colonies of Spain and Portugal as legitimate booty as long as the two latter states let themselves be taken into tow by her enemy, Napoleon I. But subsequently England was obliged to respect the transatlantic possessions of the two Latin powers, who had become in the meantime her own allies and combated the common enemy along with her.

Nevertheless, once whetted, the people's taste for liberty could no longer be restrained. In the Spanish Virreinato of Buenos Aires they celebrated their first and most lasting triumphs. There the people came to know their strength by their brave resistance to British invasion, while also noting the weakness of Spanish rule as they deposed a Viceroy without encountering reprisals. Subsequently they attempted to obtain concessions from the disorganized motherland.

The countries of the La Plata area had been under the same narrow-minded pressure and despicable colonial policy imposed in all the Spanish possessions in America. Most often the motherland sent them greedy, brutal adventurers as officials, interested only in squeezing money out of them. She drained them with high import and export tariffs and with heavy duties on all consumer goods; also prohibited was intercourse with foreigners* in order that she enjoy exclusive advantages of trade and prevent an infiltration of culture. Likewise the motherland did nothing to establish communications; in fact she even prohibited the exploitation of the most profitable branches of agriculture, so as to maintain the colonists in complete dependence. It is true that some of these measures had been relaxed in the second half of the eighteenth century, nevertheless the basic policy was still in existence by the beginning of the nineteenth. When general confusion ensued during the years 1808 to 1814 in the mother country, the system collapsed almost by itself. Little by little locally elected officials took the place of those formerly sent from Spain. Commerce was freed from its restrictions; immigration was encouraged, and contact with foreigners, Englishmen in particular, soon produced a revolution in enlightment. As the agents of the Spanish juntas of Cádiz and Sevilla, as well as those of the French, tried to propagandize among the colonists, national parties were formed whose aims were total independence.

This was not to be achieved however, without combat. The coming to power in Spain of Ferdinand VII brought to Spanish South America the prospect of wholesale reaction. The new king, who had grown up in Bourbon misjudgement of the spirit of the times, no less than in Bourbon stubbornness, simply declared the inhabitants thirsting for reform in his long undermined colonies mere rebels. He sent endless numbers of soldiers to force them back to their former obedience. The result was that bitter combat began from the Gulf of Panama to the estuary of the Silver River [La Plata].

This is not the place to describe the details of these encounters, be it sufficient to say that it was at La Plata that events first came to a head. Here the bitter feelings against the rule of the motherland soon became intensified in the form of demands: from a request for autonomy in local affairs under the recognition of Spanish sovereignty, they proceeded to

---

*Foreigners entering the interior of America were subject to the death penalty.

demand an independent kingdom ruled by a son of Charles IV, and finally they decided to break away from Spain altogether.

The ninth of July 1816 is the birthday of the United Republics of the Silver River. A congress assembled in Tucuman unanimously released a pompous declaration of independence. Ever since then geography textbooks state that fourteen former Spanish provinces at La Plata have constituted themselves as republics and united. These provinces are: Buenos Aires, Santa Fé, Entre Rios, Corrientes, Cordova, Santiago, Tucuman, Salta, Jujuy, Catamarca, La Rioja, San Luis, Mendoza and San Juan.

But during the war for independence two enemies of this union had already arisen, and they were soon to endanger not only the union's existence, but its very independence. Consequently even until the present day liberty and political order in the La Plata area are threatened.

First of all serious antagonisms developed within the United Provinces themselves, later dividing the inhabitants in the name of Federalism or Unitarianism. It is too much to say that either of the two parties was basically opposed to republicanism or independence; but the Unitarians defended the idea of centralization, that is, a strong government with firm political links which would hold the United Provinces together. The Federalists on the other hand desired a loose union only; they claimed autonomy for every single province and stood for the idea of maximum freedom, or political individualism. Such a contrast arose by necessity from the very nature of the problem in South America. It was the contrast between Buenos Aires on the one hand and the interior on the other.

The inhabitants of Buenos Aires, the so-called Porteños*, had pulled themselves up rapidly from the lethargy of a Spanish colonial town, once the Spanish pressure had slackened and contact had been made with foreigners. They discarded old prejudices and in a remarkably short time acquired European culture, even if somewhat superficial. Because of its geographic position, Buenos Aires bore the brunt of the war; still it derived the chief advantages from the abolishment of the transport restrictions. Political conditions were relatively orderly, property was fairly safe, and very soon schools were founded to provide education for its future citizens.

Conditions were very different in the interior, that is to say, in the endless plains of the pampas. This vast territory was inhabited by a sparse population, scattered in isolated farms or in small localities which were called cities. Neither culture nor political order had ever existed here, nor was there any change after the liberation from the motherland. The gauchos, accustomed to the roughest of lives as herdsmen, felt no need for such; rather they had an instinctive dislike for them. They hated

---

*The full name of Buenos Aires is: Puerto Santa Maria de Buenos Aires, thus the name of *Porteños*.

Spanish rule; in fact, they hated all rule, and either they had no education, or despised it.

Such differences between the Porteños and the gauchos soon made for harsh antagonisms between them. The former regarded themselves and their city as the natural heirs of Spanish viceregal might; they considered themselves entitled to rule over the other provinces. Ever since the first moment of the revolution they tried to hold together the former Virreinato of Buenos Aires and imposed the central power over the whole country. As much as possible they maintained the Spanish colonial system, the obstruction of river navigation and the trade monopoly; they sent troops to the provinces and removed and appointed governors at will. The inhabitants of the provinces naturally felt irritated by such procedures, and their long-standing jealousy and dislike of the capital turned into hatred, manifesting itself at times in conjunction with the partisans of Spain.

To a large degree the discord and civil wars among the states of La Plata can be attributed to these antagonisms. The groups of Federalists and Unitarians were constant rivals for supremacy, and since they were almost always ready to pounce on each other, a leader here or there was sufficient to call them to arms.

In addition to this internal strife the union was also threatened by an external enemy, namely the neighboring country of Brazil. Already under Portuguese rule Brazil had been an enemy neighbor of the Spanish colonies of La Plata. At various times she attempted to tear away from Spain the Silver River and its tributaries, which represented the trade routes for her southern provinces. Especially the Banda Oriental (now Uruguay) was the constant object of Portuguese plans for conquest. History in the 17th and 18th centuries recounts many wars fought over the Banda Oriental, followed by peace treaties in which Spain inevitably was guaranteed its sovereignty over these districts. In the second year of this century Portugal attacked again and seized the Spanish localities on the Lagoon dos Patos and the seven missions. But during the war for independence of the La Plata states and the subsequent political strife arising there, the government of Brazil judged the time opportune to execute all its plans for conquest.

Besides the desire to incorporate the northern shore of the La Plata into the Brazilian Empire, another reason for enmity became apparent as a result of the severance of the Spanish provinces from the motherland. In the united provinces and in Buenos Aires as early as 1813, slavery had been abolished, and it was decreed that every slave who stepped onto the soil of the united provinces should be free. The slave state of Brazil felt endangered by this in two ways: first, she visualized all her negroes escaping by crossing over her southern border into the Banda Oriental; and secondly, she feared that her free southern population, which was partly of Spanish origin and opposed to slavery, might be favorable to the ideas prevailing in the Union.

As early as 1816 Brazil interfered in the internal feuds of the united republics. At that time the Banda Oriental was in open conflict with Buenos Aires; she was a republic of her own, and Artigas, a chief of the Federalist Party, ruled practically with a reign of terror in Montevideo. Now, as 10,000 Brazilian troops penetrated into the Banda, Buenos Aires remained neutral. Montevideo fell in 1817; and little by little the whole Banda was occupied by the Portuguese until a *de facto* conquest was completed in 1820, that is, *de facto* because Brazil pretended that she was occupying the country only temporarily for its own security. The casting off of the mask, however, namely the formal incorporation of the Banda, followed soon after; in 1821 the Banda became part of the Brazilian Empire under the name of Provincia Cisplatina.

Until 1825 the Banda bore this dependence on Brazil, which had in the meantime lost no time in constituting herself as an independent empire. In April of that year Lavalleja, a native of Montevideo who had taken refuge in Buenos Aires, arrived in the Banda Oriental with 32 companions and unfurled the banner for liberation against Brazil. A Brazilian cavalry regiment composed of natives and led by Colonel Fructuoso Rivera went over to him; the gauchos of the province did likewise and in droves. A provisional government was formed, a constituent assembly called, and in August 1825 the independence of the Banda, along with its adherence to the United Republics of La Plata, was proclaimed.

But Brazil did not wish to lose its cisplatine province so easily. The capital Montevideo and the coastal districts were still in her power. A long drawn-out war broke out to retain these places. Buenos Aires took part in it; the General Congress of the United Republics decreed the admission of the Banda into the Union.

The scales of the fortunes of war swung back and forth for years, encounters were fought continuously, bringing glory to the Orientals but no decision, until the European maritime powers, especially France, got tired of the continuing blockade of the La Plata estuary, and urged the termination of the war. The peace was signed on 4 October 1828; Brazil gave up the cisplatine province, and the United Republics renounced admitting the Banda to the Union. Instead the Banda received its independence as the Republic of Uruguay.

Unfortunately this renunciation by the two most powerful among the warring parties was not meant sincerely nor honestly. With this peace Brazil, as well as Buenos Aires, only put off their designs on Uruguay, but did not give them up. Apparently the mania for centralization in Buenos Aires and the lust for annexation in Rio Janeiro did not die out with the peace treaty.

In the meantime however the Republic of Uruguay made extremely rapid progress. She provided a liberal constitution for herself, with Fructuoso Rivera elected as president. This man possessed no outstanding talent, was not well educated, but was of gentle disposition. Absolutely nothing had he undertaken to further the development of his young state; nevertheless he had not interfered by imposing restrictions or obstacles. He merely let matters take their course, and that was sufficient for Uruguay. Its favorable position on the estuary of the Silver River, along with the natural fertility of its soil, carried in themselves the seeds of development which did not have to be artifically fertilized. Especially Montevideo, the capital of the country, began to flourish. Immigrants arrived in large numbers; many Frenchmen, Italians, Spaniards and Englishmen settled there. As early as 1838 there were 5000 Frenchmen registered at the consulate of their country in Montevideo. The number of houses and inhabitants of the city doubled within ten years; the value of products exported to French ports was estimated at 2,215,000 francs in the year 1838.

Rivera's presidency suffered only one disturbance: Lavalleja, whom we mentioned before as the real originator of independence, was jealous of Rivera and attempted an insurrection. The danger was quickly averted when the insurrection failed, thanks to the firmness of the port captain, Don Manuel Oribe. By this act the latter merited the gratitude of Rivera and thus laid the foundation stone of the important political role he was to play from now on. He became general and Minister of war; and when Rivera's four-year presidential term expired, Oribe succeeded him (1834).

Don Manuel Oribe belonged to one of the first families of the Banda and had participated in the wars against Spain since 1811. He had the reputation of being a brave soldier, but an unlucky officer. Personally he was known to be upright, even if severe and domineering. He had some education, but was of limited intellect. When he took over the government, he tried to put more order into the administration than in Rivera's time; in particular, he attempted to introduce economy in the management of finances. On the whole these were honorable attempts, but as they were started with nervous intensity and carried out with bureaucratic severity, indeed with cruelty, they were bound to cause offense among a population just beginning to change over from total unrestraint to civilization. Within a short time dissatisfaction, particularly among the gauchos, increased into open rebellion; and this was probably encouraged by Brazilian agents.

Partly of his own free will, partly by force of circumstances, Rivera took command of the insurgents. Oribe was defeated in the battle of Palmar on 10 June 1838; he attempted to retreat to Montevideo, but was blockaded there, until he learned that he was insufficiently supported in the defense of the city by the inhabitants, especially by the foreigners, and decided to capitulate. On 20 October 1838 before the legislative bodies he solemnly renounced the presidency and left Uruguayan territory to install himself in Buenos Aires. But scarcely had Oribe reached the latter city, when he withdrew his resignation, as Rosas, the head of the Argentine Republic, recognized him as the legitimate president of Uruguay.

Rosas! Don Juan Manuel Rosas! We have to stop here to acquaint the reader with this man. In 1820 Don Juan Manuel Rosas' name appeared for the first time in the history of the internal dissensions of Buenos Aires. There the antagonisms between the Unitarians and the Federalists, that is, between the inhabitants of the capital and those of the pampas, became a permanent feature of political life. One day a skirmish occurred between the militia men of the city and those of the country right in the streets of Buenos Aires. The colonel of one of the gaucho regiments involved was named Rosas.

A native of the capital, Rosas ran away from his parents at age fifteen or sixteen, it was said because he had struck his mother and was afraid of punishment from his father. He was taken on as a farm hand on an estancia in the pampas; soon he advanced to foreman (capataz) of the farm hands, and finally became partner of the estancia with the owner. He readily took to the primitive life of the gaucho, became popular among his neighbors for his hospitality, was feared for his boldness in rustling cattle, and made a considerable fortune.

After the street skirmish of 1820, in which he was defeated with his party, Rosas retreated into the background for some years. The Unitarian Party was dominant from 1820 to 1827, and Rivadavia, the president of the United Republics of La Plata, ruled according to its policy and in its interests. However, his predilection for European ways and culture, and the very costly participation of Buenos Aires in the war against Brazil in favor of the Banda Oriental, led to a reaction. Rivadavia had to resign, the Union held together less firmly, the heads of the Federalist Party took over as dictators in some of the united republics, while in Buenos Aires itself Don Manuel Dorrego, a member of the Federalist faction, was elected governor in 1827.

Under this government Rosas reappeared. He was placed at the head of the administration of the rural territory and received the title of general. But Dorrego's rule was to be of short duration. After the conclusion of the war with Brazil the Argentinian troops returned from the Banda. Among them, particularly among their officers, Unitarian views prevailed, so that in December 1828 they were led by General Lavalle in a revolt against Dorrego. The latter had to flee from Buenos Aires but was caught in flight and shot. It was said that he had been betrayed by Rosas.

The Federalists, now with Rosas at their head, called for vengeance. For a whole year a bitter and cruel guerrilla war without decision raged throughout the Argentinian plains. At last Rosas reaped the fruits of this anarchy: Lavalle fled for his life, and Rosas was appointed governor of Buenos Aires in December 1829.

We cannot follow the long rule of Rosas in detail, or dwell on its individual phases, nor on his manoeuvers to resign, all of which ended by procuring for him ever greater dictatorial powers. Instead we have to limit ourselves to characterizing the man and his rule in general. When he took over the government he began, like most despots, by dissembling and keeping his real intentions a secret. He came to power by means of the Federalist Party and at first it seemed that he was going to pay his debt to this faction. But in actual fact he used the party only to complete the defeat of the remnants of the opposing party, who had fled to the neighboring districts. As soon as this was accomplished, he threw off the mask. He behaved as a complete tyrant; his only aim was the consolidation and increase of his power and to impose its dominance over all the other republics of the Union. He had only used the Federalist Party as a means of obtaining exclusive power for himself as an autocrat, and once he had that power, he was in fact an Unitarian of the worst kind. The idea of centralization, long familiar to the city of Buenos Aires, from now on was caricatured and embodied in the gaucho chief Rosas. He tried to centralize all affairs in his hands, while interfering in all the dissensions with the Republics of La Plata in order to further increase his influence.

Woe to him who stepped into the path of the dictator of Buenos Aires, or who even excited his envy! Whether he belonged to the Unitarian or Federalist faction, Don Juan Manuel's hatred pursued him until annihilation. While binding his friends ever closer to him by his favors, the dictator oppressed his opponents through fear. Anyone who doubted his right to absolute power appeared as an enemy to him. In the ranks of his own party a few men stood out whose rivalry he feared; they were the generals López and Quiroga. López, the founder of the Federalist Party, was Governor of the state of Sante Fé. Rosas called him to Buenos Aires and, because he was ill, had him treated by his personal physician; then, as everybody said, he had him poisoned. Quiroga was not only known to be the bravest but also the most unruly officer of the party; his home was in Entre Rios and there he exercised his greatest authority. Rosas asked him to pacify the states of Salta and Tucuman and, while en route passing through the territory of Cordova, he had him murdered. Then he feigned a pursuit of the assassins, had them imprisoned for a few years and ultimately eliminated by execution.

Assassinations, shootings and confiscations of property — these were generally the means by which Rosas attempted to strengthen his position. If few respected him, all feared him. Of uncouth habits, he indulged in low pleasures, despised culture, and aroused no sympathy among the better elements of society. But he knew how to frighten them, supported by the lowest classes and the large mass of gauchos. In this work he was greatly helped by a society, rather a confederation, founded as a kind of Freemasonry dedicated exclusively to the protection of his autocratic system. This was known as the Mashorca Society (Mashorqueros) and consisted of boorish scoundrels charged with carrying out espionage and informer services. Its members overheard conversations in public places, infiltrated families and denounced persons opposed to the dictator. Rosas took revenge on them without observing any legal procedure. Most of the time the unfortunate persons were victims of the

Mashorqueros themselves, who acted as executioners at times in public squares, or more often in nocturnal assaults, with a cold-bloodedness not unlike the slaughtering of pampas steers. And Rosas took his revenge fully, usually with ingenious cruelty, not only on the men hostile to him, but he extended it also to their wives and families. It seems that he delighted in the role of a Nero feared by all. In fact, he collected heads of his enemies preserved in alcohol, had bridles for his riding horses made from their skins, and sadistically showed off such gruesome trophies to his visitors.

By 1837 Rosas had succeeded in centralizing everything into his hands or in those of his subordinates. The legislative authority of Buenos Aires renounced its power and transferred it to him; the army, in which he had incorporated many negroes, obeyed him unconditionally; a weak and servile old man was placed at the head of the clergy, while the supervision of public education was transferred to the Jesuits.* Needless to say, in most states of the Union the most important positions were filled by his followers and favorites.

Hence this was the man to whom the ex-governor of Uruguay had fled and by whom he was influenced to declare his resignation from the presidency of Uruguay as null and void. For a long time Rosas had looked at that neighboring republic with envious and suspicious glances. She was not only the object of his envy, because of her prosperity and independence, but he mistrusted her since she served as a refuge and assembly point for his opponents, the Unitarians, who fled Buenos Aires. Now he saw Oribe's arrival as a welcome opportunity to interfere in the internal disorders of Uruguay, particularly because he himself had been admonished against such interference by British and French diplomacy.

Naturally the new government of Uruguay was resentful of the support Rosas gave to ex-president Oribe, and made common cause with the Argentinian emigrants in the country, who had just then taken up arms under the leadership of General Lavalle.

Verily the dictator found himself in a critical situation, for in addition to these opponents who rose against him on South American soil, there was a diplomatic complication* with the French government, a complication which led to a blockade of the harbor of Buenos Aires for some years. A French flotilla was stationed in the harbor of Montevideo, and the Island of Martín García, which controls the entrance to the Uruguay and Paraná Rivers, was occupied by French troops. In the meantime General Lavalle was given subsidies from France.

---

*When later he was disappointed in the hopes he had placed in the Jesuits, he took the supervision of education away from them and dissolved the order.

*The causes of this conflict were the conviction of several Frenchmen resident in Buenos Aires, robberies perpetrated on others, and the claim of the Argentinian government to draft sons of Frenchmen born in Argentina into its army.

Furthermore these allies were joined by the discontented elements in the Argentinian provinces led by Domingo Cullen, the Governor of Sante Fé and successor to the López mentioned above, and Genaro Beron de Astrada, the Governor of Corrientes. A formal treaty was drawn up in Montevideo on 31 December 1838 whereby the members of the alliance undertook to raise an army of 6000 men against Rosas.

However the first battle waged by the allies resulted in a victory for Rosas. During the murderous battle of Pago Largo the allies were defeated (March 1839); Beron de Astrada was captured and beaten to death, while Cullen fell into the hands of the victor some months later and was shot. The Argentinian troops pursued the defeated enemy and General Echague with 4000 men penetrated into Uruguayan territory to within 12 hours of Montevideo.

But soon the fortunes of war changed. Rivera won against the dictator's troops at Cagancha on 21 December 1839 and thus forced them to retreat from Uruguay. Lavalle collected important forces in Entre Rios and Corrientes, cleaned up the Paraná with the help of the French, and in the autumn of 1840 proceeded to the vicinity of Buenos Aires.

Now it seemed that according to all human calculations the days of Rosas' rule were counted; instead he quite unexpectedly got rid of his most dangerous enemy. In France a change of ministry had taken place, so that the chief command of the French squadron in Argentinian waters went to Admiral Mackau, who after brief negotiations concluded a settlement with Rosas on 21 October 1840.

This is not the place to comment on France's behavior, but the former allies of this great European power were now at the mercy of Rosas' revenge as a result of this peace. The opponents of the dictator fell into three categories: the discontented in Buenos Aires itself, the army of Lavalle, and Rivera's army stationed in Entre Rios and Corrientes. The first he liquidated quite easily: he set his Mashorqueros against them, and Buenos Aires literally dripped with blood. Against Lavalle he gathered all the armed forces he could muster and gave the chief command to Don Manuel Oribe; Lavalle was wounded and succumbed to superior forces in October 1841 at Famalla, soon afterwards he died.

Now only Rivera's army remained to take the field against Rosas. Until this time Rivera had fought successfully against the Argentinian troops, in particular inflicting defeat on General Echague at Guasu. Dissension among the allies however — Rivera on the one hand, and the governor of Corrientes on the other — paralyzed the field operations. Thus with the arrival of the victorious Oribe, here also the scales tipped in favor of Rosas. Rivera was forced to retreat to Uruguayan territory, where nevertheless, he was completely routed on 6 December 1842 at Arroyo Grande. Consequently Oribe moved up and on 16 February 1843 he began the siege of Montevideo.

With this a sad and troubled epoch began for the inhabitants of Uruguay. Until this point they had suffered little in spite of the continuous fighting. The war had been waged mostly beyond the frontiers of the Banda Oriental and had not in the least hindered the rapid development, particularly of the capital Montevideo. The population of the state had risen from 200,000 inhabitants in 1838 to 260,000 five years later; exports, national income and real wealth increased from year to year, and the war had in fact favored trade and immigration to Montevideo, since Buenos Aires had been blockaded and her trade disturbed. Now all this was changed. The fertile lands of Uruguay were overrun by Argentinian troops and became the theater of violent scenes of war and plunder. Friend and foe now vied with each other to consume or destroy the basic capital of the national wealth, the cattle herds of the campos and the provisions of the estancias. Until now the chief characters in these entanglements were a few gaucho chiefs, all of them about equally uncouth, so that it was difficult to arouse any human interest in one or the other, be it Rosas, Rivera or Oribe; but now a city came to the fore, containing a large European commercial population with an important component of culture.

That Montevideo did not fall into Oribe's lap during his first attempt, was exclusively his own fault. The city was practically unfortified by land; the walls and bastions had fallen to ruin since the peace of 1828, the artillery was mostly unusable, and the number of troops available for its defense was small. Besides, the tardiness with which Oribe proceeded to the attack gave the defenders time to put the fortifications more or less into shape. Furthermore the terrifying threats he hurled against all those who dared oppose him, only induced the peaceful citizens to resist his insolence.

While Oribe took his time in pitching camp on the hill known as the Cerrito de la Victoria, in having a fort and batteries constructed on the heights of Figarita and Tres Cruces, more than 1000 meters from the outer fortifications of the city, the inhabitants took advantage of this delay to organize a defense under the direction of General Paz, Minister of War Pacheco and Giuseppe Garibaldi. The latter's *Memoirs* report in sufficient detail the formation of the French and Italian Legions and the bloody skirmishes between the besiegers and the besieged which resulted in a stalemate, so that it is not necessary to dwell upon these topics here. The brave citizens of Montevideo showed themselves to be more than a match for Oribe; unfortunately more serious danger threatened them from another direction.

First it was the blockade of the harbor effected by Rosas' fleet which threatened Montevideo with ruin. Communications were paralyzed and trade was deviated to Buenos Aires, or to the Uruguayan coastal localities in Oribe's hands. Secondly Montevideo's complete isolation loomed in sight because of the nation's defeats suffered in the interior of the country by its troops still fighting against Rosas. After the Battle of Arroyo Grande, Rivera had succeeded in recruiting again among the rural populations of Entre Rios and Corrientes, just as the Banda itself had raised an army including some 4000 regular troops. But he was not able to maintain himself against the usurper of Entre Rios, General Urquiza. The latter received some 4000 men too from Rosas with all necessary war materiel, and it was only due to his bungling that he trailed after Rivera in the countryside for 20 months without being able to force him to a decisive battle. At last however, Urquiza overtook Rivera at India Muerta on 28 March 1845, attacked him with superior forces, and annihilated him. Rivera had been hindered in his operations by masses of fugitives and by an unwieldy baggage train. The day after the battle Urquiza had one thousand prisoners beheaded accompanied by strains of music. A thousand prisoners beheaded! Indeed this was an example of the brutality with which the war was waged. What was left of Rivera's army took refuge on Brazilian territory.

Under such circumstances the defense of Montevideo might appear almost hopeless to the reader and the fall of the city as inevitable. But in those critical times another power was already meddling in La Plata affairs, giving a different turn to events. This power was the Brazilian government.

We are familiar with the policy of this government towards Uruguay. But the Brazilian government, restrained as it was by foreign intervention, had been unable to impede the development of the young republic after the peace of 1828, although it had watched her with an envious eye. Furthermore it was barely able to prevent the secession of its own province of Rio Grande do Sul, where in 1834 and during the following years, a Republican insurrection took place under the leadership of Bento Gonçalves da Silva;* in fact, it scarcely managed to parry the attempts at a unification of the southern republics being connived by diplomatic intrigues. It let its policy be guided by the old dictum: *divide et impera* and observed with perfect satisfaction how Buenos Aires, Montevideo, Corrientes and the other states slaughtered each other ever since 1838.

Still as things developed, it was the progress made by Uruguay's latest opponents which seemed to endanger Brazil. She could not fail to see Rosas approaching his goal with rapid steps, nor to see Montevideo in the process of falling into his hands, or at least, becoming a vassal state of Buenos Aires under the nominal rule of Oribe. To prevent such an increase in power of the Argentinian dictator, who incidentally was casting glances at Paraguay as well, Brazil felt the need for urgent action in the interests of her domain. At first she tried to outwit Rosas and deprive him of his freedom of action by entering into negotiations with the Argentinian ambassador in Rio on 24 March 1843, whereupon a treaty was

---

*This was the insurrection in which Garibaldi participated.

drawn up based upon the following text: "The government of Fructuoso Rivera in Montevideo is incompatible with the internal peace of the Republic of Uruguay, as well as with the peace and security of the Brazilian Empire and the neighboring states. The continuation of his regime is not to be tolerated. Therefore, H.M. the Emperor of Brazil and the Government of the Argentinian Federated States unite against the might and authority exercised by Fructuoso Rivera in the Republic of Uruguay, as well as against the rebels of the Province of Rio Grande do Sul and the followers of said chief and rebels."

The Brazilian cabinet was so sure of its initiative in promoting this treaty that it published it in Rio at once. Rosas however thought it over just in time and refused ratification. Apparently he harbored no intention of sharing a booty which was practically assured to him alone; neither did he see the necessity of cooperating with Brazil in restoring peace to a province wherein he himself obviously entertained ambitions of expansion.

In the meantime Brazil did not give up her plans; she merely chose another course to carry them out. She turned first to the cabinet of the Tuileries and later to the Court of St. James. In 1844 the Viscount of Abrantes was ostensibly sent to Europe to negotiate a trade treaty with Prussia, but in reality to work against Rosas in London and Paris. Brazil's aims were expressed clearly enough in a memo of the Viscount to the French Minister Guizot, wherein was written: "The independence of the Eastern State of Uruguay should be maintained according to the convention of 27 August 1828. The infringement of the independence of the Republic of Paraguay should be prevented. In the name of humanity and in the general interest of trade, an end should be imposed upon the war between Buenos Aires and Montevideo, which threatens to impair the independence of the latter."

The memorandum presented by the Viscount of Abrantes found definite favor with Count Aberdeen in London, and soon afterwards France also decided to participate in an attempt at mediation. The Minister Plenipotentiary Ouseley was sent by the English government to Buenos Aires to make propositions to Rosas, while Baron de Deffaudis, admiral of the French fleet stationed in La Plata, was instructed to initiate similar negotiations. When Rosas refused to concur, the agents of the two European powers threatened him with a blockade of the Buenos Aires harbor. In fact they delivered to him an ultimatum until 31 July 1845 and when the delay expired, they left the city.

On 18 September 1845 the European allies declared the blockade, although for a long time already the commanders of the English and French naval forces had begun hostilities. On the other hand, Montevideo was besieged by land by General Oribe and blockaded by sea by the Argentinian flotilla commanded by Admiral Brown. Towards the middle of July 1845 this flotilla was seized by the Anglo-French allies and the captured ships were divided equally between them. They then turned to

207

support the operations of the Montevidean Army; the neighboring coastal localities of Colonia, Maldonado and the Island of Martín García were conquered with their help. Similarly with their support Garibaldi took the localities of Mercedes, Rincón and Salto, previously fortified by Rosas. At the same time a number of ships of the English and French fleets were stationed in the estuary of La Plata and its tributaries, so as to restore the freedom of river navigation.

Such a war without previous declaration was without doubt contrary to international law; the dictator's protest against this was well founded, and later on the western powers did recognize this by returning the captured ships. Still the intervention might have been justified on humane grounds, if it had been sufficiently strong to restore peace to the La Plata area.

However, this was absolutely not the case. The intervention was merely an ill-considered spurt which soon bogged down, as if the participants were frightened by their own temerity. New negotiations began between the Western European powers and Rosas in 1846. With field operations stopped and the MM. Ouseley and Deffaudis recalled, the preliminaries of a peace treaty were proposed by new Anglo-French agents. In the meantime the siege imposed on Montevideo by General Oribe remained unabated.

For years matters remained unchanged, that is, fruitless negotiations and attempts at mediation by the Western powers on the one hand, and fighting outside the walls of Montevideo on the other hand. To describe the happenings in more detail would bring us beyond our aim of giving a summary presentation. Therefore we will close by indicating briefly the final result.

It was not until 1850 that a treaty was concluded between the five participants, that is, the Western European powers of England and France, the Argentinian Republic (Rosas), General Oribe, and the government of Montevideo. By this treaty all participants promised to cease hostilities; the independence of Uruguay was recognized once again; Oribe's Argentinian troops were to leave the territory of the Republic; and Montevideo was to proceed to the election of a new president in the manner prescribed by the constitution.

These stipulations were carried out as agreed. Giro, the president elected by the Uruguayan people, attempted to heal by his prudent management the deep wounds suffered by the state. For those readers who may have thought that our inculpation of Brazil in the previous pages was unfounded, let us add that the administration of Giro was not a lasting one either. As early as 1852 it was overthrown once again by Fructuoso Rivera, the restless gaucho, and indeed with the help of Brazil, who exacted as the price for her aid the cession of important territories and the promise of extraditing fugitive slaves.

End of Second and Last Volume

8. Melena's home in Khalepa, Crete

9. *Hotel Adler* (the *Auberge de Napoléon*)
Ermatingen, Switzerland, where Elpis Melena died in 1899

10. Melena's grave in the Ermatingen Cemetery
Zivilstandsamt, Ermatingen

ANNOTATIONS

by the Editor

ANNOTATIONS

VOLUME I

BOOK ONE

Chapter I

1. Allusion to the day of 19 March 1852, just as his ship *Carmen* was in the throes of a terrible typhoon off the coast of the Philippine Islands, Garibaldi dreamed of his mother praying for him. His life was spared, but strangely enough, on that very day and after this incident, his mother passed away.

Chapter II

2. Nice today, but perennially *Nizza* since the 5th century B.C. when settled by emigrants from the Italian peninsula who maintained this name until it was forcibly changed by Napoleonic conquest in 1796. Restored to Sardinia, to whom it belonged prior to its seizure by France, in 1814, it reassumed its ancient name Nizza. However, by the French-rigged plebiscite of 1860, it was taken again by France and renamed Nice. Nevertheless even today many countries besides Italy, like Germany, Spain and Portugal, still recognize it only by the name *Nizza*.

3. Padre *Giaume*, not *Giauna*, as Melena writes. This is the first of Melena's misspelling of names cited in the Garibaldi manuscript, something quite incomprehensible since his handwriting was singularly well-written and legible.

4. *Angelo Garibaldi*, born in Nice in 1804, had, like all the Garibaldis, been destined for a career at sea; but soon after he dedicated himself to business, first in New York, later in Philadelphia, where he also served as Sardinian Consul. He died at the young age of forty-nine in 1853.

Chapter III

5. *Pontus*, short form of Pontus Euxinus, the sea between Europe and Asia, commonly known today as the Black Sea.

6. *Jews*; term used only in the general sense, i.e. those who overreach, deceive wilfully or cheat, and not intended in the opprobrious sense unfortunately relegated today solely to Hebrews or Jews. The long list of Garibaldi's closest associates and intimates, among whom were such distinguished Jews as Giuseppe Finzi, Enrico Besana, Major Enrico Guastalla, Colonel Augusto Elia, Lt. George Manin and others, belies any opprobrious reference to any race or particular people. More than that, Garibaldi's entire philosophy of life and subsequent actions preclude such a reference; in fact, he fought racial prejudices, as well as privileged groups.

7. The allusion is to Garibaldi's encounters of 1828 in the Greek Archipelago with Greek pirates. His only existing manuscript on these encounters is in the archives of the University of British Columbia in Vancouver, Canada. Cfr. A.P. Campanella, *Autografi di Garibaldi nella Collezione Haweis della Università della Colombia Britannica*, "Rassegna Storica del Risorgimento," Roma, A. XLVII - Fasc. IV, Ottobre-Dicembre 1960, pp. 574-604.

8. Captain Carlo *Semeria*, not Someria, as Melena writes.

9. Signora Luigia *Sauvaigo*, not Trovaigo, as Melena writes.

10. Port Mahón, Minorca, Balearic Islands.

Chapter IV

11. The identity of this person has never been established. The names of Giuseppe Mazzini and Giovan Battista Cuneo have been suggested as the most likely, but without documentary confirmation.

12. *Saint-Simonism*, or the ideas expounded by Claude-Henry, the Count of Saint-Simon (1760-1825), which had considerable influence on later Socialist thought.

13. The insurrections began in central Italy; in Modena the revolutionaries were betrayed on 3 February 1831 and on 26 May Ciro Menotti, one of the leaders, was executed; it marked the beginning of an insurrectionary chain. Two days later in Rome the liberals attempted to overthrow the pontifical government occupying the Campidoglio, or City Hall; on the same day in Bologna, the people supplanted the pontifical emblem with the tricolor; other insurrections took place in the Marches, in Romagna and in Emilia. In northern Italy the principal insurrections were in Chambéry, Genoa and Alessandria and saw the executions of the patriots Giuseppe Tamburelli, Efisio Tola, Giuseppe Biglia, Antonio Gavotti and Andrea Vochieri.

14. Giuseppe Mazzini (1805-1872) of Genoa, was the architect of Italian independence; a Republican of extraordinary political vision, his writings, probably the most prolific of any writer in any field, organized and held together the Italian independence movement, besides inspiring similar movements in Europe, i.e., *Young Europe, Young Switzerland, Young Germany*, etc. In action however, he was singularly unsuccessful and was superseded by Garibaldi, who ultimately achieved Italian unification and independence in the form of a constitutional monarchy.

15. The expedition of 1834 from Geneva into the Sardinian territory of Savoy was one of the unsuccessful attempts of Mazzini to overthrow the Savoy dynasty of Turin. General Ramorino is here blamed, although the greater re-

sponsibility was Mazzini's because of his poor organization, constant delays and lack of secrecy in his plans.

16. The seizure of the Sardinian Navy stationed in the harbor of Genoa was also conceived by Mazzini and was entrusted to Garibaldi; the action was timed to take place simultaneously with the Savoy invasion from Geneva led by Mazzini and Ramorino in February 1834.

17. Natalina Pozzo. (From the plaque in Piazza Sarzano in Genoa where her fruitshop once stood.)

18. In Europe the first floor is one flight up above the street floor.

19. Pierre Jean de Béranger (1780-1857), French lyric poet whose republican ideas first brought him imprisonment, later great popularity. Like Robert Burns, he fitted his verses to popular melodies and gained great recognition from such poets as Goethe and Heine. His *Le Dieu des bonnes gens*, here sung by Garibaldi, was one of his most popular poems put to music.

Chapter V

20. In Paris, where the French readers were not informed of the previous Dwight version which also contained this episode, some termed the episode a figment of Dumas' romantic imagination, until the boy, 25 years later and anxious to at least honor the man who had so modestly withdrawn himself after the daring act of rescue, with the dubious recompense of a ruined uniform, sent to the editor of *Le Siècle* a verification of what had taken place; it may be read in the issue of 25 June 1860, signed *Joseph Rambaud, 9 rue de l'Ecluse (Batignolles)*.

21. The devastating Marseille cholera epidemic of 1834-35 took more than 50,000 lives; cfr. *NEMESIS MEDICALE, Recueil de satires par un phocéen, A.-F.-H. Fabre. Paris, 1834-1835*. Needless to say, the risk of infection was very great among these volunteers, the cholera bacillus being transmitted readily by water, food and excreta.

22. Melena erroneously wrote Bento *Gonzales;* Garibaldi at first wrote *Gonçales,* later he changed it to *Gonçalves,* which is correct. Henceforth only the latter form will be used.

Chapter VI

23. Contrary to what Melena here writes, the Dwight, Carrano and Dumas versions, as well as Garibaldi's definitive edition of 1872, report merely that the *Mazzini* was sunk.

24. This is another incident which Alexandre Dumas was accused of inventing in his version of the Garibaldi manuscript. The fact that Melena received the latter before Dumas, proves Dumas' innocence in the matter. The Dwight and Carrano versions do not contain this incident.

25. Melena translates *tavola* into Brett or plank, which it may be; but *tavola* also means table, which obviously Garibaldi meant, as one reads a bit further in the text.

26. Of all four versions, this sentence appears only in this, the Melena, version.

27. It was the year 1837 and Garibaldi was thirty years old at the time, not twenty-five.

Chapter VII

28. Here we have an example of Melena's over-simplification of the manuscript which resulted in an apparently faulty translation. From Carrano and Dumas we see that Garibaldi first recounted how the young Uruguayan poetess also knew Italian, having recited from memory Dante, Petrarch and Tasso. Then turning to Garibaldi, she asked if he was familiar with the poems of Quintana; when the answer was in the negative, she gave him her copy in order that he might learn Spanish. Instead from Melena's translation the recitation of the Italian poets is omitted and it appears as if the Italian poems were Quintana's. Manuel José Quintana (1772-1857) was, of course, Spanish and wrote only in that language.

29. Again Melena translates *Brett,* or board; the others report a *pole,* which of course is what is intended.

30. *Lancione;* this is the Italian word for the Spanish lancha, or launch.

31. From the celebrated Italian poet Ugo Foscolo (1778-1827), *I Sepolcri* (The Sepulchres), lines 13-15, reading as follows:

> . . . un sasso
> Che distingua le mie dalle infinite
> Ossa che in terra e in mar semina morte?

Chapter IX

32. Luca *Tartabull*, not Tartabal, as Melena writes.

33. This name is unclear; the definitive edition prints *Sintoresca,* Melena *Pintosesca,* while we are inclined to believe it was *Pintoresca.*

34. The heights of *Ibicuy*, not *Hieni,* as Melena writes.

35. Don Jacinto *Andreus*, not Andreas, as Melena writes.

36. Again not *Hieni,* as Melena writes, but Ibicuy.

37. Instead of *Hieni,* as pointed out.

38. A *ronzino* is an old nag, not a small horse, as Melena has written.

Chapter X

39. *Bajada*, not Rajada, as Melena writes.

40. This sentence does not appear in any of the three other versions made from the Garibaldi manuscript and is left to the conjecture of the reader. In Dwight however, this variation appears: (in describing Captain Ventura) "a man of such a character that he had risen superior to the principles inculcated in Italian youth by their priestly instructors." A decennial later, the reference to *Israelite education* reappears in the definitive edition of Garibaldi's memoirs of 1872 (Bologna, L. Cappelli, editore, 1932, p. 51).

Chapter XI

41. *Pesente*, not Pesante, as Melena writes.

42. Silva *Tavares*, not Tanares.

43. Melena exaggerates here. The meeting with Gonçalves was in 1838, so that being born c. 1788 (the exact date is unknown), the president was around his

fiftieth year. Garibaldi, who knew Gonçalves personally, says that he was nearing his sixtieth year.

44. *Canudos*, not Canadis, as Melena writes.

Chapter XII

45. Garibaldi wrote *Camacuan;* Melena *Camacuam;* today it is called *Camaquan.*

46. In Spanish, cleared, cultivated fields are *rozas*, although Garibaldi wrote *rossas* and Melena *rossai.*

47. *Donna* is Italian, which is what Melena wrote; what Garibaldi wrote was D.a, intending the Spanish *Doña*, or title of Lady.

48. The manuscript here apparently was not clearly written; Dwight writes of the grove of *Teviva*, Carrano the grove of *Tirivà*, and Dumas mentions the little forest of *Firiva*. In the definitive edition of 1872 it appears as the grove of *Jirivà.*

Chapter XIII

49. Francisco de Abreu (or Abreus), not Abren, as Melena writes.

50. *galpón de charqueada*, a shed (from the verb *charquear*, to jerk or dry beef).

51. Charcoal is intended. Melena often used Italian terminology, as here. But in Italian *carbone* may mean either hard coal (carbone fossile) or charcoal (carbone de legno). She could only have meant the latter.

52. Again Melena's condensation of the manuscript leaves the reader confused. The incident interposed here on Griggs' death occurred on the *Laguna de Santa Catarina.*

53. All sources, including the definitive edition, show that Melena erred in her translation. Ignazio Bilbao was a *Biscayan*, not a Brescian; nor was Lorenzo's family name Natal. Garibaldi merely referred to him as *Lorenzo N.*

54. Edoardo *Mutru,* not Mistra, as Melena writes.

55. Dwight also reports 80 *Germans* took part, although in 1872 Garibaldi wrote *Austrians;* he often used one for the other indiscriminately.

Chapter XIV

56. *Itapuá,* not Hapua, as Melena writes.

57. *Zeffirino d'Utra*, not Jefferino d'Utra, as Melena writes.

58. *Northeast*, not southeast end, as Melena writes.

59. *Capivary*, not Capi Baja, as Melena writes.

60. *p.m.*, not a.m., as Melena writes.

61. *Araranguá*, not Aringue, as Melena writes.

62. Colonel *Teixeira*, not Teincira, as Melena writes.

63. Instead, all other sources, including the manuscript, report that the three ships surrendered after a short resistance.

Chapter XV

64. Much has been written about this man, Manoel Duarte de Aguiar, whom Garibaldi's detractors claim was wronged by the Italian revolutionary because he had run away with his wife, the unforgettable Anita. But despite these detractions, and what seems self-recrimination by Garibaldi here, the affair was otherwise than what it appears. Anita had indeed been married to Duarte for three years already but her marriage had been wrecked by incompatibility, both sexually and spiritually, and estrangement. Besides the differences were complicated by political viewpoints. Anita was dissatisfied with her family life, as well as the narrow, circumscribed mores of those times, and was in favor of the Rio-Grandian revolution. Contrarily Duarte, conservative and reactionary, was a staunch defender of the unprogressive and undemocratic rule of Emperor Dom Pedro II. As a matter of fact, Duarte had left the conjugal hearth in order to join the National Guard of the Emperor, leaving Anita behind instead of taking her along, as custom required. Thus when her hero appeared in Laguna in person, she, abandoned by her husband and desirous of leading a meaningful life, left voluntarily to join Garibaldi. For details and authentic documents, see: W.L. Rau, *Anita Garibaldi, o perfil de una heroina brasileira,* Florianópolis (Santa Catarina, Brazil), 1975.

65. The name the Greeks and Romans gave to the river which once flowed by Ravenna and emptied into the Adriatic Sea. Today this function is served by the Candiano Canal which connects Ravenna to Port Corsini.

Chapter XVI

66. The Laguna de Santa Catarina, not to be confused with the Laguna dos Patos.

67. In fact Garibaldi wrote "una specie di brigantino goletta," that is, a fast American type two-masted man-of-war with square rigging.

68. *Andurinha,* not Andurinka, as Melena writes.

69. Oversimplification by Melena; it should read *parapetto gabbionato,* or rampart with breastwork for the protection of the cannoneers.

Chapter XVII

70. Melena writes *Imeren*, Garibaldi wrote *Imiriù;* today it is called *Imaruhy*, which we shall use henceforth.

Chapter XVIII

71. Juan *Enrique*, not Enrigue, as Melena writes.

72. *Itaparica*, not Taparisa, as Melena writes.

73. According to the other versions and the manuscript, Griggs' face looked as if it were still alive, not asleep.

Chapter XIX

74. *Cima da Serra*, not Cinca da Serra, as Melena writes.

75. *Cima da Serra*, not Cima da Lara, as Melena writes.

76. The Pass of *Maromba*, not Morocamba, as Melena writes.

77. *Ganado:* herds of cattle which serve as the troops' only source of food

and thus relieves them of all other impedimenta.
78. *Cavalladas:* reserve horses for the cavalry.

Chapter XX

79. Major *Peixotto*, not Pecitrotto, as Melena writes.
80. *Capón*, not cappon, as Melena writes.

Chapter XXI

81. *Coritybanos*, not Coritibani.
82. *Corityba*, not Coritaba.
83. *Picada,* not piccada.

Chapter XXIII

84. Garibaldi writes *Cahó*, instead of Catin, as Melena writes.
85. *Pinheiriño*, not Pinharino, as Melena writes.

Chapter XXV

86. The original manuscript shows Menotti Garibaldi to be born on 16 (not 6) September 1840.

Chapter XXVI

87. *Foges*, not toges, as Melena writes.

Chapter XXVIII

88. In fact, Garibaldi himself wrote concerning these pilots: "Indeed, in order to deceive the enemy, I had requested and found pilots of the Uruguay River."
89. *Vallerga* (not Valberga, as Melena writes) da Loano.
90. Melena here mistakenly writes 60 cannon.

Chapter XXIX

91. *Cavallo Guatiá* (White Horse).

Chapter XXX

92. Here Melena incorrectly writes *Lijos* Pass.
93. Colonel *Esteves*, not Estiva, as the authoress writes.

Chapter XXXI

94. Garibaldi wrote instead *many*, which Melena exaggerates apparently by using *innumerable*.

Chapter XXXIV

95. This remark is probably an interpolation made by Melena. Garibaldi's manuscript does not contain it, nor do the Dwight and Carrano earlier versions. Part of it appears in the Dumas version, but since he received the manuscript from Melena, one wonders whether the latter had written it in, at least temporarily. A propos, see Chapter XVII of Dwight's version, the original and most complete of Garibaldi's memoirs. Here the scornful remarks directed against Italians, particularly by the French immigrants in Montevideo, are well described and refuted by the liberator himself. For various reasons however, principally because he magnanimously refused to bear rancor towards anyone, including foreigners, he discarded these interesting notations in later editions.

96. More of Melena's interpolations; the other versions merely speak of Bauzá as "a good soldier but very old."

97. This interesting episode in the life of Anzani appeared in the earlier manuscript prepared by Garibaldi but was removed in the subsequent revisions. Dumas (Chap. XXXVI of Vol. I) and Melena (Kapitel 34) however, retained it intact.

Chapter XXXV

98. The commodore's name was *Purvis*, not Pierce, as Melena writes; so states Garibaldi's manuscript.

Chapter XXXVI

99. Characteristic of his modesty, Garibaldi did not include, or even mention, this singular honor from the President of Uruguay to him and his Legion in his original manuscript or in his first definitive edition of 1872. President Fructuoso Rivera's offer of a donation to the Italian Legion, as well as Garibaldi's response, were first published a year later in the *Times* of London on 30 January 1846 after Giuseppe Mazzini had submitted them to the editor for his disposal. Mazzini, who was living in exile in London, but in close contact with Italian emigrants abroad, had also resented French denigration of Italians in Uruguay, and although never really upset by these picayune attacks, he accompanied the two documents with this cover letter:

[London], 1846, January 29

Sir,

The two documents which I enclose have been lying on my desk for seven months at least, without a single thought on my part of making them public. I well knew that it was no aim of my countrymen at Monte Video to seek for public praise for the fulfillment of what they believe to be their duty; but, for some time past, the French journals, which have kept silence for three years as to the existence and brave deeds of the Italian Legion, have set themselves the task of crushing it by the systematic application of the name of *condottieri** to the

---

**condottiero* (or condottiere): soldier of fortune, that is, one who follows a military career wherever there is promise of profit, adventure, or pleasure. The Italian legionaries were essentially immigrants who sought a better life in the new world; very few returned to Italy, the great majority remained, intermarried with the Uruguayans and became the largest single ethnic group in Uruguay today. [Editor's note.]

volunteers who compose it. I think, therefore, that the moment is come for the publication of these two documents, for which purpose I appeal to your impartiality. I leave to your readers to decide whether the appellation of which I complain, is owing to an historical ignorance of the meaning of the word, or to a deliberate intention of perverting the truth.

[Appended to the second document, he added:] I shall not add one word to the above document, observing only that the French Legion did accept a donation of the same nature as the one declined by my countrymen; and that when the deed of General Rivera, and the answer of their staff were officially read by the soldiers of the Italian Legion, there arose from the ranks one unanimous cry: "We are no hirelings — we are not Swiss!"

I am, Sir, your obedient servant,

Joseph Mazzini

108, High Holborn

Like Melena, Alexandre Dumas also published these two letters in his memoirs of Garibaldi, both biographers probably after having read them in the *Times.*

Chapter XXXVII

100. François-Pierre-Guillaume Guizot (1787-1874), reactionary and conservative French statesman brought up in Geneva amidst the austere teachings of dogmatic Calvinism he was at this time both Interior and Foreign Minister in the Soult Ministry and as such looked with disfavor upon all movements which might perturb the dominant powers, hence his opposition to the minority forces of the Garibaldians who would maintain the independence of Uruguay against the usurping and superior power of the Argentinian Confederation.

101. *Vivorigna*, not Sivoriña, as Melena writes.

102. *Las maneas*, not maneador, as Melena writes.

103. Here Melena mistakes *cuchilla* for knife, which it also means; but Garibaldi, in comparing the matreros of the cuchillas to the gauchos of the pampas, was referring to the mountain ridges, like Cuchilla Grande, so characteristic of the province of Rio Grande do Sul.

104. The English lieutenant's name was *Dench*, not Tench, as Melena writes.

105. The French officer who commanded the *Eclair* was Hypolite *Morier,* not Mazier, as affirms Melena.

106. Instead Melena erroneously writes *Cagebi.*

107. *Cavalladas*, not cavalcadas, as Melena writes.

108. Melena writes *curona*, which is incorrect. In his manuscript, in a footnote which Melena omits, Garibaldi explains: *Carona:* raw leather which is placed beneath the saddle. Now, by tying the four corners of this leather strip, one forms a little bark capable of carrying arms and clothing; and this little bark is tied to the horse's tail, that is, in tow of the animal, and is called the *pelota.*

109. Melena is mixed up here. Diego Lamas commanded an Argentinian division in the Salto area, hence could not have had any relations with Col. Baez. Instead it was General Anacleto Medina with whom Baez had close relations.

110. Not *tayera di Don Vincenzio*, as Melena writes. Also the tapera of Don Venanzio was not a locality but a lean-to which once formed part of an estancia and a saladero, now in ruins.

111. Melena erroneously writes *Dessellaux*.

112. Melena's names are generally incorrect; Diffaudis and L'Aine are here corrected to read *Deffaudis* and *Laine*.

113. Melena's *rodomoms* is incorrect.

114. Melena incorrectly writes *bolado*.

115. Melena incorrectly writes *Artigos*.

116. Melena here writes Gomez, obviously referring to Servando Gomez. But the latter commanded the Argentinian forces in the Salto area, the very forces which killed Col. Blanco and undid the gains made by Garibaldi and the Italian Legion.

117. Here Melena misunderstood Garibaldi's handwriting by listing together as a single name Diaz Lojes. The Colonels *Diaz* and *Tajes* had both been dismissed by Rivera for their loyalty to the cause rather than to him.

VOLUME II

BOOK TWO

Chapter I

118. Melena's Partone Street is incorrect. At that time it was called *Calle del Portón;* today it has been renamed *Calle del 24 de Mayo*.

119. This letter was written in Italian and addressed to the Papal Nuncio in Rio de Janeiro, Mons. Gaetano Bedini. It is now preserved in the Secret Archives of the Vatican, Secretary of State, Rubric 251, 1848. It was first published in the *Edizione Nazionale degli Scritti di Giuseppe Garibaldi,* Vol. IV, p. 82-85, Bologna, L. Cappelli, 1932-1937.

120. According to Garibaldi *(Ediz. Naz. degli Scritti di Gius. Garibaldi,* II, p. 234), 63 of his companions from the Italian Legion accompanied him in returning to Italy.

121. Anzani disembarked in Nice, along with Garibaldi and the others of the Legion, but he died in Genoa on July 4, 1848.

Chapter II

122. Melena incorrectly writes *Murazzone*.

123. In fact, Schönhals says: "Il fit une courageuse resistance, et quoique attaqué par des forces supérieures, il réussit, grâce à l'obscurité de la nuit et à d'excellents guides, à regagner Luino d'où il repassa en Suisse." *(Campagnes d'Italie de 1848 et 1849,* par le Général Schönhals, Aide-de-camp de Radetzky, traduit par Théophile Gautier fils, Paris, Poulet-Malassis et de Broise, 1859, p. 294-5.)

Chapter III

124. Pellegrino Rossi (1787-1848) eminent economist, criminologist and legislator, who served governments in Emilia, Geneva, Paris and ultimately the

222

Holy See where he was president of the Council in Pope Pius IX's first constitutional government. His assassination in Rome in 1848 set the way for the creation of the Republic of Rome under a triumvirate and Garibaldi as Commander of its First Division.

125. *Finanzieri*: customs officers and frontier guards.

126. *Reduci*: war veterans.

127. Here an explanation is necessary in order to fully appreciate this remark by Melena. Each time that Garibaldi's forces defeated the French, and there were some very decisive defeats like that of 30 April 1849, Mazzini, the dominant figure of the Roman triumvirate, forbade any pursuit of the enemy, lest a crushing defeat so enrage the pretentious Napoleon III that he send far greater French forces to overwhelm the gallant but vastly inferior Roman forces. Garibaldi's desire was always to drive the French invaders back to Civitavecchia, from where they came, and into the Tyrrhenian Sea.

Chapter IV

128. *emigrati*: with the founding of the Republic of Rome in 1849 many oppressed Italians from areas governed by foreigners, such as Venetia, Lombardy, Tuscany, Sicily and Campania, as well as Italians from the Apostolic Legations of the Holy See, i.e. Bologna, Ferrara, Ravenna and Forlì, flocked to Rome.

Chapter V

129. The correct spelling of this name is *Zagarolo*; Melena incorrectly writes Zargarolla.

Chapter VII

130. In fact, encircling Garibaldi and his survivors from the annihilated Roman Republic were five enemy armies, all anxious to destroy the remnants of the short-lived Republic and to restore the Papacy in Rome. They were: 1) the French Army (30,000 troops) divided into two segments, one occupying Albano, the other Civita Castellana; 2) the Bourbon Army (12,000 troops) of the Kingdom of Two Sicilies which controlled southern Italy and the Abruzzi; 3) the Spanish Army (6,000 troops), already arrived from Spain and stationed in Velletri; 4) the Austrian Army (15,000 troops) which controlled all roads and passes in Umbria and the Marches; and 5) the Army of the Grand Duchy of Tuscany under Leopold II (2,000 troops).

BOOK THREE

Chapter I

131. Ciceruacchio's correct name was *Angelo Brunetti* (1802-1849), not Peter Bruneti, as Melena writes.

Chapter II

132. The *bragozzo* is the typical Italian fishing boat of the northern Adriatic Sea, particularly to be found at Chioggia, in the Po delta and in the Romagnole ports of Cesenatico, Ravenna and Rimini. It is ketch-rigged with a lateen sail on the foremast, spoon shaped both fore and aft, and because of its wide beam amidship and heavy construction, capable of carrying large payloads. Generally they measure from eleven to fifteen metres in length.

133. Melena errs here; an inhabitant of Chioggia is a *Chioggiotto*.

134. The designation *Croats* was often used by the Italians when Austrians were intended, simply because they were commonly used by the Austrian Army for service in Italy, Croatia being the closest of the Austrian-dominated territories.

135. *Fusilare*: to shoot.

136. *Bastonare*: to beat up with a club.

137. Besides the designation *Croats*, the Austrians were also simply referred to as *Germans*.

BOOK FIVE

138. At the time of the publication of Melena's original *Denkwürdigkeiten* in 1861 this statement was, of course, true. Today however, many first-hand accounts of individuals who took part in, or witnessed, the *trafugamento* of Garibaldi from Magnavacca to Chiavari and freedom have since been published. The bibliography of A.P. Campanella, *Giuseppe Garibaldi e la Tradizione Garibaldina* (Geneva, 1971) contains more than 400 such authenticated sources. Some of the principal ones are: R. Belluzzi, *La ritirata di Garibaldi da Roma nel 1849*, Roma, Soc. edit. Dante Alighieri, 1899; U. Beseghi, *Il maggiore "Leggero" e il "trafugamento" di Garibaldi . . .*, Ravenna, Soc. Tip. ed. ravennate & mutilati, 1932; G. Fabbrini, *La morte di Anita e la fuga di Garibaldi attraverso la Romagna*, "Giornale del Mattino," Bologna, 9 maggio 1911; G. Guelfi, *Dal Molino di Cerbaia a Cala Martina; notizie inedite sulla vita di Giuseppe Garibaldi*, Firenze, Arte della Stampa, 1886; and P. Mastri, *Il passaggio di Garibaldi per Longiano, Savignano, Gatteo e Cesenatico*, "Cittadino," Cesena, 4 luglio 1907.

139. This should be *Saline Pomarance*, not Pomarana.

140. Melena here mistakes Garibaldi's maritime friend, the Genovese Francesco Carpanetto, with the Sardinian Counsul at Tangiers, Giovan Battista Carpanetti, who was also his friend. Garibaldi makes the same mistake in his manuscript.

141. The well-known story of Garibaldi having to work as a candle maker during his exile in New York is misleading, partly due to his own modest statements. In the definitive edition of his memoirs, Garibaldi writes: "I had to do something and since my friend Antonio Meucci decided to set up a candle factory, he asked me to help him." But Meucci was an engineer and inventor by profession, not a candle maker, although feeling the need to maintain some paying undertaking to cover the expenses incurred during his numerous experiments, he set up the candle factory in his garden in Staten Island. At the time Garibaldi was already famous as the *salvador* of Uruguay, as one of the precursors of Republi-

can Brazil, and now as the valorous defender of the Republic of Rome only the year before against the mighty French Army. As such, many of his Italian countrymen gave him asylum in New York. In this same spirit Garibaldi also accepted the Meucci offer, working at candle making or at any of the latter's experiments if he wished, but always feeling free to do as he pleased. A propos he adds: "I worked for a few months with Meucci, and although I was his employee, he treated me as one of the family." In fact, he lived as an honored guest in the Meucci home and often left "his work" in order to go hunting, fishing or sailing in The Narrows between that island and Brooklyn. As concerns Meucci, we know today that he was the rightful inventor of the telephone, Alexander Graham Bell having appropriated Meucci's initial patent, the experimental work for which was carried on here in the Florentine's Staten Island home where Garibaldi was a guest.

142. More than that, Garibaldi refused the greatest honor that the City of New York extends to visiting celebrities when he declined the traditional parade up Broadway. The Mayor had already announced the general desire to so honor the Hero of Two Worlds, but the Irish Catholics resident there, mindful of Garibaldi's defense of the Roman Republic against the return of the Papacy, protested. Numerous brawls took place until Garibaldi realizing that such disorder could only hurt the Italian cause, declined the honor. Thus, of all the many world-famous personalities to have been offered this singular honor, Garibaldi remains the sole individual to date to have refused it.

143. Here Melena refers to Francesco Carpanetto, Garibaldi's maritime friend and broker.

BOOK SIX

144. As is well known, when Ravenna was the capital of the Western Roman Empire it occupied a group of islands in a lagoon, similar to the layout confronting Venice, all of which formed part of the great delta of the Po River. After centuries the silt swept along by the latter and the nearby Apennine streams filled in the lagoon, as well as the surrounding area. Because of this, Ravenna finds itself today part of the mainland and 12 kilometres from the Adriatic Sea.

145. *pignoli*: pine kernels, used commonly in fine Italian cooking.

146. *Zouaves*: an infantry in the French military service which adopts the old Kabyle (Algerian) costume and emphasizes its traditional valor.

147. Ciceruacchio was a popular leader of the Romans during the Republic of 1849. He and his two sons, mere lads, joined Garibaldi in the retreat, also landed at Magnavacca on the Adriatic coast but were caught by the Austrians and executed at Cà Tiepolo in the Po delta while attempting to reach Venice and join the revolt there.

148. Ugo Bassi was a Barnabite priest but loyal to the Italian cause and a follower of Garibaldi; he joined the latter in the retreat from Rome, also landed at Magnavacca but was caught by the Austrians and executed in Bologna by order of the pontifical government.

149. *scirocco*: a Sirocco, a sultry south-east wind of cyclonic origin and generally from the Libyan desert.

150. *yatagan*: a long Turkish knife which resembles somewhat a short sword, but lacking the cross-piece at the hilt.

151. This poem was written by Garibaldi in Gualeguay, Entre Rios (Argentina), during his confinement there in the summer of 1837 after being wounded critically in the neck in the battle off the San Gregorio coast of the La Plata River near Montevideo. His friend, deputy and first biographer, G.B. Cuneo, mentioned a few lines of it in his *Biografia di Giuseppe Garibaldi* which was published in Turin in 1850 by the printers Fory and Dalmazzo, but it was not until Melena published it in her *Denkwürdigkeiten* in 1861 that it saw the light in full with a German translation. Two years before, during that memorable visit to Romagna described here in Book Six, Garibaldi had dictated it to her in the Pelican Hotel in Bologna.